Human Rights from Below

Achieving rights through community development

In *Human Rights From Below*, Jim Ife shows how human rights and community development are problematic terms but powerful ideals, and that each is essential for understanding and practising the other. Ife contends that practitioners – advocates, activists, workers and volunteers – can better empower and protect communities when human rights are treated as more than just a specialist branch of law or international relations, and that human rights can be better realised when community development principles are applied.

The book offers a long overdue assessment of how human rights and community development are invariably interconnected. It highlights how critical it is to understand the two as a basis for thinking about and taking action to address the serious challenges facing the world in the twenty-first century.

Written for students, community development and human rights workers, *Human Rights From Below* brings together the important fields of human rights and community development, to enrich our thinking of both.

Jim Ife holds adjunct positions at the Centre for Human Rights Education at Curtin University of Technology, Western Australia, and at the Centre for Citizenship and Human Rights at Deakin University, Victoria.

D1599454

Human Rights from Below

Achieving rights through community development

Jim Ife

CAMBRIDGE
UNIVERSITY PRESS

CAMBRIDGE
UNIVERSITY PRESS

477 Williamstown Road, Port Melbourne, VIC 3207, Australia

Cambridge University Press is part of the University of Cambridge.

It furthers the University's mission by disseminating knowledge in the pursuit of education, learning and research at the highest international levels of excellence.

www.cambridge.org
Information on this title: www.cambridge.org/9780521711081

© Jim Ife 2009

First published 2009

Edited by Frances Wade
Cover design by Traffic Design Studios

A catalogue record for this publication is available from the British Library

National Library of Australia Cataloguing in Publication data
Ife, J.W. (James William), 1946–
Human rights from below : achieving rights through community development / Jim Ife.
9780521711081 (pbk.)
Includes index.
Bibliography.
Community development.
Human rights.
307.14

ISBN 978-0-521-71108-1 Paperback

Contents

Acknowledgements

THE WRITER OF A BOOK can claim little credit for 'new ideas'. There are very few new ideas, but rather many old ones that are continually recycled, refined and put together in new ways. I am acutely aware of an intellectual debt to many people for the ideas in this book. As well as the cited references, there are other people who are too numerous to name, and many of whom have been half-forgotten, whose work is reflected here. Former students, colleagues and friends have made significant contributions to my thinking about community development and human rights over the years, and to this attempt to bring together these two areas that have for long been abiding concerns of mine, both intellectually and practically.

The most significant impact on this book has been that of my wife, Dr Sonia Tascón. Through many hours of dialogue, her critical and creative mind has informed many aspects of these chapters and my intellectual debt to her, as well as my personal debt, is immense. She is strongly present throughout this book.

There are some other colleagues who deserve a special mention. At the Centre for Human Rights Education at Curtin University, Perth, working with Dr Riccardo Baldissone has been an amazingly stimulating intellectual encounter and his work on the intellectual history of human rights has had a major impact on my ideas. At the same centre Professor Linda Briskman, Lucy Fiske and Dr Caroline Fleay have been long-term colleagues and friends whose critical idealism and activist engagement have been particularly influential in forming the ideas discussed here. To have been associated with this centre from its inception has been a real privilege, and the continuing resources made available by Curtin University in my retirement are also gratefully acknowledged.

In my more recent period as a resident of Victoria, Professor Susan Kenny of the Centre for Citizenship, Development and Human Rights at Deakin University has been a valued colleague. Though we share common interests and commitments, our approach to them is somewhat different and this has proved to be a valuable juxtaposition, which I have found very beneficial. I am also grateful to her, and to Deakin University, for an honorary appointment and for thereby providing the facilities to write, including office space, library and computer access.

Across the Tasman I am indebted to Gavin Rennie and his colleagues at Unitec, Auckland, where I have been privileged to hold an adjunct position. This has given me the opportunity to meet some wonderful practitioners of community-based human rights, and also to share ideas with students and colleagues, especially Gavin himself and another long-time colleague, Dr Love Chile of Auckland University of Technology.

Other colleagues and mentors, many from earlier in my career, remain important influences on my thinking, and deserve acknowledgement. In alphabetical order these include: Evelyn Balais Serrano, Jacques Boulet, Veronica Brady, Ingrid Burkett, Johan Galtung, Vic George, Riyadh al Hakimi, Adam Jamrozik, Louise Morley, Jean Panet Raymond, Stuart Rees, Graham Riches, Ailsa Watkinson, David Woodsworth, Susan Young, my many friends from my time with Amnesty International and with the Human Rights Commission of the International Federation of Social Workers, and the courageous people of Ermera and Gleno in East Timor in 1999. There are many others who could be added to the list, and I trust they will forgive their omission.

Susan Hanley at Cambridge University Press has been a patient, supportive and encouraging publisher whose belief in this project was constant, even at those inevitable times when mine was flagging, and who made sure it finally reached completion.

Finally, in hope for the future, this book is dedicated to my children, Julia and Bronwyn, my grandchildren, Ben, Emma, Joseph and Hamish, and my step-children, Trent and Isabel.

Jim Ife
Melbourne
April 2009

Introduction

THIS BOOK DEALS WITH two concepts, *human rights* and *community development*. Each of these is made up of two words whose meanings are complex and contested. One of the problems with much of the literature about either human rights or community development is that it too often treats the component words as non-problematic – indeed as self-evident in their meaning. Yet the four words *human, rights, community* and *development* are all highly problematic. Their meanings lend themselves to different interpretations, and the way in which each of them is used is highly ideological and value-laden. Therefore a book about human rights and community development explores difficult and contested territory. Part of our concern in this book will be to explore these difficult terms. Our aim is not to come up with a single 'clear' understanding of them, as all of them defy such simplistic treatment, but rather to understand some of the richness of thinking that lies behind each, and the questions that this thinking poses for anyone who claims to be concerned about human rights, or community development, or both.

As we explore the ideas of community development and human rights, what becomes clear is the common ground between them and the way in which each not only can contribute to the other, but also cannot do without the other. Those who want to further the cause of human rights must, I will argue, be concerned with community development, as community development is necessary if our human rights are to be fully realised. It is only in community that we can achieve our full humanity.

Similarly, those concerned with community development must necessarily also be concerned with human rights as the framework within which such development takes place, and which indeed gives some point to the activity of community development. Because of this, an examination of the

1

relationship between these two fields is overdue. There is value in under-standing this relationship as a basis for both thinking and taking action about the serious challenges facing the world in the early twenty-first century.

Both human rights and community development are of critical impor-tance for the world at this historical moment. It has become clear that the social, economic and political system that has driven the world in recent decades is utterly unsustainable. The ecological crisis facing humanity chal-lenges us to rethink our relationship to each other, our relationship to the natural world, our lifestyles, and indeed our very ways of thinking about humanity and whatever meaning human life has.

The economic crisis that has eventuated while this book was being writ-ten has further eroded some comfortable certainties. How long this crisis will last, and how deep it will bite, are unknown at the time of writing, but the foundations of the global economy have been called into question. How humanity will respond to these challenges is far from clear. Many 'strategies', 'solutions' or 'ways forward' are proposed; some are technologi-cal, some economic, some political, and some more philosophical. What is clear to many people, however, is that if there is to be a way forward it will involve a re-establishment of human community as the basis of our lives, our production, our consumption, our culture, our social interactions and the realisation of our humanity. Community development is likely to be a key component of the emergence of an ecologically sane and sustainable world if such a future is to be realised. It seems unlikely that ecological sanity can be achieved without strong, viable and sustainable communities. Even if this were possible, a world without community, of individuals seek-ing meaning in lives isolated from others, however ecologically sustainable those lives may be, is hardly an appealing prospect.

The imperative for human rights is also very strong. The response by many governments to global terrorism has demonstrated just how fragile is the protection of human rights that many people, at least in the West, had more or less taken for granted. Both terrorism itself and the state response to the terrorist threat have put human rights more at risk for most if not all of the world's population. In addition, the human rights abuses associated with, and indeed often required by, the increasing power of global capitalism pose a question: how robust is our commitment to human rights in an age of economic fundamentalism?

The conflict between the needs of the economy and the needs and rights of people is becoming, if anything, clearer and more dramatic. Human rights abuses in many countries remain an obscenity and an affront to any notion that 'we live in a civilised world'. When we extend human rights to include not only civil and political rights but also economic, social and cultural rights – such as the rights to education, to health care, to housing, to employment, to income security, to social support and to cultural practices – it is clear that there is a long way to go before any individual nation, let alone the global community, can claim that the rights of all citizens are fully protected and realised.

The uncertainty of the future, and the significant challenges that we seem remarkably ill-prepared and reluctant to face, raise serious questions as to whether human rights will be given a high priority by both state and non-state actors, or whether they will be sacrificed in the interests of political expediency in the apparent pursuit of a stable economy, protection from terrorism or ecological sustainability. Any of these goals, if achieved at the expense of human rights, would surely be a hollow victory.

At this time in history, therefore, both human rights and human community are under challenge, and yet the imperative for each is strong. It is in this context that this book seeks to explore the relationship between community development and human rights, and the implications of an approach that requires the integration of the two.

This book inevitably has a Western bias. It was written by an Australian, most of whose community development and human rights experience, and all of whose academic career, has been located in Western countries. This should not be taken as an assumption that the Western world view, intellectual and cultural traditions are in any sense superior to others. Indeed, it will be argued that the Western world view has limited our understandings of both human rights and community development and that broader, more culturally and intellectually diverse understandings are needed if these ideas are to retain their significance and their power. However, the fact remains that, inevitably, this is a book written by someone within the Western tradition, who sees things through Western eyes, with the inevitable blind spots and prejudices. Although many of the examples used are from the Western world, this need not necessarily be a bad thing. One of the problems with 'human rights' is that human rights violations have too often been characterised in the West as something that happens elsewhere – 'over there' rather than 'here'. It is important for people in the West to understand that their own traditions are implicated in human rights abuse, and that human rights is as much a matter of reflecting on one's own society as of righteous indignation about what may be happening on the other side of the world. An important aspect of human rights from below is to bring consideration of human rights closer to people's lived experience.

I hope that some of the ideas may be of relevance to people from other cultural traditions. Indeed it has been a pleasant surprise to find that my previous books seem to have resonated with people in other cultural contexts to a greater extent than I had anticipated. However, wherever they are applied, these ideas will need to be recontextualised. This is a task for the reader rather than the writer. This is particularly true of the final chapters, where an attempt is made to give the ideas of the book some practical application.

This book is divided into four parts. Part 1 discusses community development, with Chapter 1 concerned with issues of definition and the imperatives that have driven the current interest in community development, and Chapter 2 outlining some aspects of community development theory and issues facing community development. This represents a particular approach to community development that is not necessarily reflected in other literature but which forms the basis for the analysis in later chapters. Chapter 2 ends with a discussion of seven dimensions of community development, which together comprise the holistic approach taken in this book. People familiar with community development will recognise much of the material in Part 1, though it may be less familiar to those coming to the book with a background in human rights.

Part 2 considers issues of human rights and is structured in the same way as Part 1. Again, it represents a particular view of human rights often at odds with the perspective of human rights in other literature. Chapter 3 deals with issues of definition and the imperatives for human rights, while Chapter 4 discusses issues and theory in relation to human rights and concludes with an identification of seven dimensions of human rights that mirror the seven dimensions of community development identified in Chapter 2. These two chapters may contain familiar material for the reader with experience in the human rights field, but will be less familiar to the reader coming from a primarily community development background.

Part 3 contains only one chapter, Chapter 5, which brings together the ideas of human rights and community development, identifying principles of an emerging 'human rights from below'.

The two chapters in Part 4 have a more practical orientation. They focus on the 'practice' of human rights from below, whether by paid community workers or by unpaid citizens. Chapter 6 examines the seven dimensions of community development and human rights, bringing together the ideas from earlier chapters, and Chapter 7 is concerned with a number of specific issues relating to 'practice'.

As with my previous books, I would be happy to receive feedback from any reader who wishes to engage in constructive dialogue about these issues. Those familiar with my previous work will notice that in a number of respects my ideas have changed, and they will undoubtedly continue to develop in the future. This book, like any product of intellectual work, remains very much a work-in-progress, a point on a journey rather than an arrival. Human rights and community development are fields where there are many questions and only tentative answers. It is only through dialogue that we will be able to find ways forward, to refine the questions, to ask new ones and to clarify some directions for further inquiry and practice.

Part 1
Thinking about community development

We must not be ashamed that we are capable of love, friendship, solidarity, sympathy and tolerance, but just the opposite: we must set these fundamental dimensions of our humanity free from their 'private' exile, and accept them as the only genuine starting point of meaningful human community.

Vaclav Havel, *Vaclav Havel: Open Letters*, p. 267

1

Definitions and imperatives of community development

DEFINITIONS

COMMUNITY

Although the word 'community' is commonly used and generally has positive connotations, the term itself is problematic. It is used in many ways (Bauman 2001, Chile 2007, Bryson & Mowbray 1981, Ife 2002, Ife & Tesoriero 2006, Kenny 2006). Before we start making sense of the idea of *community development*, therefore, we need to examine the idea of community itself. Just what is it that we are aiming to 'develop'? When we examine the following usages of the word 'community', we find that it conveys a variety of meanings:

- community care
- the Australian community
- a community centre
- widespread community debate
- the academic community
- the Google Earth community
- the Muslim community
- the needs of the local community
- consulting community representatives
- the global community
- community mental health
- community grassroots initiatives.

A word used in so many ways defies strict definition. It is more appropriate to think, instead, about all the meanings that it has in its different contexts. Ultimately, 'community' is subjective. It means what the person using the word decides it will mean. It is therefore important to look at this constellation of meanings.

The first thing to note is the positive connotations that the word 'community' has for us. Community is generally seen as a 'good thing': as something to be valued or desired. Although there can be no doubt that communities have been and can be oppressive, this negative view is usually far outweighed by the good feelings the word seems to generate. In part, these are associated with a nostalgic longing for a past that is felt to be more meaningful than one's present experience, such as one sees portrayed in idyllic TV costume dramas about village life or hears in the reminiscences of elderly relatives. This evocation of 'community' expresses a reaction to the perceived threats and emptiness of contemporary life and a wish for a certainty and a security that is imagined to have existed in times past.

This idealised past is far from the lived reality, of course. Those idyllic villages could impose a rigid conformity and could exclude the outsider or anyone who was thought to be too 'different'. Life in villages was not all friendship, nurturing, kinship and conviviality. For many it amounted to apparently endless toil with little reward and constant insecurity. People were always at the mercy of the weather, the feudal lord or master of the estate and armies that roamed the land and claimed the right to take food and pleasure as they wished (Samuel 1975).

Despite this, the vision and the hope conveyed by the ideal of 'community' remains strong. Loss of community may have brought the benefits of industrialisation, mobility and wealth at a level undreamed of by the villagers of yesteryear, but in the modern mind these benefits were purchased at a loss of something valuable in terms of personal relationships, collective responsibilities and social cohesion. A perceived emptiness and loss of meaning in modern industrial or post-industrial life has resulted in a longing for something which, while largely imaginary, is nonetheless a powerful vision and motivation (Bauman 2001). There is certainly a feeling that something called 'community' has been lost and that we are the poorer for it. We feel a need to rediscover, or more realistically to reconstruct, a stronger and more robust form of human community than is our current experience.

This idea of loss of community was a recurring theme in sociology in the twentieth century. Classical sociologists, most notably Tönnies (1955) and Durkheim (1933), took considerable trouble to trace the decline of traditional community and its replacement by a more atomised, individualistic and superficial form of society (in Tönnies' terms, from *gemeinschaft* to *gessellschaft* or, in Durkheim's, from *mechanical solidarity* to *organic solidarity*).

This sense of loss of something valuable called 'community', and the corresponding positive value associated with the word, has led to its being used indiscriminately to give a positive spin: for instance in 'community mental health', 'community corrections' and 'community service'. Governments, politicians and advertisers understand the power of the word and use it accordingly, often with little substantive meaning beyond the 'feelgood' factor (Bryson & Mowbray 1981, Craig 2007).

However, 'community' has more meaning than this. One of the meanings associated with it is the idea of the collective. 'Community' implies people acting together in some way as a group, and the whole meaning more than the sum of its parts. A community is not just a collection of individuals; those individuals are part of something bigger, which has meaning for them and for others. The idea of valuing the collective is somewhat at odds with the dominant individualism of modern post-industrial capitalist societies, but it has played an important part in the human experience throughout history and across all cultures. In this sense modern post-industrial capitalist societies are the exception rather than the rule. Collective consciousness, collective understandings, collective experiences and collective action are all important in other societies. Perhaps it is this understanding of the collective in contrast to individualism that is at the heart of the nostalgic wish to recreate the idealised communities of the past.

But community is evidently about more than simply the collective. There is, in most understandings of community, some idea of *membership* (Bauman 2001). This idea of membership is important. Membership implies not just a certain status but also rights, privileges and responsibilities, and some level of common purpose. To be a member of an organisation one normally has to agree to the aims and goals of that organisation, to undertake to not work against those aims, and to uphold the good name of that organisation. There is an implied level of commitment and a willingness to contribute in some way to the furthering of the organisation's goals. That the phrase 'member of a community' is so readily accepted suggests that the idea of membership is an important part of the construction of community. With membership goes a feeling of belonging, and this seems to be an important component of community. Often when people talk about the need for community they will cite the importance of this feeling of belonging; of a place where one is recognised and included (Ife 2002). These aspects of membership are important if we are to understand the symbolic significance of community in contemporary society.

Another common association of 'community' is an idea of human scale. The experience of community is seen as a corrective to the alienation and atomisation of the large-scale and impersonal structures of modern society. Society can just seem too big and too impersonal and there appears to be considerable appeal in the idea of something on a more human scale. Despite the apparent economic imperatives for things to happen on a large scale, the phrase 'small is beautiful', coined by E.F. Schumacher in the 1970s (Schumacher 1973), continues to resonate. Humans, after all, evolved as hunter-gatherers, and it could be argued that the small group necessary for the hunter-gatherer lifestyle is the most 'natural' form of human social interaction (Diamond 1998). Although it would be a mistake to pursue such a biological determinism too far, it is through small groups, whether based on the tribal group or on the extended family, that people have defined and realised their humanity throughout human history. The large industrial societies of the last century or so (predominantly only in the West) represent the exception rather than the norm. The persistent wish for things to happen at a more manageable, personal and 'human' scale is a powerful reason for the persistence of community as an ideal, and this forms an important part of the common construction of community.

The idea of community, therefore, has certain associations – the collective, mutual rights and responsibilities, membership and belonging, and human scale – which are generally seen as diminished within the context of modern (or postmodern) industrial (or post-industrial) societies but are positively valued. There are, however, some other issues associated with community that are more contentious.

One issue that will be explored in more detail in subsequent chapters is the multidimensional nature of community, which has inevitably led some community development workers to concentrate on some dimensions of community to the exclusion of others. Perhaps most notorious in this regard are the advocates of community economic development. While economic development is clearly important, there is sometimes a tendency for community economic development workers to assume that, so long as a community's economy is strong, everything else will somehow work out. This is a form of economic fundamentalism, familiar in the workings of global capitalism, which devalues other aspects of human and community experiences. In later chapters a multidimensional approach to community will be discussed, which incorporates the social, the political, the cultural, the environmental and the spiritual as well as the economic. The idea of human community, if it is to have value, should reflect these different aspects of the human experience. To concentrate on any single one to the exclusion of the others is to reduce community to a unidimensional experience.

It has long been common to draw a distinction between geographical communities, defined in terms of specific geographical location, and functional communities, where there is some non-geographical basis for the definition; for example, the Italian community, the Christian community or the business community (Ife 2002). In complex industrial or post-industrial societies, functional communities may be more significant for many people than are communities based on a town, village, suburb or region. Strong functional communities have been made possible by relatively easy mobility; people are no longer confined to a single geographical area but can travel to meet others with similar interests. At the time of writing it is becoming doubtful whether such high levels of personal mobility can be sustained in the future, as the likely rise in oil prices and the need to reduce carbon emissions significantly affects people's ability to travel as far and as often as they wish. This may well result in a re-emphasis on the local, and hence geographical communities may become more significant.

The other significant development is that of virtual communities, in which people are connected through the internet and may never have actually met face-to-face. The internet has made it possible for people with common interests to establish 'communities' even though they may be widely separated by physical distance. Such vastly dispersed communities are not a new phenomenon, however. Scientific communities are a good example of people forming a community despite wide physical separation, and these existed well before the development of the internet. They were connected through the mail, through reading and participating in exchanges published in scientific journals, and through occasional conferences. Other functional communities have also been maintained largely through the apparently ubiquitous newsletter. The internet, however, has made such community experiences widely available to many more people, and the ability to communicate and respond instantly through email, rather than waiting for conventional letters to be delivered or for newsletters to be mailed out, has allowed the new virtual communities to function in a way that was previously only possible in a face-to-face encounter. It has made communities that are not based on any geographical definition more viable and more numerous than ever before.

This rise of virtual communities has clear benefits. People are more able to participate in communities of interest without the limitations of travel. This has considerable advantages, especially for those with mobility problems, those who live in remote locations and those without ready access to transport. However, as with most technological innovations, it also has its problems. One of the advantages of geographical community is that it is potentially inclusive. Everyone has to live somewhere (even homeless people will live in a city, a town or a municipality) and so everyone has a legitimate claim to belong to a geographical community – in some cases, to more than one. Functional or virtual communities, however, can be exclusive and it is easier for people to be left out and marginalised, especially those without the necessary computer access or computer skills.

A further problem with virtual or functional communities is that they devalue a sense of place, or of connection to a physical locality. This assumes greater importance in a world where the environmental crisis has reached alarming proportions. If ever there was a time when people needed to feel a connection to the physical world, to a sense of place, it is surely now. Yet virtual communities enable people to have an experience of community that is removed from the physical world, and in which a sense of physical place can be completely absent. This is hardly conducive to a sense of obligation to care for one's environment and, as indigenous people the world over have insisted, it removes a vital component of our humanity (Knudtson & Suzuki 1992). For us to realise our full humanity, indigenous people will argue (and many non-indigenous people will agree), we need to feel a profound sense of belonging to the land and a connection to a specific place where we 'belong'. Later it will be argued that this represents an essential component of community; hence the virtual community experience not only discourages environmental awareness and responsibility but will only ever be a partial experience of human community.

For these reasons, it is important that the physical, geographical basis of community not be abandoned. Virtual communities and functional communities can be important for many people but, in the sense in which it is used in this book, the idea of 'community' will generally be treated as including some notion of physical location and of connection to the natural world.

Another important and contentious area is the issue of sameness and difference. It is usual for people to understand 'community' as implying that people are brought together by something they have in common. Community is perceived as being built around common characteristics, as a place where people can experience and reinforce the things they hold together. This is particularly true of functional communities, in which people have sought community membership on the basis of some common element, and also of communities built around a cultural identity.

While the motivation for such communities is obvious, it also needs to be pointed out that there are dangers around this tradition of building communities out of commonality. The most obvious of these dangers is the danger of exclusion. When a community is built around commonality, a person or a family that is different is likely to be excluded, formally or informally. This is particularly problematic where geographically based communities are organised around commonality. The locally based community that is proud of its history and its cultural heritage, and has worked hard to preserve and strengthen that heritage and sense of 'identity', is likely to reject and exclude a new arrival who is seen as somehow 'different': the refugee family, the person from a different religious faith, the person with a different ideology or the gay or lesbian couple, for instance. This is the basis for racism and other forms of discrimination, and for exclusion on the grounds of culture, of which there are all too many examples in contemporary Western societies. For a geographical community, the only thing that its members should be expected to have 'in common' is a connection to that particular locality; no other criteria for membership of the community should be required, formally or informally. (It is usually the informal exclusion of the 'other' that is the more common, and the harder to address, than the formal.)

Communities that are consciously and deliberately built around commonality are particularly dangerous at times of perceived crisis or risk. Such communities are likely to react against anything they see as a threat by reinforcing exclusivity and shutting out the stranger. They will seek security and comfort in the familiar and reject the unfamiliar as endangering their perceived community strength. This has been experienced at a national level in the popularity of 'border protection' and communities at the local level can react in similar ways, readily resorting to xenophobia, racism or scapegoating in response to the perceived threat that the stranger brings to their construction of their 'way of life'. For many social and political 'progressives' the idea of a strong community built on pride in cultural heritage is valued positively, while exclusion and border protection are criticised as dangerous and oppressive. Yet there is little difference between the two, and there is a natural and inevitable connection between strong communities built around commonality and the practice of exclusion and 'border protection'. Because of this, community development that fails to address issues of diversity and access can actually help to reinforce prejudice, racism and cultural arrogance.

Another problem with communities built on commonality is the danger of sterility. Where the experience of community is one of constant contact with people who are similar and familiar there is little room to grow or develop, as one is not exposed to new, different ideas and experiences that can challenge existing preconceptions and suggest alternatives. In such communities this constant reinforcement of the status quo can lead to a boring and static conformity – hardly the ideal environment for the full realisation of the human experience. There is little point in talking only to people who think the same way as we do. It may be comforting but we are unlikely to learn very much, and it will simply perpetuate already-existing stereotypes and world views.

For these reasons, there is a significant problem with the idea of building community around commonality and this needs to be addressed. It is important for communities to be open to change, to be able to accept and indeed welcome difference, to be inclusive rather than exclusive. Rather than building community on commonality or sameness, it is important to explore the building of community on difference. This has been emphasised by postmodern writers, who have stressed the significance of difference rather than sameness and have identified the Enlightenment origins of an obsession with sameness and uniformity (see for example Carroll 2004 and Kumar 1995, among many).

Following the thought of Jean-Luc Nancy (1991), communities built on difference can be far more resilient and viable than communities built on commonality. Indeed, for Nancy, ultimately the only thing we have in common is our difference. Instead of being something to avoid in communities, difference is something to be accepted, promoted and celebrated. It is out of our differences, rather than our similarities, that we will develop and grow. Strong communities must therefore be built on diversity rather than uniformity; must welcome the stranger because of what she or he can bring; and must include rather than exclude.

This in turn involves a questioning of the boundary around the community in line with the postmodern mistrust of clear categories and impermeable boundaries. For community development, the border needs to be problematised (Tascón 2009) and perceived as excluding. Instead of simply accepting conventional definitions of the boundaries of a community (including geographical communities), we need to see such borders as constructions that should be open to question and never regarded as settled. Above all, however the boundary of a community is constructed, there needs to be an emphasis on the permeability of that boundary so that both people and ideas from 'outside' are embraced rather than spurned.

Community, then, is a problematic concept that not only defies neat definition, but itself also requires critical reflection. Indeed, part of the process of community development is to reflect on the meaning of 'community' for the individuals and groups involved, rather than starting with a 'clear' definition of a 'community' that needs to be developed.

DEVELOPMENT

Like 'community', the word 'development' has positive connotations, though these are often counterbalanced by the poor reputation of many 'development projects' and the perception that a good deal of harm has been done in the name of 'development', especially in the so-called 'developing world'. However, these criticisms do not generally reflect on the positive value of development; rather they suggest that the way in which development has proceeded has been flawed. Such critique is usually accompanied by the advocacy of some alternative form of development, named variously 'sustainable development', 'appropriate development', 'people-centred development', 'bottom-up development', 'human scale development' and 'holistic development' (Peet & Hartwick 2009, Shiva 2005, van Ufford & Giri 2003). The idea of development, it seems, is almost universally valued, even though the way in which development has been implemented is widely criticised. However, this critique of the forms that development has taken suggests that development by itself is not sufficient to bring about a desired result. The way in which development is implemented is crucial, and in this sense there is a similarity with community. 'Community' too can have its negative manifestations, despite its generally positive connotations.

One of the key dimensions of development is the distinction between top-down development and bottom-up development (Ife 2002). The former is development that is directed by the 'experts': those with superior wisdom, knowledge and expertise, who have clear ideas about how development ought to proceed and who seek to implement development programs accordingly. Where the 'expert' comes from a cultural or national tradition that is different from that of the community, this top-down development is essentially colonialist in that the external expert knows best and seeks to impose their world view on others. However, top-down development can also operate from within a nation or culture; here the 'expert' may be a government agency or an NGO, which again assumes superior wisdom to that of those who are to be 'developed'. Such top-down development is in contrast to the bottom-up tradition, which recognises wisdom and expertise located in the community itself and seeks to validate that wisdom and to provide resources so that the pace and direction of development can be directed by those most affected.

Of course, most development projects are a mixture of both the top-down and the bottom-up. Many top-down projects acknowledge the importance of 'empowerment' and 'participation' of the people concerned, and similarly many bottom-up projects make use of external expertise, especially when that expertise is not available in the community itself. Some projects that claim to be bottom-up are in reality largely top-down: they can be constrained by management and accountability requirements, the need for demonstrated outcomes, the requirements of funding bodies, and so on. In such projects, talk of 'empowerment' and 'self-determination' is often empty rhetoric to disguise the top-down and essentially colonialist and exploitative nature of the development activity, and the 'participation' of the people is token consultation rather than genuine engagement.

It is partly the mix of top-down and bottom-up models that gives 'development' a bad name. Most if not all of the criticism of development is aimed at top-down approaches, which seek to impose on a community someone else's view of what is appropriate development and thereby deny people's right to self-determination and perpetuate structures of oppression and disadvantage. Such inappropriate and undemocratic top-down development takes its extreme form in the neoliberal programs of 'structural adjustment' imposed by the World Bank, the IMF and other apparent economic 'experts', often despite the express wishes of the people concerned – so much so that they can only be implemented with the help of military or security forces and the abuse of human rights (Klein 2007).

By contrast, bottom-up development is criticised less often. The most obvious criticism of bottom-up development is that it can seem haphazard and piecemeal because it tends to be process-driven rather than outcome-driven, and hence tends not to deliver clear, predetermined outcomes of the kind much favoured by managers. It also tends not to fit into previously determined time-frames required by funders. Participatory democracy can be messy and time-consuming, and from within the framework of modernity it can seem inefficient and unreliable. However, genuinely bottom-up development tends not to attract the same level of political criticism as does the top-down approach.

The issue of top-down and bottom-up development will be discussed in later chapters. It is central to understandings of *community* development, and it also has significant implications from a human rights perspective. It will be argued that one of the reasons why human rights has often been less than effective is that it has tended to adopt a top-down, legally driven approach rather than a bottom-up perspective, and that if we are to take a community development approach – implying the importance of bottom-up development – human rights, in both theory and practice, will be cast in a rather different light.

Another important issue in discussing the idea of development is the relationship between development and growth. Often, especially within economics, the two are used interchangeably, as if 'development' is simply another word for growth, or as if the achievement of growth implies that development has also been achieved. This is in part a consequence of economic rationalism or economic fundamentalism: when everything is seen purely in terms of economics, economic growth must be, by definition, a good thing, and so growth becomes a readily measurable criterion for determining the success of 'development'. Indeed, from this perspective, development would be impossible without growth. Within this world view it is easy to assume that growth equals development equals good, and hence to ignore the important differences in meaning between 'growth' and 'development' (Daly 1997).

This conflation of 'growth' and 'development' is particularly problematic at a time when ecological imperatives are requiring us to reconsider our previous attachment to growth, and to recognise that there are necessary limits to growth in a finite world (Meadows et al. 2004). Too much growth produces negative rather than positive consequences. These are plain to see in the impact of global warming, over-fished and increasingly polluted oceans, a crisis in the supply of clean water, the impending crisis of peak oil, the destruction of wilderness and the extinction of species.

It therefore becomes imperative that the idea of development be uncoupled from the idea of growth, and we need to be asking how development can proceed without growth (Daly 1997, McKibben 2008, Shiva 2005). That the two are different is obvious. In the human life cycle, for example, growth only occurs during the first two decades of life, but development (including intellectual, social, moral and cultural) can continue until the day we die. Growth can be equated with quantitative change – simply getting bigger; whereas development implies qualitative change – getting better – which can be transformative or renewing. While growth and development can go together, this is not a necessary or universal connection. Sometimes bigger is better, but at other times small is beautiful. Indeed, as was indicated above, the interest in 'community' represents in part a reaction to the negative consequences of growth when small communities were replaced by large-scale 'societies'. Development and community go together in a way that growth and community do not.

'Development' then, like 'community', is both problematic and contested. As with community, we will not attempt a clear, rational definition for the purposes of this book. As with community, the contested nature of the concept makes it an important focus for reflection in any community development process. Development can, and will, mean very different things in different contexts; what represents good development for one community may be bad development for another. Helping people to think about and define what 'development' means in their context is an important part of a community development process. Indeed, by the time a community group has reflected on what 'community' means for them, and then what 'development' means for them, a community development process may be well under way.

SOME ALTERNATIVE WORDINGS

There are four other terms that are sometimes used interchangeably with 'community development', but which carry subtle but important differences in the way they denote the idea of working with communities.

COMMUNITY ORGANISATION

In the United States, the term 'community organisation' has a long tradition. The dominant narrative of community organisation was established in a classic and much-cited typology by Rothman from the 1970s, which constructed community organisation as having three strands: locality development, social planning and social action (Rothman 1974; later editions added a fourth strand of policy/administration). The idea of community *organisation* gives a rather different emphasis from 'community development' as discussed here. With the emphasis on organisation, there is less natural inclination towards organic development and more emphasis on purposeful action towards clear outcomes. Rothman's typology further suggests that community development may be equivalent to 'locality development' and is therefore simply a subset of 'community organisation'; it is thus linked with social planning – with an inherently top-down perspective – and with social action. While community development as understood in this book can involve some aspects of both planning and activism, and indeed of 'organising', these two elements are seen here as subservient to the overall goal of *development*, and this is a reversal of the Rothman typology.

The tradition of organising comes in part from the labour movement. Labour organising was influential in the historical development of US community organisation, especially through the influence of Saul Alinsky

(1971). While this tradition has valuable contributions to make to understanding community development, and particularly community political development (see Chapter 2), it is a more limited and less holistic or organic concept than community development as discussed in this book.

COMMUNITY BUILDING

The term 'community building' is also sometimes used to describe working with communities. The use of the word 'building' implies a linear, ordered activity, in which one step comes after another as a cumulative process and something is gradually but steadily 'built'. This is a characteristic formulation from within modernity, with its search for order. It is in sharp contrast to the more postmodern experience of community development, which is characteristically messy, disordered and unpredictable, but rich in its diversity and disorder. The idea of community building has a connotation of 'putting the pieces together', as if messiness and chaos – the reality of community life – is to be resisted and ordered if possible.

COMMUNITY CAPACITY BUILDING

A variation on 'community building' that has become popular since the 1990s is 'community capacity building'. This term has been adopted in relation particularly to international development projects. The idea is that the development process is meant to 'build capacity' so that a community is better able to achieve its goals (James 2001, Plummer 2000, Smillie 2001). However, the language also changes the meaning (Craig 2007). The word 'capacity' carries with it an idea of what the community is supposed to accomplish. The outcome is implicitly defined; the role of community work is then to help build the 'capacity' for this to be reached. Without some implicit notion of that outcome the idea of 'capacity' is meaningless, as every community has capacity for many different things, including self-destruction, exclusive border protection, fragmentation, racism, violence and oppression of minorities; presumably these are not the 'capacities' that are meant to be 'built'. This implicit assumption of outcome is contrary to the idea of community development. Also, despite the rhetoric that is commonly associated with community capacity building, it can too readily lead to a deficit approach to community, which concentrates on the weaknesses or deficits of a community – where 'capacity' is lacking – as opposed to a strengths perspective that seeks to build on the strengths that are present in any community (McCashen 2004).

SOCIAL ENTREPRENEURSHIP

The more recent movement for 'social entrepreneurship' (Bornstein 2004, Nicholls 2006) has resulted in the reformulation of community development using the vocabulary of private enterprise, adopting a set of ideas about ways of working that are very different, and which rest on a different value base. While there may be some commonalities between community development workers and entrepreneurs, such as creativity, flexibility and commitment, the aims of the two are not the same. Entrepreneurs are concerned with making money and individual profit, while community development workers are concerned with the interests of the community. Social entrepreneurship rests on the assumption that ideas and skills from the business community can be usefully applied to community development and that people from the private sector, or at least using a private sector model, can improve outcomes for communities. To use the vocabulary of one and apply it to the other is misleading, confusing and potentially dangerous, and can undermine the very essence of community development.

CONCLUSION

In summary, language is important. The language of capacity building, social entrepreneurship, community organisation and community building therefore carries with it certain assumptions about the world in which it is practised (Craig 2007). To move from the language of community development to the language of these other terms thus involves a subtle shift to a language, and hence a world view, more consistent with the outcomes-driven, ordered, managerial approach of modernity, and carries with it the danger of betraying some of the most important characteristics of community development theory and practice as understood in this book.

IMPERATIVES

The generalised feeling of loss of community, as discussed in the previous section, has long represented a strong imperative for community development. If community development can indeed re-establish a sense of community and of belonging in some human-scale group, then it is naturally regarded as an important and worthwhile approach. However, there are other imperatives for community development that make it a particularly attractive proposition at the present time.

One such imperative is the perceived need for more human-scale activity as a basis for human services, including health, education, housing, income security and personal services (Ife & Tesoriero 2006). The large, impersonal welfare state has proved to be alienating for both service recipients and service providers alike. This was part of the impetus for privatisation, but market-based human services have also proved to be problematic in that they can exacerbate rather than ameliorate social and economic inequality, and services delivered by large bureaucratic private sector organisations are scarcely less impersonal and alienating than services delivered by government. The apparent 'customer focus' of the private sector is often more myth than reality. The primary concern of the private sector is necessarily for shareholders rather than for customers, and the profit motive means that the relationship with the customer inevitably has an element of exploitation, however much this may be disguised by 'customer focus'. In such a relationship, altruism and genuine care for another human being will necessarily be devalued, and this is felt by those receiving the service. Indeed in this context the term 'service' is a misnomer, as it becomes a commodity or 'product' to be purchased rather than a service to be given.

Because of these perceived inadequacies of both state-provided and market-provided human services, there has been an ongoing attraction to the idea of human services being located within a human community. This suggests that the problem is neither the market nor the state, but rather that both have tended to involve top-down delivery of 'services' by large and often impersonal organisations, causing the person receiving the service, whether labelled 'customer' or 'consumer', to feel relatively powerless and to have little sense of agency.

The need for services to be delivered at a human scale has led to an interest in 'community-based' services and the fact remains that you cannot have community-based services unless there is a strong and viable community in which those services can indeed be 'based'. Hence community development becomes a necessary component of the move towards community-based human services. As will be explored in later sections, some professionals engaged in human services have found that a community development perspective can be a significant basis for the way services can be delivered.

In this regard, it is not surprising that many people who practise community development come from a background of human services, including health workers, social workers, teachers and recreation workers. While this has undoubtedly brought much richness to community development, too close an identification of community development with human services can lead to a narrowing of community development and a devaluing of other disciplines and perspectives. As an example, in the USA, Canada, Australia and New Zealand (though less so elsewhere), community development has been regarded as simply one aspect of social work, along with casework, group work and other activities such as policy and administration. It is therefore seen as a subset of social work, and this can restrict a community development worker with a social work background in taking a broader perspective and seeing community development as encompassing more than human services. Community development can be an important basis for human services, but it is also about much more than just human services and extends into other areas of the human experience. In this book human services will be seen as a subset of community development, rather than *vice-versa*.

Another impetus for community development comes from the evident failure of the global economy to meet local needs. Many local communities are not well served by the global economy, which may simply extract wealth from the local community, which is then expropriated as profits for shareholders who may be on the other side of the world, or who may see no value in a local community and will simply bypass it altogether. This has led to an interest in establishing stronger community-based local economies, either through the encouragement of local enterprise or through locally based barter or currency systems (Meeker-Lowry 1996, Shragge 2000). Such community economic development has a different tradition from the human service-based development discussed above, and represents a very different strand of the imperative for community development. However, in a world so dominated by the economic, it is particularly significant in driving the movement for reinvigorating local communities.

A further strand of the impetus for community development comes from community cultural development. This has several sub-strands. One is the importance that can be attached to a particular community being proud of its cultural heritage and wishing to express that as part of its identity. This is particularly so with indigenous communities, or with communities of people from particular ethnic or national backgrounds that are perceived to be different from the 'mainstream'. Another sub-strand of cultural development has been the perceived importance of cultural expression – art, music, dance, theatre, storytelling – in the life of a community, and the recognition that this is so often missing because of the commodification of culture. When cultural experience is confined to buying a DVD or CD, watching a movie, going to a concert, watching TV or listening to an iPod, it becomes passive consumerism. A move to community cultural development seeks to emphasise the importance of active participatory cultural experiences as an important component of our humanity.

A third strand of community cultural development is the emphasis on inclusive communities: community as the site for the acceptance and inclusion of refugee families, for example. This leads to the valuing of cultural diversity as being important for newly emerging cosmopolitan visions of a good society, and hence the valuing of culturally diverse and inclusive communities as the basis for this.

Another important imperative for community development comes from reaction to the ecological crisis, which has now become evident across a number of issues such as global warming, peak oil, water supplies, food shortages and toxic pollution. A number of writers have argued that an adequate response to these ecological crises must include decentralisation, localisation and the revitalisation of local communities (for example see Hines 2000, Hopkins 2008, Mander & Goldsmith 1996).

It has become clear that the easy personal mobility that those in the affluent West have come to enjoy through the use of the motor car and frequent and low-priced air travel is unsustainable and will be soon brought to an end by peak oil and the consequent rise in fuel prices (Hopkins 2008, Roberts 2004). Similarly, the ready transport of all kinds of goods, including food, over long distances from production to point of sale is also unsustainable and increasingly unaffordable. While alternative fuels and energy sources may make some difference, it appears unlikely that the days of really low-cost transport, whether of people or of goods, will ever return. Inevitably, things will need to be produced and consumed locally.

This will represent a major shift in the nature of economics, but also in the kind of social relations that accompany economic activity. An increase in local activity at a community level has not only been advocated by writers from the ecological tradition as an important development; it is also increasingly being seen as a necessity for survival. In this context, local communities and community development become a major priority in thinking about the future in a world beyond the oil economy and beyond carbon emissions.

Another imperative for community development comes from a more anarchistic tradition. This is the perspective that mistrusts top-down structures and hierarchies and emphasises the capacity of people at the grassroots level to take charge of their own destiny. This resonates with much popular mistrust of 'them': those who are seen to be in authority and who more often than not seem to make stupid decisions because of their lack of connection to 'the real world' or the 'real' problems of 'real' people. These sentiments can be found regularly expressed in the popular media, on talkback radio and in similar forums.

The anarchist tradition, however, has a more solid intellectual background than a simplistic mistrust of 'them'. There is a long tradition of anarchist writers who have argued that the imposition of structures from above denies the expression and realisation of our true humanity, and that such structures should be minimised or dismantled (Marshall 1992). This tradition has been important for different political ideologies. The 'new right' ideology of Thatcherism argued for the dismantling of the state so that free market forces could be allowed to flourish and individual choice could predominate over central government decree. There is also a strong tradition of anarchist thought from the left arguing, contrary to Stalinism, that justice and equality can only be achieved if the weight of state domination is lifted from people's lives (Marshall 1992). Anarchist writing also resonates with some strands of green ideology, especially through the writing of Thoreau (1983). A community development approach fits naturally with this anarchist tradition, a tradition that quietly celebrates whenever those in authority make a mess of something, and that seeks to enhance grassroots activism and empowerment.

At a more theoretical level, community development is very consistent with a postmodern approach that critiques the 'one size fits all' ordered meta-narratives of modernity and seeks instead to accept chaos, messiness, confusion and contradiction (Kumar 1995, Seidman 1994). While modernity encourages conformity in its heroic quest to fit everything into a single unifying system, postmodernity values and celebrates diversity. Such a postmodern view is much more consistent with the diversity of different communities, and indeed within communities, as discussed in the previous section in relation to communities of difference. In this sense, we can understand the continuing interest in community development as a reaction to modernity and as a search for ways to move beyond the certainty and order of modernity to a more organic and diverse, though less predictable, future. We will return to postmodernism in later chapters.

Alongside these apparently positive or progressive influences towards community development, it is important also to mention three that are perhaps less benign. One is the tendency for governments, aware of budgetary limitations and the apparently unending demands on the state, to use 'the community' and community development as an excuse for either reducing public services or for not increasing them to keep pace with demand or need. Relying on 'the community sector', accompanied by persuasive rhetoric drawing on the positive connotations of the word 'community', governments can use the justification: 'This service is better provided by the community than by government.' In reality, this means relying on voluntary labour, or the poorly paid workers of 'the community sector', to do the work that governments perhaps ought to do themselves, but which would cost more if it was incorporated into the public sector. The argument in favour of community development – that things are generally better done at a community level if possible – can readily be applied by governments as an excuse to avoid, at least in part, their responsibility for the provision of human services. Thus governments can advocate community development for less than fully noble reasons.

Another less desirable motivation for community development is its capacity for control. Community development, or at least a bastardised form of it, can be used to control rather than to empower a community. The experience of token consultation is perhaps the classic example of such control: apparently participatory and consultative community processes that in fact are used to give an already taken decision the appearance of democratic participation. Using community development as a form of control is particularly significant in the international arena, where 'community development' can become a way of driving a colonial agenda. The external 'experts' come into a community to control a set of community processes that are really designed to lead to a specific outcome that is in the interests of the external body, whether this is a government, a corporation or an NGO, rather than in the interests of the community itself. When processes are owned or controlled by external agents, the danger of colonialist control is very real; this will be further discussed in later chapters.

A third questionable imperative for community development comes specifically from the private sector. There has been a lot of interest in 'partnerships' between the private sector and the community sector, and this has in some places led to the corporatisation of community development. While there may be some benefits from such partnerships, the concern is that they are all too often an excuse for the imposition on the community sector of a particular ideology, with its inherent managerialism and profit motive, that is not really compatible with community development, at least in the form in which it will be discussed in later chapters.

There are, then, a number of imperatives for community development and the motives for advocating community development programs are mixed. Hence community development has taken several different paths in different contexts. Community economic development, for example, has tended to be separate from community cultural development, and these are different again from community development inspired by a vision of local ecological sustainability. While one may see such diversity of approaches as advantageous, it is perhaps also unfortunate that this tendency for community development to proceed along different paths, with different vocabularies, has led to a fragmented approach and has worked against a more holistic understanding of what community development might be. This sort of holistic approach would emphasise how these various strands of community cannot be understood in isolation and would seek to emphasise their connectedness. It is such a holistic approach that is behind the vision of community development that is discussed in the next chapter.

2 | Principles and dimensions of community development

PRINCIPLES

As WE SHALL SEE, the very nature of community development precludes specific 'how to' procedures for 'doing' community development. However, it is certainly possible to derive a number of higher-level *principles* which, while not being narrowly prescriptive, can nevertheless provide a framework within which community development takes place.

The perspective on community development outlined in this book is not necessarily shared by other writers. Specifically, the approaches to community development based on predetermined outcomes, top-down planning or program implementation and step-by-step processes are incompatible with the more organic and 'from below' perspective developed here.

Community development can be regarded as a way of thinking, as a philosophy of practice, rather than merely as a process for building stronger communities. In this sense, many people who are not specifically labelled 'community development' workers can still work from a community development perspective. Health professionals, teachers, development workers, social workers, lawyers, recreation workers, artists, planners, librarians and researchers are just some of the occupational groups that can, and in many cases do, work from a community development perspective by incorporating some or all of the principles discussed below into their work. Similarly, community members who may be out of the workforce for a variety of reasons (unemployed, retired, parenting or caring for a relative) or who may be employed in jobs that have nothing to do with community development, can still engage with their community according to these principles and can play key roles in community development. The approach to community development outlined below is not restricted to 'community workers'; it is potentially for everybody.

It must also be recognised that the discussion below is not a thorough or exhaustive treatment of community development principles. Rather it is a brief survey of the territory so as to ground the later discussion of human rights and community development. Readers wishing to pursue these principles in more detail are referred to more extensive texts on community development, which explore the issues in more detail than is possible here (Ife 2002, Ife & Tesoriero 2006, Kenny 2006).

BOTTOM-UP DEVELOPMENT

The distinction between top-down development and bottom-up development is obvious. Community development as understood in this book is clearly a bottom-up process. It is based on a premise that local knowledge, wisdom, skills and understandings are necessary for the experience of human community, and need to be valued above top-down wisdom and experience. This may sound like a simple principle but, in the context of modern industrial society and its manifestation in modernity, it is a radical position. Organisations are typically structured on a bureaucratic model, which assumes that superior wisdom resides at the top of the hierarchy, or at the centre rather than at the periphery, and that it is the implementation of this superior wisdom that is the task of political, administrative and community processes.

This is reinforced by the dominance of managerialism: the view that sees good management as the secret to effective organisations, whether those organisations be government departments, corporations, prisons, universities, hospitals, sporting clubs, political parties, churches or communities (Considine & Painter 1997, Rees & Rodley 1995). Managerialism holds that any problems these organisations may experience can be resolved by good management; hence its obsession with organisational restructure, the appointment of yet more managers and apparently endless rounds of planning.

The top-down perspective is very powerful and is characteristic of modernity with its search for certainty, order and predictability, even though the world in which it operates is characterised by unpredictability and chaos. To impose order on chaos and to impose predictability on uncertainty requires a level of control, and often coercion, that can stifle individual or group creativity and initiative. It is the antithesis of community development, where such initiatives 'from below' are not only allowed, but are encouraged.

The notion of bottom-up development is at the heart of community development and is related to some of the other principles below, which simply spell out what this over-arching principle of bottom-up development can mean in practice. It is a simple principle, but one that challenges many of the taken-for-granted assumptions of modernity.

VALUING WISDOM, KNOWLEDGE AND SKILLS 'FROM BELOW'

Valuing the wisdom, knowledge and skills of community members is an essential part of bottom-up development. Too often people feel that their experience and wisdom are marginalised or denied by those who, because of their position, claim to 'know better'. Community development will always try first to find wisdom, knowledge and skills in the community itself; only if these are lacking in the community will there be any attempt to find wisdom elsewhere. This is in contrast to the 'get a consultant' mentality, which is all too common. There can be an important role for the external consultant, but not if it means devaluing the expertise that is in the community already.

Local knowledge will be contextualised in a way that external expertise can never be. The people of a community will know more about what is feasible and what is not, what will offend and what will not, and what is likely to work best. This local knowledge is necessary if community processes are to work or be effective (Hines 2000, Shiva 2005). The construction of knowledge as universal, applying everywhere regardless of context, may be appropriate for the laws of physics, chemistry or biology, but not for processes that are located in, and influenced by, culture, place, history and tradition (Midgley 2001). Indeed, the effect of applying knowledge as if it is universal and context-free not only produces solutions that do not work very well, but also marginalises and devalues the knowledge, wisdom and expertise of local people. The very way in which knowledge is commonly understood – as timeless and context-free truths that are learned in a university – has significant impacts on people's lives and is a major cause of disempowerment. This is another way in which community development, a non-problematic concept on the surface, is in fact quite radical. It challenges conventional wisdom about what should count as legitimate knowledge and it requires a significant reconstruction of the nature of expertise.

This is not to say that there is no role for external knowledge or skills. There will certainly be occasions where such external expertise is necessary. However, a community development perspective requires that local expertise should always be the first, and preferable, option and that external expertise should only be called on where the necessary expertise is not available locally. This is in contrast to the more conventional top-down situation, where external expertise is valued first and local expertise is only allowed to contribute either through a process of 'consultation' (more often than not an exercise in tokenism) or where local views are forced on the planners, managers and politicians by concerted citizen activism. In each case the local voice is reacting, rather than initiating, driving or setting the agenda; that agenda is set elsewhere and the local role is simply to react to a process that has been set up by others.

SELF-RELIANCE, INDEPENDENCE AND INTERDEPENDENCE

A related principle is self-reliance. The idea of self-reliance has been appropriated by the ideological right as a way of justifying the withdrawal of state services and of blaming individuals for their misfortune. This, however, is a highly individualised form of self-reliance. In a community development context, the idea of self-reliance is applied to communities rather than to individuals. Consistent with the idea of valuing expertise from below, self-reliance suggests that a community should where possible seek to rely on its own resources rather than becoming dependent on other communities or on some central authority. This, indeed, is advocated by writers from within green political theory, according to which relatively independent, self-reliant communities are seen to be more sustainable (Bryant 1995, Carter 1999, Hines 2000, Hopkins 2008).

Thus ideas of self-reliance and independence become reconstructed within community development as values that need to applied to communities rather than to individuals. When applied to individuals, self-reliance and independence become the cornerstones of capitalism and are consistent with the increasingly atomised society that so many people find alienating. Rather than advocating independence at an individual level, it is important to emphasise our *interdependence*, as in reality we are all dependent on each other in a myriad of ways, including the economic, the social, the cultural, the political and the material. The isolated autonomous individual, despite being the basic unit of economic theory, is a myth; community development not only recognises but affirms, celebrates and encourages interdependence among people.

At a community level, however, the value of self-reliance becomes more possible and more significant. It is impossible for any community to be totally independent and autonomous, but communities that lack a level of self-reliance can become economically, socially, politically, culturally and environmentally disadvantaged. There is therefore a clear distinction to be made between the individual experience and the community experience, and the values of autonomy and self-reliance apply much more to communities than to individuals. Fully self-reliant *individuals* are effectively an impossibility, but in a future characterised by uncertainty, crisis and the failure of the state, self-reliant *communities* become a necessity.

ECOLOGY AND SUSTAINABILITY

Ever since the publication of the Brundtland Report in 1987 (World Commission on Environment and Development 1987) the terms 'sustainability' and 'sustainable' have become so overused and abused that they have lost much of their meaning. That politicians and economists continually talk about 'sustainable growth', which is clearly a nonsense in a finite world, indicates the extent to which the idea of sustainability has been bastardised for political purposes. The adjective 'sustainable' is frequently used in conjunction with both 'community' and 'development'. This suggests that the term, despite its problems, has to be a central concept for the purposes of our discussion.

To assert that community development must be sustainable requires a longer-term perspective. It involves thinking about the future beyond the next few years and seeking to ensure that whatever community development takes place can be sustained in a longer time-frame. This requires care with the use of physical resources, especially those that are non-renewable, and means that community development must have a consciousness of the physical environment within which it operates and the limits that this environment imposes. It also requires the establishment of processes and structures that can be maintained, not just in the short term as a response to immediate imperatives but also in the longer term. For this to happen, there must be flexibility and the capacity for adaptation, and a willingness to look at likely futures and the challenges that they will pose.

The need for sustainability has been brought about by the imperatives of the ecological crisis. Rather than trying to define the increasingly meaningless term 'sustainable', it is preferable to look at an ecological perspective and what a more ecological understanding of the world implies within a community context. An ecological perspective incorporates a number of subsidiary principles such as holism, diversity, organic change and the importance of equilibrium (Ife 2002). These are reflected in the discussion below. However, one of the most important principles of sustainability, and of the ecological perspective, is the harmfulness of growth. The ecological crisis has brought home the reality that we live in a finite world, with finite resources and a finite capacity to absorb the by-products of human activity, and that in such a world growth without end is an impossibility.

Yet growth is a fundamental value of modern capitalism. Industries must grow, populations must grow, consumption must grow, profits must grow, incomes must grow, and in general there is an equation of growth with health and prosperity. 'Sustainable growth', despite its apparent attractiveness to economists and politicians, is surely an oxymoron in a finite world, and the value of sustainability clearly challenges our obsession with growth at all costs. However, despite increasing evidence that growth beyond a certain level has negative rather than positive outcomes, that more is not necessarily better and that owning and consuming more is no guarantee of increased happiness (Hamilton 2003), it appears that the human worship of growth, at least in Western countries, is still an ingrained habit and one that seems likely to lead to disaster as the limits to growth are reached and then exceeded (Meadows et al. 2004).

These issues of sustainability and the ecological crisis are the greatest challenges facing humanity at the start of the twenty-first century. They raise critical questions and require a radical rethinking of the nature of human activity and of the relationship between humans and the natural world (Macy 2007, Shiva 2005, Spratt & Sutton 2008). For this reason an awareness of them is vital for community development. In the views of a number of writers, community development can indeed be part of the solution (see, for example, Hines 2000). It is more likely that these challenges can be adequately addressed if there are strong and viable human communities, seeking and evolving a diversity of sustainable approaches to living together while treading lightly on the earth.

DIVERSITY AND INCLUSIVENESS

As we discussed earlier, the tradition of basing community on commonality can be questioned, and the idea of basing community on diversity seems much more robust and enriching (Nancy 1991). An important ecological principle is that of diversity. It is from diversity that we grow and develop, and it is diversity that enables us to be exposed to other ideas, other world views, other cultures and other practices.

How we handle diversity represents a major test of any society, nation, culture or world view. Diversity is at the same time exciting and threatening. It opens up possibilities for growth and development, but it also opens up possibilities of danger and the 'shock of the new', with the potential to undermine our security and our familiarity. Too often a society will react by seeking to eliminate diversity, or by keeping the threatening stranger at arm's length; sometimes it will amount to active persecution. Fear of diversity can be used by politicians to create a feeling of insecurity and a corresponding wish to vote for the party that will offer reassurance by keeping the stranger away. The fear of diversity is an all-too-common experience. We have seen it in Nazi Germany, Apartheid South Africa, border protection policies, action against immigrants (especially those deemed 'illegal'), persecution of the Roma in Europe, conflict in the Middle East, tribal conflicts in Africa, oppression of indigenous people in many countries, and Islamophobia in the United States and other Western nations.

All these examples leave the majority nation or group poorer and meaner, and at the same time oppress and disadvantage the scapegoated group. The resentment, anger and suspicion thus created can last for generations. It can have many unfortunate consequences, not the least of which is terrorism, which only reinforces feelings of insecurity and threat, thereby continuing a cycle of fear and exclusion.

If community development is to be the site for the renewal of humanity, it must not merely tolerate and accept diversity, but must actively promote and celebrate it. Rather than accepting the bland assurance that 'in unity is strength', it is necessary to build community development around the understanding that 'in diversity is strength'. This requires an approach that is based on inclusiveness rather than exclusiveness: an approach that welcomes the stranger as someone worthy of acceptance and as someone who can enrich rather than threaten the community, and that welcomes and encourages dialogue and mutual learning.

The principle of diversity applies not only within communities but also between communities. It suggests that communities should not try to be the same as each other; rather that the differences should be positive and allow for communities to learn from each other's experiences. As a community follows its own development path, there is no reason why it should try to be like any other community, though there is obviously value in learning from the experience of others and applying those lessons in one's own context.

One of the legacies of modernity has been the pursuit of sameness, the view that there must be one right or best way to do things (often called 'best practice'). This can lead to boring uniformity as managers and politicians try desperately to fit everyone, and every community, into the same mould: a one-size-fits-all community development. By valuing and promoting diversity, community development stands against that world view of modernity and instead seeks the greater richness, though also the greater unpredictability, of difference.

THE IMPORTANCE OF PROCESS

One of the most important principles of community development is the valuing of process. This is directly contradictory to the emphasis on outcomes that is so dominant in Western managerial thinking. Many social programs are now defined exclusively in terms of their outcomes rather than their processes. It is results that are important, and how they are achieved is immaterial. The world of targets, deliverables, outcomes, performance indicators and so on devalues process. Much managerial language is even couched in military terms, which treat the process as some kind of battle involving 'strategy', 'tactics', 'campaigns', obstacles that need to be overcome, and a struggle that has to be endured if we are to reach our goal. The pervasiveness of this perspective can be seen in the way these military metaphors are so often adopted in community development, where one would have hoped the process would be very different.

Such a perspective makes a clear distinction between means and ends. In this world view it is the ends that are important, and the ends justify the means. The choice of means is to be determined by criteria such as efficiency and effectiveness; the aim is to achieve the goal by whatever means is most cost-effective. Means, or process, becomes devalued.

Such a split between means and ends is both flawed and dangerous. It is flawed because the distinction is never clear cut. Means can become ends, and ends can become means to further ends. Is 'democracy', for example, an end in itself or simply the means to achieve a peaceful and prosperous society? The same question could be asked of 'the free market', 'sustainable communities', 'free and independent media' or 'human rights'.

The distinction between means and ends is dangerous because it can lead to the choice of means being only a rational, 'objective' choice, using criteria of efficiency and cost benefit, and with values confined to the choice of ends. Thus the ends are determined through a political process in which values and ideology play an important role, but the choice of means is taken out of the political debate and left to the technical experts. The fallacy of such an approach is seen in economics: important decisions that affect people's lives are deliberately removed from the arena of public debate and left to the 'expert' economists (who frequently disguise their debates with jargon that is impenetrable to many) and the governors of independent central banks. This is done because these decisions are seen as instrumental, as concerning means (the end being economic prosperity, however that is defined) and therefore the realm of the technical expert.

In contrast to this view of the separation of means and ends, the Gandhian tradition emphasises the linking of means and ends and maintains that the two cannot be separated (Gandhi 1964, see also Fay 1975). From this perspective, the means is as important as the end, and the end does not necessarily 'justify' the means. Corrupt means are not acceptable, even if they lead to a worthy end, and corrupt means will inevitably corrupt the end as well. This is in line with the Kantian tradition of valuing humans as ends and never only as means (Appelbaum 1995), as opposed to the utilitarian view (simplistically characterised as 'the greatest good for the greatest number'), which readily justifies dubious means if they lead to a desired end (Goodin 1995). This tension between Kantian philosophy and utilitarianism is at the heart of many debates in the area of human rights, and it will be discussed in Chapter 4.

The approach to community development taken in this book rejects the justification of means on the basis of ends and takes a more Gandhian approach that sees means and ends as necessarily linked, and insists that the choice of means is itself significant. In community development terms, this position implies an emphasis on process. Indeed, for community development the process is more important than the outcome. Community development is essentially about process. It holds that, if a community is able to embark on a process of self-determination in which people are actively involved in determining the direction they wish to go, and involving the genuine participation of all, there is no need for predetermined goals, objectives, targets or outcomes. These will emerge naturally from the process and, if the process is sound, the outcomes will also be sound.

Thus the idea of process is critically important for community development. It is the process rather than the outcome that is the focus of community work. The role of the community worker is not 'to ensure a good outcome' but rather to ensure a good process. Most of the principles of community development therefore relate to process rather than outcome, and one of the most important lessons for community development workers is to 'trust the process', which is not always an easy thing to do when a community seems to be moving in a different direction from the one that the community worker sees as ideal.

However, this does not mean that outcomes can be ignored. To the extent that outcomes become processes (ends becoming means to further ends), they are themselves important. There is also the issue of what happens when an outcome is unacceptable on the grounds of ethics or human rights (for instance, if a community develops processes that entrench racism and exclude the outsider). This will be considered in later sections. (It is, in fact, one of the reasons for bringing human rights and community development together in this book.)

ORGANIC CHANGE

A natural consequence of the emphasis on process is the idea of organic change. This can best be described by analogy with the natural world, where change takes place slowly and on a number of dimensions at once, as in the growing of a plant, the aging of a human, the evolution of a species or the growth of an embryo. It is true that sudden and catastrophic changes also occur in nature, such as earthquakes and volcanoes, but these are relatively rare.

It is steady organic change that is the norm: a number of small, incremental events on a number of fronts that together result in both qualitative and quantitative change. Such an approach to change is in contrast to single-event radical change, where a single action brings about major (and often catastrophic) outcomes. Community development, because of its process orientation, is more consistent with notions of organic change, and it is often a reaction against sudden radical change (such as a proposed freeway through a community) that can most readily motivate community-level action.

Sudden radical change, of course, is sometimes necessary or unavoidable, as happens when the challenges are posed by climate change and peak oil (Hopkins 2008, Roberts 2004, Spratt & Sutton 2008). In such cases major change is required with very little time for it to be achieved, and then community development processes can be easily compromised. However, if a community has been made aware of the importance of these issues (as is the case with many community groups; for example, climate action groups), a community development response involving more sustainable and low-consumption lifestyles becomes feasible.

This perspective on change may appear to be conservative, and in the true sense of conservatism – valuing what is, and seeking incremental rather than radical change – this is largely true. However, this does not mean that significant change is impossible with community development. On the contrary, it can be argued that it is only through community development processes that such significant change can be achieved without disastrous human (and other) consequences. The important point is that community development insists on the importance of process in implementing change. This process involves the active, genuine and informed participation of all and is likely to proceed in incremental steps. It can be argued that, accepting the necessary link between means and ends, ecological change cannot be achieved unless the methods employed to reach it are themselves ecologically sound. Seeking to impose ecological change through a non-ecological process would be doomed to failure.

An important consequence of this approach to change is that community development processes cannot be hurried. The expectation of quick and immediate, or at least time-specified, outcomes is characteristic of the modern managerial approach. This does not sit well with community development, since it could bring about a fatal compromising of process. It is one of the reasons why a community development approach is often not favoured by policy-makers. Community development must be allowed to take its course and cannot be circumscribed by deadlines. To use the phrase often ascribed to indigenous processes, 'it takes as long as it takes'. Good community development cannot be rushed. Community development in this sense is perhaps more consistent with the 'slow movement', which maintains that we live our lives at too fast a pace and need to slow down to achieve more (Honoré 2005). Of course in reality there are often compromises that need to be made in this regard, such as when there is a deadline that has to be met, but this does not negate the importance of the principle. When things need to be rushed beyond their 'natural' pace it needs to be remembered that this is done at a cost.

PARTICIPATION

Participation is a key feature of community development. Community development processes can only operate if there is a high level of genuine participation by community members, however they may be defined. Nevertheless, participation has been particularly problematic for community development (Stiefel & Wolfe 1994). Many community workers have found it difficult to achieve high levels of participation, and all too often 'community processes' involve only a small number of people.

There are several reasons why participation is problematic. The first is the dominant discourse of individual consumerism, which suggests that happiness is to be found in the role of private consumer rather than in public action. There is a tendency to see community participation as a duty, something that we 'ought' to do; something that takes us away from the preferable joys of the flat-screen TV, the computer game or the iPod rather than something that is enjoyable and has its own rewards. Despite the strong rhetoric about the benefits to be gained from community participation, the world of the private passive consumer is marketed as the way we can best achieve our true humanity. In the light of such strong pressure, low levels of community participation are understandable.

Another problem is that much of what happens in the name of participation is little more than tokenism. Often this takes the form of 'community consultation' when there is already a well-worked-out proposal and the 'consultation' is simply to gauge what level of opposition there may be and to attempt to placate angry opponents. People can readily see through such games and every experience of such sham participation makes it less likely that they will bother to show up next time. For participation to work, people must have a genuine opportunity for meaningful input, and this must be clearly evident.

A further reason why participation is so problematic is that too often the form of expected participation excludes people. Typically, the public meeting held in the evening at the town hall is a good forum for articulate, confident people with few family commitments who are readily able to attend the meeting and who are comfortable speaking in that environment. It effectively excludes those who are not confident speaking in public, those who are not fluent in the dominant local language and those who cannot easily attend a meeting at that time, perhaps because of lack of affordable child care. It is necessary for a community worker to think beyond the public meeting and to recognise that there are other ways for people to participate: morning coffee sessions, story-telling groups, blogs, engagement with cultural expression (such as singing, dancing, theatre or art), sporting clubs, service clubs and informal groups or networks.

Participation, in fact, should extend beyond a specific task to include all aspects of community life. A healthy community is an active, participatory community where many people can participate in different ways. The person who makes the tea for supper after a community meeting is as important as the chairperson of the meeting, and can be seen to be making an equally significant contribution to the community. Recognising that there are many ways to participate, and valuing all of them, results in a community that is active and engaged and moves away from the uni-dimensional approach to participation that characterises much traditional community work thinking.

Related to the question of participation are ideas of *participatory democracy*. Although democracy is an ideal that is highly valued in most societies, the experience of democracy is very limited (Held 2006, Saward 1998). For the most part, democracy is equated to some form of *representative* democracy, where we elect our leaders every few years and then leave them to get on with the job unless we particularly object to something, in which case we may be roused to some form of protest. The role of the citizen is therefore largely passive, and active only in opposition.

By contrast, ideas of *participatory* democracy include a much more active role for the citizen. Here people have an active role in decision-making and, as a consequence, have to carry more responsibility for their decisions. Participatory democracy can be cumbersome and it is clearly impossible in a complex modern society for every citizen to be involved in every decision. There is an obvious need to delegate some decision to a smaller group, and so some degree of representative democracy is inevitable, but it is also possible to increase the level of participation in decision-making, thereby creating a more participatory form of democracy. One form that this can take is *deliberative* democracy, where groups of people can be engaged in the intricacies of the policy process and hence contribute actively to the outcome (Roemer 1999, Saward 1998, Uhr 1998, 2000).

These forms of democracy can operate at a community level, and in fact it is at that level that some form of participatory democracy becomes more possible. The idea that democracy means more than voting – and that indeed voting is a relatively minor part of the democratic process – is a significant component of community development, even though it means having to counter the strong pressures against citizen participation as outlined above. We will return to a fuller discussion of democracy in Chapter 5.

CONSENSUS/COOPERATION AND CONFLICT/COMPETITION

In much of the earlier community development literature it was common to draw a distinction between conflict and consensus approaches to community work (Alinsky 1971, Craig 1993, Ife 2002). A consensus view naturally values cooperation, while a conflict approach naturally favours competition, and they were typically seen as two opposing perspectives.

This led to their being considered as a binary – an 'either/or' – which involved debate about what was the more appropriate way to go about community development. Such a binary distinction, so characteristic of modernity, masks the simple fact that both conflict/competition and consensus/cooperation are a part of life and are inevitable aspects of community and of community development.

Darwinism in its various manifestations, including social Darwinism, has given impetus to the conflict perspective. It leads naturally to a world view in which human achievement is seen as attributable to competition and where conflict is not only inevitable but is actually beneficial. Such a view is reinforced by the dominant narrative of capitalism and competition in the market, which has come to be seen as somehow 'natural'.

This high value attached to conflict and competition masks the fact that cooperation has been just as important in human achievement. Modern societies may be seen to be motivated by competition, but they only function because of people's ability to work together and to cooperate, whether in teams, formal organisations, families, civil society organisations, social clubs, religious groups, or in simple day-to-day interactions with others.

It is also evident that most people will prefer consensus over conflict where possible. When a group of people meet to make a decision there is usually some attempt to reach agreement by consensus rather than having to cast a vote that will result in a majority 'defeating' a minority. Often at a meeting there will only be a formal motion requiring a vote after there has been general discussion and some form of informal consensus has been reached. This enables a motion to be worded in such a way that it can be supported (or at least not opposed) by everyone. While conflict is a normal part of life, most people will seek to avoid it if possible, and if this is so in Western societies it is even more true in those societies with a more collective or Confucian tradition. Where conflict cannot be avoided, we often seek to confine it within prescribed bounds, such as the rules of formal debate, or through regulation and legislation. Indeed, the entire legal system represents an attempt to prescribe and contain conflict within carefully regulated institutions.

Communities themselves will often be in conflict with other institutions or organisations; for example, over environmental issues where a community is resisting a development that will degrade the local environment or destroy the existing community. To do this effectively, a community group needs to be able to engage in conflict and be skilled in ways to do this. However, it will only be able to do so effectively if there is minimal internal conflict within the group. This capacity to deal with both competition and cooperation together is part of living in modern society, where both are constantly being negotiated. The ultimate example of this tension is team sports, such as football. The dominant narratives associated with football emphasise the importance of an extremely competitive and conflictual approach to dealing with opposing teams and the equal importance of team harmony, bonding, team-building and friendship. A football team will only be successful if it is good at both conflict and consensus.

Community development inevitably has to deal with both conflict and consensus, within the community itself as well as in relation to external bodies, and so processes of both competition and cooperation will be evident in community groups. While it is impossible to avoid conflict, the principles of community development discussed above are clearly much more consistent with a consensus-based, cooperative approach. These principles involve valuing all participants whatever their views and seeking to resist the institutional and structural violence that is associated with conflict and competition, where there are inevitably winners and losers. Community development, therefore, will strive to achieve consensus and cooperation wherever possible and will seek ways to avoid conflict. In doing so it again conflicts with a dominant narrative of Western capitalism, which holds that competition and conflict are not only inevitable but also desirable.

The emphasis on consensus and cooperation has a major impact on community development processes, how they are planned and how they are implemented. There are a number of ways to go about building consensus and supporting cooperation, which are dealt with in the literature on community development but which cannot be dealt with in detail here (see Ife 2002 for a fuller discussion). The important point for present purposes is to identify ideas of consensus and cooperation as central to community development and to recognise that any attempt to understand human rights within a community development framework must seek to incorporate such principles.

DEFINITION OF NEED

The definition of need is critical in community development. In fact, community development can be regarded as a process whereby a community is engaged in defining its needs and then working to have those needs met. Often, however, the needs of a community are defined by others: planners, researchers or managers who undertake some form of 'need assessment'. In doing so, they claim to know the needs of a community better than the community itself does. While researchers and planners have a certain expertise that can help in needs definition, a community development perspective requires that the community itself in some way be involved in the process of defining its needs. As will be discussed in Chapter 5, the right to define one's needs is significant in human rights terms, and to deny members of a community a voice in defining that community's needs is to infringe on that right.

The idea of need is often treated as if it is straightforward and non-problematic; however, a closer examination of 'need' reveals that this is far from the case. An analysis of 'need' is central in the approach to human rights from below as developed in later chapters, and a more detailed consideration of the problematic nature of need will be deferred until then.

THE GLOBAL AND THE LOCAL

While community development may be regarded as a particularly local idea because of the identification of community with locality, in an era of globalisation it is necessary also to consider the global aspects of community development and to understand community development in a way that seeks to connect the global and the local. The problems that may affect communities, however 'local' those communities may be, will inevitably have global dimensions, and to seek to understand communities, and community development only within a local frame of reference is clearly inadequate. Not only can the global impinge on the local, but similarly the local can impinge on the global. Global interconnectedness, through the internet and other media, makes it possible for individuals and communities to interact with global issues in ways that were not thought of twenty years ago. The capacity for communities to form part of 'globalisation from below' (Brecher & Costello 1994, Falk 1993, Shiva 2005) has potentially made community groups more powerful and influential. Not only do they have instant access to expertise and information, but they can also become part of global or regional lobby groups or action groups, and can play a role in education and consciousness-raising well beyond a community's own boundaries.

The phrase 'think globally, act locally' is now outdated. The very idea that one can think locally and act globally draws a sharp distinction between thinking and action that is unwarranted. For the community worker, thinking and action go together and to separate them is to deny that each must be grounded in the other. Similarly, to separate the local and the global is to create an increasingly false dichotomy. In the newly globalised world the two are necessarily connected. This will be discussed further, in relation to both community development and human rights, in Chapter 5.

Global issues such as global warming (Spratt & Sutton 2008), world poverty (Pogge 2008), the reaction to terrorism (Pojman 2006), peak oil (Hopkins 2008, Roberts 2004) and water politics (Barlow 2007) will impinge on the daily life of communities in many ways, and it is necessary for any community development process to be aware of them, for example by reducing the community's carbon footprint. Communities can find ways in which to help address these issues by linking with other groups and by joining various global coalitions for action around such topics.

Community development, of course, has for a long time had an international component. Many community development programs have been part of the aid and development agendas that have been implemented in the developing world. Such community development cannot be understood in isolation from a global analysis, including colonialism, Western imperialism, the politics of aid, conflicts over territory and resources, independence struggles and so on. With the exception of colonialism and Western imperialism (see below), these issues will not be discussed in detail here.

COLONIALISM

There is a strong danger of colonialism in any practice of community development. This does not apply merely to community development undertaken as part of an international aid program, but also to community development undertaken within any society.

In this sense, colonialism represents the attempt to impose a culture or world view on any individual, group or community (Larsen 2000, Said 1993, 1995, Young 2001). Colonisation does not proceed only through the activities of a conquering army or through military or security coercion. Often more effective colonisation is achieved through less overtly violent means, though the violence perpetrated on the culture or world view can be just as devastating. This is colonisation that is achieved by teachers, missionaries, social workers, aid workers and indeed anyone who seeks to 'enlighten' those assumed to need such enlightenment.

In fact the modern form of colonialism had its genesis in the era known as 'the Enlightenment' in the eighteenth century, when the achievements of Western civilisation, science, reason and humanism were held to be progressive and an improvement on all other, more superstitious and 'primitive' world views. The idea of 'civilisation' was equated with the society of Western Europe (later followed by that of the USA) and this provided a perfect justification for the imposition of this form of civilisation on all others. This of course allowed Western economic interests to predominate and allowed for the economic exploitation of land and resources, justified by Western views of religion and education, which were imposed on local societies 'in their own best interests'. Although the days of colonialist expansion in the name of nation states are largely over, the same processes continue, normally justified in the name of economic development rather than in the name of religion or education.

It is important to emphasise that colonisation often proceeds from the best of intentions. Those involved in the colonial project will often genuinely believe that they are doing the right thing, and are bringing benefits to the people with whom they are working. This makes the danger of colonialism subtle and insidious. It can also mean that someone criticised for engaging in colonialist practice will most likely react strongly against such criticism and find it both hurtful and unfounded. Another insidious aspect of colonialism is that the ideology of colonialism is held as much by the colonised as by the coloniser. People will assume the natural superiority of the colonisers and seek to be like them. For this reason, those struggling against colonialism and seeking to reaffirm the importance of their own cultural traditions have found it necessary to engage in education and consciousness-raising, as well as to oppose the colonising forces.

Postcolonial analysis (Schwarz & Ray 2000, Young 2001) seeks to identify such colonialist exploitation and to question the dominance of the white, Western, patriarchal world view that still seeks to impose itself on others, on the assumption of its self-evident superiority. This still manifests itself in the assumed superiority of Western universities, Western economics, Western philosophy and the English language, which still embody the aspirations of many people in the developing world.

It also finds its way into community development. Indeed any community development project, if undertaken by someone from outside the community concerned, can fall into the trap of colonialism, even if it is apparently local and within a cultural group. Cultural groups themselves can be stratified, and the view of an elite may not represent the view of the majority. It is so easy for a community worker to assume superior knowledge and wisdom and to seek to impose their world view on others, with the best of intentions. A postcolonial analysis is therefore important in any community development program. There are several ways to guard against colonialist practice, but one of the most important is to remember that community development is founded on the value of wisdom from below, from the community itself, rather than the wisdom of the external expert.

COMMUNITY DEVELOPMENT AS POSTMODERN

From the above discussion it will be clear that community development sits uncomfortably with modernity. The classic characteristics of modernity – certainty, uniformity, neat classification, hierarchical organisation and predictability – are all challenged by community development in one way or another. Community development also challenges the single meta-narrative, instead allowing for multiple realities to be validated both within and among communities.

Community development, therefore, is more compatible with postmodern understandings, which not only accept difference, chaos and unpredictability but also welcome and encourage them (Kumar 1995, Seidman 1994, Touraine 1995; readers unfamiliar with postmodernism will find a fuller account in Chapter 5). The postmodern valuing of pastiche – in which different elements do not need to fit together, show consistency, or work in harmony, but can be disjointed and can contrast with and disturb each other – allows for communities where difference is valued rather than communities where difference needs to be eradicated. Postmodernism is also very compatible with the emphasis in community development on wisdom and change from below. If 'reality' is constantly being constructed and reconstructed, if a single text is open to multiple readings, and if it is the reader rather than the author of the text who 'makes sense' of it, then multiple wisdoms 'from below' will be valued rather than single, unifying world views imposed from above.

Community development, then, at a theoretical level draws heavily on postmodern thinking and embraces something of a postmodern world view. This puts it at odds with two of the most powerful narratives of modern Western society, namely managerialism and the law.

Managerialism, the urge to manage and control everything and to make life predictable and certain, is the essence of modernity, whereas community development, as understood in this book, presents a markedly different world view. This accounts for the difficulty many community development workers have with the constraints imposed on them by managers and organisational imperatives.

It is a similar case with the law. The legal system, as generally understood, is thoroughly grounded in modernity. It seeks to apply a single set of rules to everyone in a consistent, predictable way, fitting everyone into the same system, and sees this as evidently desirable. This point is particularly important for this book, which seeks to bring together human rights and community development. Human rights, as will be discussed in Chapters 3 and 4, have been heavily influenced by the law, legal processes and legal definitions. Lawyers are often seen as the 'natural' human rights practitioners, and human rights have been understood as being defined and enacted through the legal process. If human rights are understood in this way, they are fundamentally incompatible with community development ideas; therefore, a radical reformulation of human rights is required if human rights are to be understood in community development terms. That is a major task for later chapters.

STRUCTURAL ISSUES AND SOCIAL JUSTICE

One of the dangers of a postmodern approach is that it can lead to a devaluing of any notions of social justice or human rights, which are seen as meta-narratives that need to be disregarded. This represents a simplistic understanding of postmodernism, at least in its more affirmative manifestation (Rosenau 1992). There are ways of understanding postmodernism that allow for ideas of human rights and social justice, and postmodern writers such as Derrida were deeply committed to such values (Beardsworth 1996). The important point here is that any approach to community development requires a framework of social justice or human rights. If such a framework is not present, community development can lead to practice that violates social justice principles, entrenching oppressive or unfair practices and excluding minorities, all in the name of a community being self-directing.

Two good examples of this are the Hitler Youth and the Red Guard. Judged by many of the usual criteria for community development, they would be regarded as successful programs. They encouraged a high level of commitment by young people; they gave them a strong sense of self-worth, purpose and achievement; they achieved high levels of participation. Judged in a value vacuum, they would be success stories. Yet, understood from a perspective of social justice or human rights, they rightly earn strong condemnation.

The way in which such a framework is most commonly understood is in terms of social justice, another term that is interpreted in different and conflicting ways (Boucher & Kelly 1998). In this context it is usually informed by a structural analysis based on dimensions of structural inequality such as class, gender, race, ethnicity or sexuality. Community development needs to ensure that it takes such analyses into account, as the very nature of structural oppression is that any program that does not specifically address, or at least acknowledge, these issues is likely to reinforce or entrench such forms of structural disadvantage rather than challenge them. This is critically important for community development and ensures that community development does not exist in a value or ethical vacuum. Community development cannot be regarded as a value-neutral or objective activity. It must rest on a value, ethical, moral or ideological base, and one of the aims of this book is to explore human rights as such a base for community.

Conventional structural analysis is somewhat out of favour among those who prefer a more poststructural approach and seek to understand the way in which power and oppression are constructed and enacted discursively and are present in all human experience (Foucault 1986). However, this does not negate the importance of class, race, gender, ethnicity and sexuality as significant dimensions of disadvantage. Whether one takes a structural or a poststructural perspective, analysis of those key issues of social justice is vital for any community development program that does not wish to repeat the injustices of the Hitler Youth or the Red Guard, though in a less extreme and obvious way.

CONCLUSION: COMMUNITY DEVELOPMENT AS A WAY OF THINKING AND WORKING

The approach to community development outlined above can be applied to a much wider range of human endeavour than simply to programs labelled 'community development'. As shown at the beginning of this chapter, many people engaged in other activities, especially in the human services more generally (such as health, education and social work) can and do incorporate some or all of these principles in their practice or in their day-to-day lives. In this sense we must understand community development in a broad sense, as an approach to working, living and progressive change and as a way of thinking, rather than simply as an occupation or a set of practice prescriptions.

This has significant applications well beyond traditional community work settings. A clear example can be found in the environmental movement and in the various responses to the environmental crisis facing the planet. Many of the responses implemented by governments or advocated by lobby groups are characteristically top-down. They have great faith in new technology or market mechanisms and pay little attention to wisdom from below (indigenous wisdom in particular is largely ignored), to broad community participation (where it is seen as a 'policy' problem for the experts), to diversity (where there is a constant seeking for the one right or 'best' way to do it) and to the need to work in harmony with nature rather than to tame and exploit it. These are the same attitudes that brought about the problem in the first place, and so are hardly likely to achieve a satisfactory alternative. From a community development perspective, it will be no surprise if these measures turn out to be less than fully successful, as the whole approach to the problem has been flawed.

Another example is economics. This discipline, so significant in the way it affects the lives of everyone, is constructed and practised in a way that negates community development principles. It is seen in top-down terms, as a matter for experts, and is dressed in inaccessible jargon. It has no place for broad participation and constantly seeks or affirms one true way to run economies. Economics from a community development perspective would look very different, as has been outlined by various alternative economists who are commonly regarded with suspicion if not disdain by their professional peers (such as Bello 2002, Daly 1997, Diesendorf & Hamilton 1997, Ekins & Max-Neef 1992, Henderson 2006).

Community development as outlined above defies neat definition, but the idea involves much more than a simple linear process of 'how to develop a community'. It is a perspective which, in the opinion of this writer, the world needs to embrace as a matter of urgency if it is to address the challenges facing humanity in the twenty-first century. However, the aim of this book is more modest, if no less important. It is to examine how such a perspective can apply in the field of human rights and how it can advance the cause of human rights, both in terms of understanding the concept and in terms of human rights practice.

DIMENSIONS

The experience of human community is multidimensional, and hence the process of community development must reflect that multidimensionality. Elsewhere (Ife 2002, Ife & Tesoriero 2006) I have identified six dimensions of community development and argued that community development needs to take each dimension into account. These are *social development, economic development, political development, cultural development, environmental development* and *spiritual development*. Here I will consider each of them briefly, both as an aspect of the experience of community and also as a dimension of community development, and will also discuss a seventh – *survival-based development* – which was not covered in earlier works. This dimension addresses some important aspects of community that are omitted from the other six categories, and that have a particular relevance to the integration of community development with ideas of human rights.

The order in which the seven dimensions are discussed does not reflect an order of priority; in fact at the end of this section we will consider the way in which some of these have come to dominate, and whether there should be any re-prioritising in the current context. The discussion below is a summary of each, rather than a detailed treatment, and the reader wishing a more complete discussion is referred to the citations above. We will return to these dimensions in more detail in Chapter 6.

SOCIAL DEVELOPMENT

To say that community is social is to state a truism. The very idea of community requires interaction between people, and therefore social interaction. The evident 'loss of community' in modern societies might be represented as a wish for social bonds between people to be strengthened.

Community social development involves a number of aspects. One, a very common experience in community work, is the identification of community needs followed by efforts to meet those needs, either through the establishment of new community services or through the expansion of already existing agencies to provide the necessary services. Examples are community action to establish a child care centre, a recreation facility, improved public transport, police services, a women's refuge or an aged care facility. Such needs may be the result of a needs assessment or may simply emerge from people's perceptions, from their daily experience of what services could improve the life of their community.

However, while this is a very common community work activity, it is not the only aspect of social development. Also included are programs aimed at helping people to meet each other and at strengthening community ties. Examples include a welcome scheme for new arrivals, bringing people together for a picnic, festival or other social event, a visiting program for people who are housebound, or establishing a variety of educational, leisure or recreational activities to encourage people to become involved. Such programs may run from a community centre or from some other community facility such as a school, a recreation centre or a church, mosque, synagogue or temple.

There is, of course, a limitation on how much community bonds can be 'forged' through such programs, as the initiative ultimately has to be taken by people themselves rather than by a community worker. However, it is certainly possible for community development to provide space for those interpersonal connections to occur and to grow by creating non-threatening, friendly environments where people can seek out others in relative security.

The encouragement of participation is a central feature of all community development but it is particularly significant in social development, as it is out of direct participation that people are able to connect with each other and feel a sense of belonging. This requires that there be a broad-based approach to participation, as discussed earlier in this chapter, where the participation of the person who makes the tea or the person who drives the vehicle is valued as much as the participation of the person who chairs the committee or the person who leads the demonstration. This means that participation needs to be valued as an end in itself, rather than simply as a means to some other end. It is not just that high levels of participation bring about a 'better' result, but that high levels of participation are themselves important and that participation in its own right is worthwhile, quite apart from what outcomes it may or may not achieve.

Much of the literature on social development, especially in the international context, juxtaposes social development with economic development (Midgley 1997). It is an important plea for 'development' to be understood not merely in economic terms, but also in terms of the impact on people's lives and the need for development in non-economic aspects of living. While this is a necessary corrective to economic rationalism as applied to development, it also has the effect of categorising all non-economic aspects of community life and human existence under the term 'social'. Social development is understood here in a narrower sense, as about 'the social'; that is, interactions between people. Other aspects of development – cultural, political, environmental and spiritual – deserve to be discussed in their own right and have their own characteristics, which tend to become lost if they are all included under the single rubric of 'social development'.

ECONOMIC DEVELOPMENT

As mentioned in the previous paragraph, economic development is often seen as the only, or the most important, aspect of the development process. If the economy is healthy, the argument goes, the rest will follow, as a strong economy and high levels of prosperity mean that people will be able to purchase the things they need to live a full and healthy life. Such a view is characteristic of economic rationalism or economic fundamentalism, which sees the economy as the major priority in personal, national and international life. In government, economic policy is seen as the most important area of government activity and the economic portfolios are regarded as the most important positions in a cabinet, rather than health, education or even defence.

Such a view can also be applied to community development and there is a tendency, as noted in Chapter 1, for those engaged in community economic development to see this as the foundation of a successful community and to argue that, if a community has a strong economy, everything else will follow. This is clearly untrue. Many of the most economically advantaged communities have low levels of cultural activity, social connection or citizen participation. The valuing of individual consumption, so characteristic of successful capitalism, is counter to the experience of strong community. Economic development is important, of course, but it is only one dimension of community development.

Community economic development (Shragge 2000) can be classified into two broad areas: the conservative and the radical. Conservative community economic development involves helping a community to benefit within the existing economic order, while radical community economic development involves the establishment of an economic system that represents a genuine alternative. In the former category are included various attempts to make a community more competitive and more profitable. These generally involve seeking new industry or external investment so that economic activity in the community increases and more money is generated which remains in the community.

Such an approach to community economic development depends, of course, on the health of the wider economy. It seeks to make the community a better player in that economy, but if the wider economy suffers then so does that community's economic base. Attracting industry may seem like a good idea, but there is always the risk of that industry being forced to close or to relocate if there is a slow-down in the economy more generally or in that industry in particular. And sometimes industry can only be attracted by offering such major concessions that the net community benefit remains questionable. In any case, much of the profit from that industry will not stay in the community, but will be transferred to the bank accounts of shareholders who may be on the other side of the world.

There are also problems in the case of tourism, so often touted as the answer to a community's economic troubles and a classic case of conservative community economic development. Tourism can erode community, as there is a danger that community activity becomes subordinated to the needs of the tourist. There are particular problems with building strong communities in areas with high levels of tourism and the economic benefits of the tourist industry can have negative effects on other aspects of community life, as will be discussed further in Chapter 6.

Radical community economic development, by contrast, seeks to establish a local economy in some form that is less dependent on external forces and is locally sustainable. This includes establishing small-scale local industry and also establishing some form of local economic system, such as a barter system or LETS scheme. LETS (variously referred to as 'local employment and trading scheme', 'local energy transfer scheme' or 'local exchange and trading system') involves the creation of a local currency, which is traded among local people and businesses so that the benefits of local economic activity remain in the community itself (Kennedy & Kennedy 1995, Meeker-Lowry 1996).

Such schemes have the advantage of relative isolation from the increasingly fickle global economy and of establishing a strong community economic base, even for communities largely ignored by the global economy. The capacity for community development not only to react to current problems but to pioneer viable sustainable alternatives is important, and more radical community economic development represents one aspect of this. Such schemes challenge the dominant economic order and so may meet with resistance if they become too successful or too widely implemented, but their importance in articulating alternatives must not be underestimated.

POLITICAL DEVELOPMENT

The political aspect of community, and of community development, is concerned with political relationships – that is, relationships of power – both within the community (internal political development) and between the community and the larger society or other communities (external political development). Internal political development, concerning politics within the community, is concerned with establishing structures and procedures that allow some form of participatory democracy and ways of making decisions whereby people feel that they have a genuine role in the decision or that they are satisfied with the process others have used in decision-making (recognising that some decisions may need to be taken without everyone's direct input).

This aspect of community development is therefore concerned with the way decisions are made and the importance of the process of decision-making, rather than the outcome. Attempts to 'steamroll' a decision, to 'get the numbers' and to ride roughshod over others, though endemic in party politics, are hardly conducive to good community development processes. Participatory forms of democracy are not easy to implement, at least in Western societies, given people's familiarity with representative democracy and their unfamiliarity with formalised consensus decision-making. Yet some form of participatory democracy is essential for good community development, as it ensures high levels of participation and ownership of decisions.

External community political development focuses on the community's relationship with the external environment. Communities often have to negotiate around issues such as resources, planning, property developments, recognition and the environment. This can involve submission writing, tendering, lobbying, networking, use of the media, social action, civil disobedience and the like. How, when and where to engage in such actions, and which actions are appropriate, is an important aspect of community life, and it is necessary for communities to develop their knowledge and skills in these areas. Good community development will seek to have these skills shared among a broad group of community members, rather than leaving them in the hands of a few, and this requires training programs for people so they can develop their competence in the broader political arena.

One aspect of a healthy community is a high level of engagement in political issues, generated by a high level of political awareness. This can be seen in the existence of local groups concerned with such issues, for example a climate action group, an Amnesty International group, a refugee support group, local action on behalf of NGOs such as Oxfam, World Vision, CARE or religious aid groups, campaigns around rights for indigenous people and local branches of political parties. The support and encouragement of such groups can be an important aspect of community development work.

CULTURAL DEVELOPMENT

In modern societies, much of what we call 'culture' has become commodified and is purchased and consumed rather than performed. With ever more sophisticated audio equipment, from the hi-fi to the iPod, music has become something that, for most people, is listened to rather than performed. In the face of the excellence of the recorded musician, most people feel thoroughly inadequate and would be reluctant to allow anyone to hear them sing or play an instrument. Yet for earlier generations music-making, whether at a family or a community level, was common and there was widespread pleasure in active performance as well as in passive listening.

The same can be said of other forms of cultural expression such as theatre, dance and art. In all these, the emphasis is now on the excellence of the elite practitioner and the role for most people is to be the passive consumer who purchases the product, whether it be a CD, a DVD, downloaded music or movies, a ticket to a rock concert or the theatre, a painting or print, or a TV program. Much the same can be said of sport, where the era of the elite sportsperson is fast replacing mass participation in sport at a community level.

One aspect of community cultural development is to try to reverse this trend and encourage active participation in cultural expression. This involves the establishment and support of, for example, local drama groups, local music groups (rock bands, gospel choirs, symphony orchestras, African drumming), dance groups (ballet, ballroom, belly dancing), the legitimisation and support of graffiti and street art, sculpture, pottery, weaving, creative writing, story-telling or local film-making. Such community-level cultural expression enriches a community in a number of ways, not least by bringing people together to practise and celebrate their own talents. It can also give people a feeling of self-worth and enables them to meet others with similar interests. Performing at a community level can assert the value of the community and can promote further community activity. This aspect of community cultural development can be seen in the work of community arts workers, as well as in the work of community developers more generally.

Sport is another aspect of community cultural development. Like other aspects of culture, sport has become highly professionalised and commodified, with elite sports people performing while the rest of the population consumes the packaged product, either as spectators at a game or by watching on TV. However, sport can, and does, still play an important role at the community level, where it represents a way for a community to come together and be active participants rather than passive consumers.

For some community workers the competitive aspect of sport contradicts the more cooperative approach of community development. However, this is a simplistic view of community-based sport. In some instances, for example in social tennis or bowling, winning and losing can be relatively unimportant. In other sports the competition can be real and earnest, but the social event after the game is at least as important in bringing people together. In team sports a competitive team is only possible through a high level of cooperation and teamwork among team members. The competitive aspect of sport can also be a way for a community to assert its identity and its feeling of solidarity when it competes against another community. In rural areas in particular, there can be no doubt that sporting events play a vital role in community life and are seen by many as evidence of community strength. This is in sharp contrast to professionalised sport, where a franchise may have little connection to the local community and may be moved if it is not sufficiently profitable. Most players in professional teams do not come from the locality but may be from other cities or, increasingly, other countries. In this way professional sport has cut its ties to the local and to the community, but this is not true of more local community-based amateur sporting activities, which remain an important aspect of community life.

Another important aspect of cultural development relates to cultural diversity. The importance of community-in-difference (Nancy 1991) and of strength in diversity has been discussed above as a critical component of community development. This is particularly true in relation to culture, and it is essential that community development both allow for and encourage cultural diversity. This is often harder to achieve than it sounds. Too often attempts to facilitate cultural diversity have extended no further than hosting multicultural festivals and eating food from different cultural traditions. These are important in themselves, and should not be underestimated. Indeed, the eating of food is such a significant human activity, with so much cultural meaning attached to it, that sharing food from different cultures can be a powerful symbol.

However, while this is important, it is not sufficient. The experience of multiculturalism needs to extend beyond the symbolic to enable people from different cultural backgrounds to meet in a spirit of dialogue and to learn from each other at a more fundamental level.

While it is clear that such dialogue is potentially very rewarding, it is also potentially very threatening, since to meet in a spirit of dialogue requires moving out of one's comfort zone and becoming vulnerable to influence from the other. Typically, efforts to improve 'cultural understanding' do not require this of people from the majority or dominant culture, though this is clearly the expectation on those from the minority culture or the culture labelled as 'different'. In this way the encounter is unequal and, at heart, assimilationist; people from the 'different' culture are expected to learn more about the dominant culture, while those from the dominant culture feel that they are 'helping' the other to understand and to accommodate to the dominant culture, and are becoming more 'tolerant' without exposing themselves to the possibility of change.

Genuine cross-cultural or multicultural dialogue must move beyond this, as anything less is essentially a form of colonialist practice. This is one of the most important challenges facing community development at a time of high levels of mobility and at a time when the dominant Western world view is increasingly under question and its way of doing things can no longer be held up as the 'right' or 'superior' way.

The idea of dialogue will be discussed further in Chapter 5, as it has a central place in the synthesis of human rights and community development. There will also be a further discussion of cultural difference in Chapter 4, where it will be considered in relation to human rights and in the debates about universalism and cultural relativism.

Another aspect of community cultural development, which can be in conflict with the need to embrace diversity, is the valuing of cultural heritage. A community will have a history. Sometimes (especially with non-geographical communities) this may be very brief, but in other cases that history can stretch back for centuries or even millennia (most notably with indigenous communities). History is important. It is the story of the community, its traditions, its myths, its shared meanings, its pride and sometimes (though often this is expunged from the collective memory) its shame. Members of the community will in part define their identity in terms of that heritage (Castells 1997), and will see the heritage as worth preserving and celebrating. This aspect of community is seen in local museums, in stories, in buildings, in written histories, in film and in monuments such as statues and war memorials. Celebrating and preserving a community's heritage can therefore be important in community development, and this is especially true when a community perceives its future as under threat.

However, there are dangers associated with this. A community's history may not always be worth celebrating, especially if that history includes violence, abuse, exclusion, racism or other forms of discrimination. In considering its history, a community may need to reflect on that history, not in the form of uncritical celebration of everything that happened in the past, but rather of thinking about how the story may have been distorted over the years, denying or underplaying the negatives while exaggerating the positives, and thinking about the voices that may have been silenced in the process. Such a reflection on a community's history may be a painful experience, but it can also lead to a new appreciation of the past and discussion of how that past should be represented. Selecting and designing the displays for the local museum, for example, can be a critical process, and if it involves broad community participation it can be an extremely valuable community development process. Without such critical reflection, celebrating a community's heritage, while it may at first sight seem both important and harmless, may work against the aims of open and inclusive community development.

ENVIRONMENTAL DEVELOPMENT

The environmental aspect of community development has become more significant with increasing awareness of the environmental crisis facing the planet. Global warming, toxic wastes, air and water pollution, top-soil degradation, desertification, depletion of fisheries and the resource crisis present challenges to humanity, at a global level, on a scale never before experienced. Whether humanity will be able to respond to these crises adequately remains to be seen, but for the purposes of our current discussion the ecological crisis underlines the critical importance of the environment in community development. This is seen first in the impact of environmental degradation on a number of communities exposed to toxic wastes, harmful air pollution, declining fisheries, drought and natural disasters.

There is a long history of local community action in response to environmental challenges, including decisions as to whether to stand up to powerful political and economic forces through advocacy and social action or to develop stronger, more sustainable and cooperative local structures to cope with environmental uncertainty. Indeed, environmental threats represent one of the most potent focal points for community organisation, which can lead to other forms of community development as a community comes together and builds its solidarity and identity.

A number of critics from the environmental movement have advocated decentralised communities as a preferred model of sustainability (for example Bello 2002, Hines 2000, Hopkins 2008). They have pointed out that the centralising tendencies of modernity have not taken account of very different local conditions, and have suggested that decentralised structures have the best chance of responding appropriately, and sustainably, to environmental change. This is because of the ecological principle of diversity. Change will be more effective if it is addressed in different ways in different local circumstances, rather than through a single 'blueprint for change'. Local communities will also be more aware of their immediate environment and will be able to respond more appropriately to its needs. Such critics suggest that large structures are, ultimately, unsustainable and that it is in strong local communities that a sustainable future lies. From this perspective, community development is important not only for reacting to environmental challenges, but also for the more proactive task of building an alternative, sustainable society.

Jared Diamond's widely read study of the way in which societies react to environmental challenges (Diamond 2005) suggests that those who succeed in making the necessary changes towards sustainability do so either because of strong leadership from above – from rulers or political leaders, for example – or because of strong leadership from below – from citizen action and initiatives as people at the grassroots level become aware of the significance of the crisis and the need for change. Current political leaders are, sadly, demonstrating their inability to deal with climate change and other environmental challenges with the necessary level of urgency (Lovelock 2006, 2009, Shiva 2005, Spratt & Sutton 2008).

Because of the realities of the political process and the mechanisms of international diplomacy, action on climate change will almost inevitably be too little and too late. The warnings of scientists have been diluted by 'political reality': by the need for compromise, by pressure from powerful economic interests and by the demands of electoral politics. Government policies therefore only address the issues partially, and international action is confined to talk of non-binding targets, market-led process, blind faith in new technologies and continuing compromise.

To hope that such leadership alone will adequately address the challenge of the impending ecological crisis is naive indeed. If there is to be change that achieves a more sustainable future the initiative must come from the grassroots, from local initiative, with politicians being forced to follow the lead of the people. The idea of change from below, a central tenet of community development, has perhaps never been so important in human history, and the future of humanity may well depend on the adequacy of community-level leadership. For this reason, environmental concerns must play a central part in community development.

More radical voices from the green movement have suggested that sustainable development and new technology are not enough. Rather, they call for a new relationship between humans and the natural world, emphasising our connection to other species and to the non-living environment. The Gaia hypothesis of James Lovelock (1987, 2006, 2009) has perhaps expressed this most strongly in the public arena, though other writers have also been calling for a less anthropocentric and a more ecocentric approach (Eckersley 1992). From this perspective, it is important that we learn to work in harmony with nature, rather than continuing in the Enlightenment tradition of trying to dominate and exploit nature.

The Gaia hypothesis sees human violence as something that is imposed on the natural world as well as within the world of human beings, and insists on a non-violent approach to both. Some deep ecologists have taken the argument even further, into a more spiritual realm, in seeking to articulate a new relationship with nature (Drengson & Inoue 1995, Macy 2007, Naess 1989, Seed, Macy & Fleming 2007). This strand of ecology suggests that continuing to seek yet more sophisticated technological means of 'mastering' nature for our own purposes is doomed to failure, and that small-scale technology that is both human-friendly and nature-friendly should be the goal.

It also suggests that, rather than seeking the answers from science and technology, we should be seeking the wisdom of indigenous people (Knudtson & Suzuki 1992), who have more wisdom than Western 'civilisation' about how to live in harmony with the natural world. This perspective has the potential both to be realised through community development processes and also to inform our understanding of community and of community development. Our relationship to the earth, to the natural world, is of critical importance at this stage of world history. In this light, understandings of community that are confined to cyberspace, severing any link to place and to the earth, must be treated with caution.

SPIRITUAL DEVELOPMENT

The next dimension of community development that needs to be considered is the spiritual. Spirituality has not been afforded much prominence in the secular world of modernity and the Enlightenment, which has been the context for the theoretical development of both community development and human rights, but despite this it has remained a key element of our experience of humanity. For some this finds its expression in organised religion, while for others spirituality is a more personal matter, which may be experienced in nature, in music, in physical work, in sex or in a variety of other pursuits.

As doubts grow about the adequacy of Enlightenment modernity to meet our needs, spirituality is achieving something of a revival. It is now receiving attention in professions and academic disciplines that previously thought it outside their legitimate interests (Gale, Bolzan & McRae-McMahon 2007). Although in some societies attendance at traditional religious services has declined, there has been an apparent rise in more fundamentalist forms of religious activity, perhaps as a way of seeking certainty in an increasingly uncertain world. There has also been considerable interest in less traditional forms of spirituality, including various New Age practices and, perhaps most notably, in indigenous understandings of spirituality that serve to reconnect people to the natural world.

For these reasons, it is important to consider spirituality as an aspect of community development (Macy 2007). For many people, the experience of community might be seen to be a form of spiritual experience; certainly intense experiences with others, such as through dance or music, can be profoundly spiritual. Organised religion also provides a community experience; membership of the local church, mosque or temple can give an important sense of belonging to a community, and the practices of 'religious communities' perhaps represent an experiment with community in its purest form. For centuries in Western societies the local priest or vicar played an important role in community development and the local community was based on the church parish. The mosque has occupied a similar position in Islam and the synagogue in Judaism. Community is closely connected to both religion and spirituality, and it is therefore important to consider the spiritual aspects of community development.

Spirituality, of course, overlaps with some of the other categories of community development outlined above, in particular cultural development. While some would see religion and spirituality as part of culture, for others they are more extensive and relate to all other aspects of life. For this reason also spiritual development deserves to be considered as a distinct aspect of community and of community development.

Community development, understood more generally, needs to allow space for the expression and experience of spirituality in a variety of forms. It is important that this be inclusive rather than exclusive. One of the dangers is that the more fundamentalist adherents of a particular tradition will claim superior wisdom and will not accept or even tolerate alternative expressions of spirituality (Armstrong 2000, Howland 1999, Sim 2004). While communities based around an exclusive understanding of religion may be strong, resilient and cohesive, whether they be the Amish communities of the USA, Muslim communities, Jewish communities or New Age communities, ultimately the test of a strong community is its capacity to be inclusive, to welcome strangers and to seek to learn from others. There are traditions of such acceptance within all major religions; it is exclusive fundamentalism rather than religion *per se* that is the problem. Rather than reinforcing such exclusivity, community development can encourage inter-faith dialogue, which has proved to be very rewarding in many communities as people learn more about each other's experiences of spirituality, rather than staying locked within their own.

As previously indicated, indigenous spiritual traditions are particularly important, especially given the need, discussed above, for a closer relationship with the natural world. In many places, the descendants of indigenous people who have lived in a location for a very long time and who know the land in a very special way will be able to participate in community events and provide that connection to the land and its stories. In countries such as Australia, Canada, Aotearoa/New Zealand and the USA there is increasing involvement of indigenous people in formal ceremonial roles, welcoming people to their country, being acknowledged as the traditional custodians of the land and sharing their wisdom. This can only be done within the spiritual traditions of the indigenous community. For many indigenous people land, nature, climate, food, drink, music and dance are so interconnected with the spiritual that they cannot be thought about in isolation from their spiritual dimensions, and community development that genuinely includes indigenous people must, of necessity, incorporate the spiritual.

SURVIVAL-BASED DEVELOPMENT

It is a common experience that at times of threat – from natural disasters or from human causes such as military invasion – communities tend to pull together. People will help each other at times of crisis and will comment on the increase in social solidarity in the face of a common risk. These are situations when the very survival of individuals, families and communities is at stake and a perceived common threat to survival can often bring about a collective response. In countries where basic survival rights – for food, water, shelter, clothing and basic health care – are not adequately met, the resulting insecurity can be a powerful stimulus for community development that is based on these very significant survival rights.

However, community development that is based on survival need not be confined to war, natural disasters or situations of third-world poverty. Stronger communities are better able to cope with such threats, and planning community responses in the possible event of such disasters can be a powerful focus for a developmental process. In rural Australian communities, for example, volunteer fire and emergency services are a focus for community volunteering and in turn can be a very practical avenue for community participation, helping to make the community both stronger and safer in the event of bushfire, flood or earthquake. Such development focuses on specific ways in which a community can prepare for a potential disaster, both in terms of prevention (clearing fire breaks and building flood levies) and in terms of response (having effective and prompt emergency services available, ensuring a supply of food and clean water and so on).

In this regard it is also important to mention community development as a response to stress and trauma. Trauma recovery need not be simply an individual matter, to be dealt with by counselling in a very private and personal way, but can also be addressed at a community level. There are different ways in which a community can go about trauma recovery. The memorial service, for example, is a community-level response to trauma where people together seek to come to terms with what has happened. For many years in predominantly Christian countries it has been a very important way of responding to the aftermath of disasters. However, it has to retain its community focus if it is to be of value. In an interesting example, after the severe bushfires in Victoria, Australia, in February 2009, when more than 170 people died and over 2000 homes were lost, the state government held a special memorial service at a stadium in Melbourne, the capital city of Victoria, providing free transport for all those affected by the fires who wished to attend. However, the event at the stadium was not well attended, other than by dignitaries, political leaders and celebrities, and the buses were not needed. Instead, people chose to watch the service together, in their local communities, on large-screen televisions. The memorial service made more sense if it was experienced in the local community context, where the fires had done the damage and where the people of the community could be together, rather than in a stadium in Melbourne.

The memorial service is not the only community-level response to trauma. In different contexts, community art, music and theatre have been used as ways for people to address together the issues thrown up by traumatic events (McCowan 1996). In communities that have experienced severe human rights abuses (such as in South Africa, Rwanda, Cambodia and East Timor) some form of truth commission can be very powerful in helping a community come to terms with what it has experienced (Tutu 1999). Again, this is more effective if undertaken at a local community level, as was done in Rwanda, for example, rather than in the courtrooms of a remote capital city. The form that such a truth and reconciliation process takes will vary with different cultural contexts and traditions. What works in one location will not work in another, as is the case with most community development. However, although each experience of community-based trauma recovery will be unique, the fact remains that the application of community development principles can significantly assist the trauma recovery process.

INTEGRATED COMMUNITY DEVELOPMENT

These seven aspects, or dimensions, of community development are all important. Good community development needs to take account of, and incorporate, all seven. There is little point in concentrating exclusively on one, for example economic development, to the exclusion of the others, as such an approach will not even begin to tap the richness and the many layers of community experience. It may well be that a community will have stronger needs in one area than another – for example, a community may be economically well developed but culturally and spiritually weak – and this can help to set priorities for community development; but it is always the case that all seven dimensions need to be understood and addressed. In this way they are not unlike the 'triple bottom line' often alluded to in business and government, which argues that economic profit alone is not sufficient, but that social and environmental goals are equally important. While the triple bottom line, in a business context, can be criticised (in a capitalist society, profit for a business must of necessity take precedence over all else), in a community context it makes more sense. Here, however, we have added the political, the environmental, the spiritual and the need for basic survival to the trinity of the triple bottom line.

It can also be argued that, in different historical and material contexts, different aspects of community development will be seen as more or less important. At the present time, for example, environmental development is seen by many people to be critical – much more so than would have been the case twenty years ago. However, the necessary interconnection between the seven requires us to think holistically about community development; successful community development can never be unidimensional. In this regard, it is important to note that there is considerable overlap between the seven, and it would be wrong to draw rigid or impermeable boundaries between them. The spiritual overlaps with the cultural; the economic is clearly political; social and cultural development are closely related; the environment is political; and so on. They are not clear, distinct categories, but rather represent different foci, or centres of understanding, in thinking about community development.

CONCLUSION

This brings to an end the discussion of community development. It has, of necessity, been a summarised and somewhat sketchy account. Readers wanting to know more are referred to the many specialist books and journals on the subject. The purpose has not been to give a complete picture of community development, but rather to present some of its more salient features, to support a discussion about the relationship between community development and human rights. It is, inevitably, one person's view of community development. Other writers or practitioners would no doubt take issue with the picture of community development that has been sketched here, and would wish to emphasise different aspects; it is a rich and diverse field, with different interpretations and emphases, which cannot be fully contained in any single account. For the purposes of this book, however, the account presented here outlines a particular approach to community development which, it will be argued in later chapters, links well with human rights.

There has been virtually no discussion of actual community development practice in this section. This has been a deliberate omission, as a discussion of practice is the aim of the last section of this book, which will revisit the seven dimensions of community outlined above and consider ideas of human rights-based practice within them.

Part 2
Thinking about human rights

This is the nature of humanity:
Destroying all it establishes
Establishing all it destroys
Until the day it repents.

Murad Mikha'il, 'Three Flags'

3 | Definitions and imperatives of human rights

DEFINITIONS

'HUMAN'

As WITH COMMUNITY DEVELOPMENT, attempting any clear definition of human rights is not easy. To understand why, we need to start with the two words themselves. *Human* and *rights* are both words that defy easy definition, and the definitional issues around each of them cloud any overall understanding of something called 'human rights'. In the human rights literature there has been more concern with the problematics of the term 'rights' than there has been with the problematics of the term 'human', and this has downplayed the importance of a very contested idea.

The word 'human' may at first sight seem unproblematic, but it needs to be remembered that over time there have been different constructions of who, or what, counts as human (Foucault 1970, Hunt 2007, Taylor 1989). One reason the Nazis were so readily able to persecute Jews was that Jews were regarded as a somehow 'sub-human' species. In times of war it is common to 'dehumanise' (that is, see as less than fully human) the enemy, which makes it easier to hate and to kill; examples include British newspaper cartoons depicting Germans during World War I, similar portrayals of Japanese people during World War II and the language used by US soldiers in depicting the 'enemy' in Vietnam. In each instance the dehumanising implied that the people portrayed as 'sub-human' were not entitled to full 'human rights' and so did not need to have those rights protected.

Similarly, the European colonists tended to regard the indigenous people they encountered in Africa, Asia, the Americas and Australasia (that is, most of the world) as less than fully human, and treated them accordingly in a remarkable display of Eurocentric arrogance. While there were debates over whether indigenous people should be treated brutally or humanely (Reynolds 1998), it was easy and convenient for people on both sides of those debates to assume that indigenous people represented a lower form of humanity and that indigenous cultural expressions of that humanity did not need to be taken seriously other than for the purposes of scientific study of the exotic 'other'.

People with severe intellectual disabilities, brain damage or serious dementia have also often been regarded as not fully human, and are sometimes referred to as 'vegetables' to underline their difference from the 'human'. People showing characteristics that are seen as not conforming to the 'standards of humanity', such as extreme antisocial behaviour or uncontrolled aggression, may be referred to as 'animals', which similarly defines them as somehow not fully human. Such labelling tends to imply that these people do not 'deserve' to be 'treated like humans' and are therefore not necessarily entitled to the full range of human rights. Most controversially in modern Western societies, problems of defining the meaning of 'human' arise in debates around abortion and the rights of the unborn. Indeed, the abortion debate might be characterised as a debate about the definition of 'human' and at what stage in the development of the human being 'human rights', including the right to life, may be said to apply.

Children represent another category where people's full 'humanity' is sometimes questioned. If someone is 'only a child' they can be seen as somehow less than fully human, and indeed a number of 'human rights', which by definition should belong to all humans, are not applied to children: the right to vote, the right to work, the right to freedom of movement, the right to freedom of association and so on. If these are human rights, and yet children are not perceived to have these rights, the inevitable conclusion is that either children are not seen as fully 'human', or we construct their 'humanity' rather differently. The question of who counts as 'human' and of how we construct the idea of 'humanity' is therefore at the heart of any understanding of human rights.

The contemporary discourse of human rights is grounded in Western humanism. The humanist tradition was an important part of the Western Enlightenment, which arose as a reaction to the religious wars of sixteenth- and seventeenth-century Europe (Carroll 2004, Foucault 1970, Hunt 2007, Taylor 1989). The Enlightenment attempt to substitute human reason for divine revelation as the key to human understanding, and as determining how we should treat each other, had the effect of marginalising religion and placing 'man' rather than God at the centre of human affairs.

Know then thyself, presume not God to scan;
The proper study of mankind is man.
Alexander Pope, 1688–1744, from *An Essay on Man*

The centrality given to the human as the ultimate form of evolution, as the 'natural master' of the world, as the source of superior wisdom and as the 'proper study of mankind' in place of seeking God's will, was a major change. Instead of 'man' being considered a part of nature and as interconnected with other living beings, 'he' was instead considered to be above nature and having a special value. The valuing of the human in his or her (usually just his) own right became a central tenet of philosophical and ethical argument (Macy 2007, Saul 2002). Thus the very idea of 'humanity' and its significance became redefined and human reason was regarded as superior to superstition, divine revelation or emotion in working out the way the world should work and the way people should behave towards each other and towards other species. The assumptions of humanism are still very much part of the Western world view and go unchallenged in mainstream discourse (Baldissone 2009).

The humanist tradition, however, valued a particular construction of the 'human' as the ideal. The ideal human was a white, European, adult male, able-bodied, of above-average intelligence and with a high level of education. Other people (who of course constituted the overwhelming majority of the human species) were expected to aspire to this ideal. This was reflected in education, literature, politics and indeed throughout society, including business, recreation, the military, media and popular culture (Young 2001). Humanism, despite its important advances in the valuing of humanity, was also inextricably bound up with the agenda of patriarchal Western imperialism/colonialism. It valued the human, but in such a way that inevitably some humans were seen as more worthy and important than others. Thomas Jefferson, a great advocate of human rights at the time of the American Declaration of Independence, kept slaves and presumably had no conflict in doing so.

Women, until recently, were simply treated as appendages to 'man'. The language of the 'rights of man' suggested that women somehow did not count as fully human and entitled to the same rights, though this has been challenged by feminist writers not only in recent decades (Brems 2003, French 1992, Peterson & Parisi 1998), but also back to the times of Mary Wollstonecraft (1759–1797) with her seminal publication *A Vindication of the Rights of Women* (Wollstonecraft 1975; see also Hayden 2001). As well as its gender bias, the language of human rights also had an individualist bias; it valued 'the rights of man' rather than 'men' (let alone 'men and women'), and the humanity that was so valued was valued in individual terms rather than as a human collective.

Human rights are often regarded as having a basis in humanism, and indeed the very use of the word 'human' in the term implies a secular humanist orientation. Although there are elements of various religious traditions that reflect human rights values, the contemporary mainstream philosophical formulation of human rights has tended not to draw on them, but instead to rely on the work of a range of thinkers from Hobbes (1968), Locke (1967), Rousseau (1968), Mill (1906), Kant (Appelbaum 1995) and Marx (1954) through to Gandhi (1964), Nelson Mandela (1994), Martin Luther King (1969) and Vaclav Havel (1991, 1992). While many of these had personal religious beliefs, their advocacy for some form of rights derived primarily from reason, argument and personal conviction rather than from divine revelation. (Though Locke and King, in particular, did see rights as God-given, they nevertheless developed their political philosophy from rational argument about what those God-given rights implied.) Hence the philosophical basis for human rights rests firmly within the secular humanist tradition and, as the above list demonstrates, a particularly male version of that tradition.

There is insufficient space here to discuss further the topic of humanism and its impact on human rights, though we will return to it in Chapter 4. In this chapter we simply need to emphasise that the word 'human' is far from neutral and unproblematic, but rather (as we saw with 'community' and 'development' in the previous section) that it is contested and raises significant questions about any use of the word, including in 'human rights' (Baldissone 2009). 'Human' is not a static concept. It is redefined in different contexts and for different purposes, and is continually being reconstructed according to the needs of the moment.

Before leaving our discussion of the word 'human' it is important to note that its use in 'human rights', and indeed the whole Enlightenment humanist tradition, results in a separation of humans from the rest of the natural world, which from a contemporary ecological perspective cannot be sustained (Macy 2007, Shiva 2005). The dominance of Western anthropocentric thinking has been challenged by writers from a more green or ecological perspective, who emphasise that we are part of the biosphere and interconnected with other species (Eckersley 1992). This view is unremarkable for indigenous people but is a challenge for Western modernity, which treats humans as separate from the natural world. This view has undoubtedly contributed to a devaluing of the environment and an exploitation of the natural world that have reached a point where the very survival of the human species (and many others) is at stake. A more ecological approach requires that we not only be concerned for human rights, but also for the rights of other species. The relationship between human rights and animal rights is important, and although there is no space to discuss it further here, this subject will be raised again in Chapter 4 in relation to the important area of environmental rights.

'RIGHTS'

The problematic nature of the idea of 'rights' is more immediately obvious than is the case with the term 'human'. Defining 'rights' is a task that has challenged social and political philosophers, and it would be fair to say that there is no clearly accepted definition (Gewirth 1996, Hayden 2001, Herbert 2003, Orend 2002). Are human rights part of 'human nature'? Are we born with rights? Can rights be said to 'exist'? If so, how do we establish the 'existence' of a right? Does a right 'exist' prior to a responsibility being established, or is a right only determined out of our obligations to others? Does a right only 'exist' if it is somehow guaranteed in legislation or regulation, or do rights exist independently of any legal framework? If someone claims a right, what evidence is required for that claim to be justified? Can rights belong to some people and not others? Are rights merely constructions (whether social or legal) that are entirely dependent on context?

These are just some of the questions regarding the definition of rights. Some of them will be taken up in later chapters. However, for the moment it will be sufficient to identify three traditions in the ways people have thought about human rights. These three traditions can be called the *natural rights* tradition, the *states obligations* tradition and the *constructed rights* tradition.

NATURAL RIGHTS

The first of these, which emphasises 'natural' rights, rests on the ideas of John Locke (1632–1704) and of various religious formulations of humanity (Hayden 2001, Locke 1967). It sees rights as something we are born with, as part of our natural state of being. In this sense, rights are derived from our very humanity and are a quasi-objective aspect of the human condition. Such a view of rights requires that, by their very nature, they are universal (that is, owned by all people, everywhere) and inalienable (that is, they cannot be taken away from us). This thinking is often associated with the gift of a creator God. This was certainly so in Locke's conception and is also mirrored in the famous words of the US Declaration of Independence:

> We hold these truths to be self evident: that all men are created equal; that they are endowed by their Creator with certain unalienable rights; that among these are life, liberty and the pursuit of happiness.

If these truths are to be held as self-evident, there is little more to be said and the natural rights tradition is established as self-evident truth.

The idea of natural rights accepts that rights exist in a quasi-objective sense and hence that they can be identified, established, described and measured. This tradition is strong in much of the rhetoric of human rights (of which the US Declaration of Independence is just one example), though when we need to move beyond rhetoric to action it proves not to be very powerful or useful. Relying on the natural rights tradition alone means that, to understand human rights, we must understand what it means to be human or what the 'essence' of humanity is. This renders human rights as primarily a field for philosophical or theological discourse.

While such philosophical analysis is important, indeed essential, in our understanding of human rights, by itself it can leave the human rights practitioner or the human rights activist confronted by the reality of human rights violations and feeling relatively powerless, as there is no obvious necessary connection with action. Within this tradition, human rights practice usually consists of educating people about their rights and activism to ensure that those rights are realised. Practice has no role in defining or constructing rights, but is only concerned with their realisation.

STATES OBLIGATIONS

The *states obligations* tradition of human rights regards human rights as imposing obligations on governments to provide for the protection or realisation of those rights. Rights in this sense only exist when such mechanisms are in place. Commonly these are in the form of bills or charters of rights; legislation to ensure that certain rights are protected and can be guaranteed through the courts; adequate, efficient and accountable police and court systems; and government programs to ensure that a range of rights to such benefits as education, health, housing and social security are realised for its citizens.

The effect of this tradition is to link human rights to the law, to legal mechanisms and processes and to government policies. This legal approach to human rights has been very influential in the way human rights have been implemented throughout the world. It has been behind much of the United Nations human rights program, which is aimed at ensuring that member states of the UN institute and maintain such legal and policy mechanisms. It also has the consequence that human rights tend to be equated with national citizenship; it is out of our national citizenship that our rights are derived, realised and protected.

This entails certain problems, which will be discussed later, as it does not do a good job of protecting non-citizens such as refugees and migrant workers, nor does it mean that all humans have the same rights. The citizens of one state will have more rights than those of another state, depending on different legislation, and this is hardly compatible with the idea of universal human rights. Hence universalism has no place within this tradition, as rights are determined within different legal jurisdictions. This problem is addressed by either advocating adherence to universal human rights law, or persuading different governments to adopt comparable laws and policies.

The states obligations tradition has caused human rights to be strongly equated with the law, and lawyers have therefore tended to play a dominant role in human rights work (Meckled-García & Çali 2006). The work of lawyers, and the mechanisms of the law, are important for human rights and must not be undervalued. However, the approach to human rights in this book suggests that, while such legal work is important, indeed necessary, it is far from sufficient if we are to achieve a society based on human rights for all (Woodiwiss 2006).

With some rights, such as the rights to education, health, employment and income security, the law is not enough in the states obligations tradition. Here the role of the state is not only to legislate but to provide in the form of public services, which may be state-run or, alternatively, state-funded but run by the community sector (NGOs) or the private sector, which tender for government contracts. This is a more positive role for the state than simply regulation; the state also has an obligation to provide, or to otherwise ensure the provision of, basic social services.

One weakness of the states obligations tradition is that it does not fully take account of the role of non-state actors in working for human rights. It tends to leave primary (if not sole) responsibility in the hands of the state, whereas it can be argued that there are also important roles for other actors such as the family, civil society, business and the global community, quite apart from any role they may have contracting for government services as indicated above. The role of non-state actors, such as NGOs, tends to be limited to lobbying and pressuring the state to meet its responsibilities (as is the case with Amnesty International and Human Rights Watch, for example) rather than taking an active role in meeting human rights themselves. In an era where the power of the state is being eroded by the dual forces of globalisation and privatisation, other actors will need to accept some responsibility for human rights if those rights are to be taken seriously.

The emphasis on the nation state as holding primary responsibility for human rights is further reinforced by the approach of the UN, which has taken the lead on human rights through the Universal Declaration of Human Rights, the many subsequent UN human rights treaties and covenants and the role of the UN Human Rights Council. By its very nature, the UN (United *Nations*) is only able to deal directly with nation states, and therefore it locates responsibility for human rights with nation states. When human rights become equated with the work of the UN, they will inevitably be constructed within the states obligations tradition. While the work of the UN has achieved a great deal in furthering human rights, its very success has limited our understanding of human rights to something for which the nation state must take primary responsibility.

CONSTRUCTED RIGHTS

The third tradition is the *constructed rights* tradition. This suggests that human rights are constantly being negotiated, defined and redefined at all levels of the society. Human rights from this perspective do not stand still, whether as part of 'human nature' or in constitutions and statute books. Rather they emerge from our shared and negotiated understandings of what it means to be human, how we should treat others, and how we can expect to be treated ourselves. Hence those disciplines that are concerned with identifying these shared understandings, such as anthropology or sociology, play an important role in the study of human rights (Goodale 2009, Goodale & Merry 2007, Wilson & Mitchell 2003).

In this tradition human rights are contextual and dynamic, rather than universal and stable, but they do not necessarily lose their power as a consequence. They are firmly grounded in lived experience, and indeed we can think of everyday life as a constant negotiation and renegotiation of shared assumptions about human rights and human responsibilities. From this perspective, it is developing a *culture of human rights* that is important in human rights work, not just the passing of legislation and the strengthening of legal mechanisms and forms of accountability. Such a

	Natural rights	States obligations	Constructed rights
Origin	Human nature, God-given	Legislature, UN	Lived experience
Discipline for study	Philosophy, theology	Law, political science	Anthropology, sociology
Universality	Universal	Subject to jurisdictions	Contextual
Practice	Education, activism	Law, policy development, advocacy	Community development

Three traditions of human rights

perspective raises difficult questions about universality and context, which will be discussed in Chapter 4. However, it also has more potential for spreading the responsibility for human rights throughout the society, and for giving more people a sense of agency when it comes to human rights protection and realisation.

SUMMARY

The three traditions are summarised in the above table. This outlines the different assumptions about the origin of human rights, the disciplines or fields of study that naturally lend themselves to each tradition, the way in which universality is dealt with in each tradition, and the kind of human rights practice that each tradition implies.

In the rest of this chapter, and more particularly in Chapter 4, an approach to human rights will be outlined which, while acknowledging aspects of all three traditions, is most heavily reliant on the third: the constructed rights tradition. This approach to human rights allows a natural synergy with ideas of community development, as discussed in previous chapters, and this will form the basis of the subsequent exploration of the integration of community development with human rights. However, the natural rights and the states obligations traditions of human rights are also important in developing a more holistic approach to human rights and community development, and will be incorporated into the discussion in this and later sections.

IMPERATIVES

Although it is possible to identify human rights traditions in religious and philosophical traditions that go back centuries (Hayden 2001, Ishay 1997), and although there is a long tradition of philosophical writing about the concept of rights, the term *human rights* is of relatively recent origin. Discussion of 'the rights of man' dates from the Enlightenment and the American and French revolutions in the late eighteenth century (Hunt 2007, Ishay 1997, Lewis 2003, Paine 1994), consistent with the humanist tradition as discussed above with its limited understanding of 'man'. However, the term 'human rights' only made its appearance in the twentieth century.

The main impetus for the modern Western human rights movement was undoubtedly the Holocaust. The Holocaust was not the worst atrocity of the twentieth century in terms of numbers of deaths (more people died in Stalin's gulags than in Hitler's death camps), but it caught the Western imagination in a way that other atrocities and genocides did not. This was, at least in part, because the Holocaust was genocide committed by a Western nation – indeed a nation that for many represented the peak of Western culture and civilisation, the land of Beethoven, Bach, Goethe, Schiller, Kant, Hegel and many other great figures. As a consequence, it was harder to rationalise this massive human rights violation as the activities of a 'less civilised' nation – something that happened 'over there'. The West, and Western civilisation itself, was implicated.

It might be argued that the Holocaust was simply the natural extension of the humanist quest for the perfectible human, a form of amoral humanism. Certainly there were people in other European nations who were broadly in sympathy with the ideology of Hitler's Reich, including members of the aristocracies of European nations, though they subsequently kept quiet about it. Seen this way, the Holocaust was not simply an awful aberration, but was rather embedded within the Western Enlightenment humanist ideal, which had already shown its ugly side in colonialism and now was turned on the Jews of Europe, whose intellectual and creative achievements within the Western world could not be denied. This meant that the West had to treat the Holocaust more seriously. It was forced to examine its own soul rather than criticise somebody else.

The human rights movement, led by Western nations and the Western conscience, may therefore be seen as an attempt by the West to redeem itself (Tascón & Ife 2008). It was able to emerge from the ruins of World War II as the moral leader of the world, asserting the value of human rights and condemning the Nazi regime as an aberration that was the anathema of Western values, rather than as a tragic consequence of the Western pursuit of order, rationality and the perfectible human being.

Despite such origins, however, the achievement of a global 'consensus' on human rights, as enshrined in the 1948 Universal Declaration of Human Rights, remains one of the great achievements of the twentieth century. It is true that the historical time was ripe for such an initiative. It is hard to see such a document being given universal assent by the nations of the world at any subsequent time, and most certainly not at the time of writing when, for some governments at least, 'human rights' has become a highly suspect term. However, the origins of the Universal Declaration, at a time when the impact of an extreme amoral modernity was intensely felt, also suggest that the human rights movement, and the Universal Declaration itself, are more than merely the West seeking to redeem itself. They also suggest a genuine attempt to reintroduce morality to the world of modernity, to make it the basis of international law and to find ways to limit the worst excesses of modernity by appealing to the values of humanity (Cassese 1990, Laber 2002, Sellars 2002).

In this sense, we can see the human rights movement both as a child of modernity and also as a means to limit and question some aspects of modernity (Bobbio 1996). Its relationship to modernity is therefore somewhat ambivalent, and this ambivalence is at the heart of some of the contradictions of human rights that will be discussed in Chapter 4. While questioning modernity by introducing a moral dimension, human rights nevertheless seek to operate largely within the constraints of modernity itself, using mechanisms that are characteristic of modernity (for instance rational/legal authority, laws and regulations, rationality and objectivity). This is a weakness of the mainstream human rights discourse. One of the aims of this book is to develop a more organic approach to human rights that is able to step outside the bounds of the pure rationality and legal reasoning of modernity.

Such analysis, however, can fail to acknowledge the appeal of human rights to many people simply because it reflects values they see as important. These values include respecting the rights of others, ensuring that people are treated with dignity, respect and fairness, and seeking to treat people not as members of a particular class, race, nation or community but rather as people in their own right, whose very humanity is sufficient basis for ensuring that they be treated in certain ways. This broader appeal, beyond national or cultural borders, represents a reaching out to connect with others through a common or shared humanity.

Despite the ready temptations of colonialism and the propensity to impose a Western view of 'how people ought to be treated' on others (Douzinas 2007, Pereira 1997) the concept of human rights can be, and has been, a powerful force for change. It is a discourse that has enabled people to work in solidarity with those suffering oppression or discrimination and has helped to overthrow Apartheid in South Africa, to eliminate racially discriminatory laws in the USA, to support the people's movement for independence in East Timor and to make a difference in many other situations. The Universal Declaration has served as an inspiration to many people and has been the basis of human rights education programs that have helped to make people more aware of the idea of rights and what they mean (Lauren 1998).

One of the attractions of human rights in the last two decades of the twentieth century and the early years of the twenty-first is that it represents one of the few legitimate alternatives to the dominant discourses of neoliberalism, unbridled capitalism, economic globalisation, individualism and the free market. With the decline of socialism as a legitimate discourse of opposition, human rights remains one of the few oppositional voices. It has been used by many groups seeking to oppose, or to promote an alternative to, the dominant conservative discourse. Hence anti-globalisation protesters have found it useful to emphasise how economic globalisation results in human rights abuse, for example in poor working conditions in 'sweatshops' and in the way economic interests are maintained, if necessary, by security forces using torture and intimidation to deny voices of opposition (Klein 2007).

Similarly, environmentalists have been quick to point out how lack of concern for the environment by governments and business results in human rights abuse. This includes health problems caused by toxic waste; displacement of large numbers of people to make way for dams and other major construction projects; the use of police and security forces to protect the interests of global capital in spite of the will of local people and allowing them to use oppressive force to achieve this; and the threatened loss of homelands for people from Bangladesh and some Pacific Island nations from rising sea levels caused by global warming (Brysk 2002, Monshipouri et al. 2003, Shiva 2005, Zarsky 2002).

Human rights, because of their strong appeal, have become an important part of these campaigns and have lent legitimacy to them. Human rights have proved to be a powerful discourse and have been readily harnessed to many progressive causes. Those wishing to oppose the existing order, for whatever reason, are often able to appeal to human rights as an alternative discourse of opposition at a time when socialism lies discredited in the disasters of the Soviet system and when social democracy, in the English-speaking nations at least, has been thoroughly discredited by the compromise and evident corruption of 'third way' politics as espoused by 'New Labour' in the United Kingdom. Human rights remains one of the few remaining discourses of opposition, along with environmentalism, and it is common for the two to be linked in political campaigning.

Another reason for the appeal of human rights, in the West if not else-where, has been the decline of the influence of religion. Just as socialism has lost its power as a vision of an alternative, so too, in an increas-ingly secular society, has religion become less significant as a source of ideas about how we should treat each other, and there has been instead a need for some form of secular ethics to take its place. Human rights fills this gap well. In line with the Enlightenment tradition discussed above, human rights represents an attempt to derive moral and ethical behaviour not from a position of divine revelation, but from human rea-son. It represents a form of secular humanism that has considerable appeal to those seeking some form of universal, or quasi-universal, morality in a secular age.

Another impetus for human rights lies in the importance of internation-alism and universalism. The twentieth century was the century of interna-tionalism, as international travel became faster and more readily available to more people and as communications technologies revolutionised ways of exchanging information, money and opinion.

The era of international NGOs began in the late nineteenth century with the establishment of the International Red Cross. This was followed by Rotary International, the first service club, in 1905, and then through the twentieth century by many other NGOs such as the ILO (International Labour Organisation), Amnesty International, Oxfam, Save the Children, World Vision, Greenpeace and the Women's International League for Peace and Freedom. The League of Nations was formed after World War I and the UN after World War II. The UN in turn established a number of global bodies, such as UNICEF and UNESCO.

These were all part of the response to the world growing 'smaller' and an increasing recognition that the world's problems were global in scale and needed to be dealt with in global forums if they were to be successfully addressed. In such a context it is not surprising that ideas of 'the rights of man' as advocated in previous centuries, largely through national approaches, should become a more genuinely international idea, and that the term 'human rights' should come to imply an international universalism that is consistent with the internationalism of the twentieth century (Korey 1998).

In considering the appeal of human rights, it is also important to identify its limitations. 'Human rights' is often used as a synonym for 'social justice'. This can devalue some important aspects of a social justice perspective. Writers on social justice have long been concerned with issues of structural disadvantage, where people must be understood as belonging to particular social groups that are either relatively advantaged or relatively disadvantaged in comparison to others (Boucher & Kelly 1998). The most commonly discussed dimensions of structural disadvantage are class, gender and race/ethnicity, though other dimensions such as age, (dis)ability and sexuality are also obviously important markers of privilege or disadvantage. A human rights discourse can marginalise such structural considerations, as it tends to treat all people as one. It is a discourse of human unity rather than of human diversity, emphasising our membership of a common 'humanity' from which our rights are derived, and hence can readily ignore such factors as gender, race, and class. A human rights discourse that is devoid of analyses based on class, race, gender and so on is likely to reinforce such structural inequality rather than address it.

Discussions of the human condition, whether in the disciplines of philosophy, sociology, psychology, anthropology, history or politics, are likely to emphasise either discourses of unity or discourses of difference. It needs to be recognised that human rights lends itself naturally to a discourse of unity, built around ideas of a common humanity, and the things that unite, rather than divide, human beings. This needs to be balanced with analyses that emphasise diversity, difference and structural disadvantage. Hence there is a considerable literature about human rights and gender, specifically arguing that women are often excluded from the human rights agenda (Ashworth 1999, Brems 2003, Peterson & Parisi 1998, Rendel 1997) and also about human rights and race within the broader literature around human rights and cultural difference. (Both gender and cultural difference are to be discussed in Chapter 4.) There has been less theoretical discussion about human rights and class beyond literature that deals with workers' rights.

The position taken in this book is essentially similar to the position taken in previous chapters in relation to community development, namely that structural considerations are necessary in order to maintain some essential balance between discourses of human unity and discourses of human difference. How ideas of human rights can cope with ideas of diversity is a familiar sticking point for those concerned with human rights

(Caney & Jones 2001), and it will be a recurring theme in the following chapters.

Community development has addressed and come to terms with diversity more effectively than has human rights discourse. This represents an important area where community development can contribute to human rights, as will be discussed in more detail in subsequent chapters. One way in which this has been done is through the incorporation of ideas from poststructuralism and postmodernism, which attempt to move beyond conventional structural analyses – characteristic of modernity – to more fluid and multiple understandings. This has not been discussed to any great extent in the conventional human rights literature with the exception of the work of Costas Douzinas (2000, 2007), but will be addressed in more detail in Chapter 5.

In summary, this chapter has outlined the imperatives for human rights, attempting to account for the significant increase in interest in human rights in recent decades. There is a clear attraction in the idea at this point in history and there is little doubt that, despite its conceptual difficulties, which will be discussed more in the next chapter, it has been a powerful progressive force in the world and the world would be a poorer place without the human rights movement. It must be emphasised that this book does not seek to devalue the idea of human rights, but rather to affirm it and to find ways in which it can become more powerful and effective by embedding it within human community.

4 | Principles and dimensions of human rights

PRINCIPLES

Human rights are commonly considered to be:

- universal; belonging to everybody regardless of race, nation, culture, sex, age, ability, beliefs or behaviour
- indivisible; unable to be separated from each other, but belonging together as a package
- inalienable; unable to be taken away from an individual or group
- inabrogable; unable to be given away, voluntarily or as a trade-off for some other privilege.

In reality, none of these principles applies in the way we understand and enact human rights. Perhaps the most contentious of the four is universalism which, if applied uncritically, can lead to a denial of the importance of culture and diversity and the imposition of one form of human rights (usually a very Western construction) in cultures that do not accept its assumptions (Douzinas 2000, 2007, Pereira 1997). Such an approach to universal human rights can become part of a colonialist agenda.

Clearly there is a need for a more nuanced approach to universalism (Brown 1999), taking account of cultural context while at the same time not succumbing to the dangers of an extreme relativism, which is as untenable as an extreme universalism. This issue of universalism and context is one of the most contentious in human rights discourse and it will be discussed in some detail later in this chapter. A naïve and uncritical universalism is problematic, and hence the assertion that human rights are universal cannot be allowed to go unchallenged, and is not always observed in practice.

The indivisibility of human rights is also potentially problematic. The human rights field has consistently divided rights into categories (see below), and has always treated some rights as different from others. Civil and political rights have been traditionally seen to be separate from economic social and cultural rights (this will be discussed later in the chapter), and there has been disagreement as to the relative priority to be given to each (Freeman 2002). Similar debates have emerged about 'individual' and 'collective' rights (Lyons & Mayall 2003).

Indeed, the very idea of a 'clash' of human rights (for example, the rights of parents and the rights of children; the right of free expression and the right to be free from verbal abuse; civil rights and the right to be free from 'terrorism') implies that specific rights can be treated in isolation, rather than as something that comes in a single, unified package. It also implies that human rights can be in conflict, thereby denying the possibility of indivisibility. The notion of indivisibility is indeed a powerful tool to unsettle some traditional understandings of human rights and to require a redefinition of rights so that they do not conflict with each other.

Clashes of rights usually occur when one actor seeks to exercise their claimed right in such a way that it impinges on the rights of others. If human rights are indeed understood to be indivisible, such excessive exercising of rights becomes itself a violation of rights. Therefore there need to be limits placed on the exercise of rights so that they do not impinge on the rights of others. This is a common argument from within the liberal discourse of human rights (Mill 1906) and it is this liberal notion of exercising rights only insofar as they do not impinge on the rights of others that is at the heart of ideas of indivisibility.

Human rights are also, in practice, not always inalienable. We do take people's rights away from them in certain circumstances. For example, when someone is sentenced to prison their rights of freedom of movement and of association are removed. Similarly, in a number of workplaces (such as the military) the right to join a trade union is denied. Children are denied a number of human rights that adults take for granted, such as the right to vote and the right to earn a living. It is also common to hear rhetoric to the effect that a right needs to be 'earned'. This is in reality an argument that there are responsibilities that go with rights, but the implication is that if people do not meet their responsibilities then they effectively 'forfeit' their rights; such a view is hardly compatible with the idea of rights being inalienable.

Finally, the idea of human rights as inabrogable is also frequently contradicted. It is common for employees, whether in the public or the private sector, to be required to sign confidentiality agreements, thereby abrogating their right to freedom of expression. This is an example of a human right being traded away; this could not occur if human rights were truly inabrogable. And freedom of expression is often not the only right that has to be traded in order to gain employment (itself a human right). Freedom of movement, freedom of association, the right to work in a safe and healthy environment, the right to free time with one's family and the right to be treated with dignity may be abrogated in order to be employed, depending on the labour laws, the labour market and accepted employment practices of the state concerned.

Thus the conventional characterisation of human rights as universal, indivisible, inalienable and inabrogable is not consistent with the way human rights are enacted. Such a view of human rights represents perhaps an ideal to be worked towards, rather than a description of reality. However, many conventional human rights education programs will insist that human rights 'are' (not 'should be') universal, indivisible, inalienable and inabrogable, and this is a cause of confusion and ambiguity. It sets an ideal that is not attainable in reality, and that can result in human rights being readily dismissed as idealistic dreaming, or 'not in the real world'. This conventional approach fits more closely with a positivist view of rights as 'existing' within the natural rights tradition, rather than as constructed.

In the world in which people struggle to define and achieve human rights things are much more messy, complex and contradictory than the certainties of conventional discourse would suggest. Human rights in people's lived experience are not universal, indivisible, inalienable or inabrogable, even though we may wish them to be. As 'principles' of human rights they represent a normative ideal rather than a valid description.

In the pages that follow, the approach to human rights will be more consistent with the constructed tradition and will seek an understanding of human rights that is more embedded within, and consistent with, people's lived experience. For this purpose, we need much more than pious statements about rights being 'universal, indivisible, inalienable and inabrogable'.

BEYOND THE NATION STATE

One of the important characteristics of the idea of human rights is that it extends our rights well beyond the boundaries of the nation state. Commonly, we think of our rights as being defined by our national citizenship and guaranteed by national bills of rights, constitutions, conventions and so on. This is partially modified in Europe, where the European Union has begun to replace nation states as the guarantor of citizenship rights.

However, there are problems with the nation state, or even with a regional grouping such as the EU, acting as guarantor of the rights of the citizen. In an increasingly globalised world many people are living in nation states where they do not hold citizenship, and most of these people are the ones who are at the most risk of human rights abuse: refugees, asylum seekers and migrant workers. If rights are guaranteed as a result of our national citizenship, such people have limited protection and risk being overlooked by a nation's human rights regime.

Another problem with national citizenship rights is that, in the age of globalisation, many human rights violations are caused, directly or indirectly, by international actors (such as transnational corporations) which are often effectively unaccountable to the governments of the states within which they operate. The power of national governments to regulate and control the activities of transnational actors is strictly limited, especially in the case of large and powerful corporations.

In this regard, it has been common for governments to seek to ensure 'human rights' through national legislation, bills of rights or constitutions. This is, undoubtedly, a worthy aim, but it poses a problem for any notion of universal human rights. It results in one person's rights being different from another's because they hold different national citizenship. This is hardly an adequate regime for 'universal' rights. The United Nations seeks to overcome this by requiring that states that have signed UN conventions on human rights should include those rights in their legislation and ensure that they are adequately realised and protected. However, this has had less than complete success and human rights protections are very different for people living in different states. If people's rights vary according to their citizenship, they can hardly be said to be 'human' rights, held by all people in common.

To counter these problems, there have been attempts to incorporate the idea of global citizenship into the concept of human rights. We derive our rights not from our citizenship in a nation state, or even in a regional grouping such as the EU, but from our common humanity or membership of the 'human race' (Douzinas 2007, Falk 1993, 2000a, 2000b, Falk, Ruiz & Walker 2002, Keck & Sikkink 1998, Rajagopal 2003). This becomes a more important agenda in the era of globalisation as the power of nation states becomes eroded and as global forces that threaten human rights require global responses to address them.

It is not only the threat to human rights that can be wider than nation states. With global private operators in areas such as health care and education our rights to health and to education may be met (adequately or otherwise) by global rather than national actors. It seems likely that the nation state as a guarantor of human rights will become less adequate and less relevant if globalisation continues. As transnational corporations claim global 'rights' to act as they wish regardless of national governments, it becomes necessary for citizenship rights to be similarly guaranteed at a global level if people are not to fall victims to the vagaries of unaccountable global markets. Human rights represent a platform from which this can be achieved, and an organising idea for the development of 'global citizenship'.

At present the only people able to call themselves 'global citizens' are the powerful: those whose wealth, power, recognised ability or celebrity status are in demand, who are welcomed wherever they go, and for whom national borders are readily crossed. For others, however, global citizenship is a dream and if they try to cross borders they risk being turned back or detained, or at best given minimal accommodation in refugee camps. There are global citizens and global non-citizens, but human rights, at least in theory if not in practice, demand that the rights of global citizenship be extended to all, regardless of wealth, property or ability.

JUSTICIABILITY OF RIGHTS; THE RULE OF LAW

Another important characteristic of human rights discourse is the idea of justiciability. This is the notion that human rights need to be protected by law and that, for a right to be justiciable, it has to be able to be defended through legal processes. Traditionally some rights (such as the right to a fair trial) are more readily justiciable than others (such as the right to be treated with dignity), but the idea of justiciability has led some human rights advocates, especially lawyers, to try to find ways to make all rights justiciable (Meckled-García & Çali 2006). If the right to health care, or to education, were truly justiciable, people who believed this right had been denied (for example through poverty or through poor teaching) could take their case to court and receive adequate compensation.

Whether all rights can be made justiciable, however, is open to question. There is no doubt that some are more readily justiciable than others, and too strong an emphasis on justiciability may mean that some rights are marginalised or ignored and human rights can become over-legislated. This represents an argument against justiciability, but on the other hand it may also be argued that if a right cannot be legally protected there is not much point in having it.

Such an argument for justiciability, however, privileges the legal world view over others. A purely legal world view suggests that the only things that count are those things that are defined or protected by law, and that laws form the basis of all human interaction. This is, for most people, a gross overstatement of the importance of laws. It is obviously false to think that we only do things because the law says we must, and only refrain from doing things because the law forbids them. Human activity, and how we treat each other, is determined by a complex variety of motivations, including our socialisation, genetic endowment, morality, religion, emotions, peer pressure and cultural expectations as well as the law. For most people, most of the time, the law plays a very minor part. If human rights are justified only on the basis of law, they surely do not adequately reflect the full reality of how and why people behave towards each other in the way they do. Relying on the law alone to achieve human rights is a limited view indeed.

In particular, the law does not deal well with 'low-level' forms of human rights abuse, especially within the domestic arena (which will be discussed more fully below). For example, it is possible to legislate against verbal harassment of a racist or sexist nature, and many states have such legislation. However, it is effectively impossible to legislate against ongoing low-level harassment within a family, which may not be severe enough to be covered by abuse legislation but may be extremely demeaning in the long term for the person concerned. Even in the public arena, for example in the workplace, legislation can deal with significant (even gross) human rights violations, but not with ongoing low-level harassment, which may take subtle forms that cannot be demonstrated by 'evidence' but which effectively deny or violate an employee's rights in terms of her or his own lived experience.

In matters of human rights, the law is effectively a blunt instrument. It can deal with clear, substantiated cases of significant abuse, but it is not able to deal with more subtle, complex or ambiguous situations in which human rights are daily denied or violated.

The dominance of the legal view of human rights privileges one particular world view and marginalises others. It is part of the dominance of the law, and legal rationality, in all aspects of life. It has given lawyers key leadership roles in the field of human rights and has led to human rights often being simply categorised as a specialisation in law. Lawyers are usually called on to lead human rights commissions or inquiries and human rights books are usually found in the legal section of bookshops or libraries. The definition of human rights has been regarded as an exercise in law and, because of the very nature of the law, this has led to a top-down view of human rights in which human rights are defined by experts and imposed on others, rather than the bottom-up approach that is the perspective of this book.

This is not to say that there is no role for lawyers or the law in human rights from below. The legal profession should not be seen as holding a dominant position in relation to human rights, but it should be seen as one of a number of professions and occupational groups that can play a role in human rights work. There have also been significant attempts to reconstruct law 'from below' (Goodale & Merry 2007, Rajagopal 2003), and these are much more compatible with the community development approach to human rights, which will be discussed in later chapters.

RIGHTS AND RESPONSIBILITIES

Another important issue that is central to human rights is the relationship between rights and responsibilities, duties and obligations. It is obvious that rights imply responsibilities: responsibilities on others to ensure that one's 'rights' are realised or protected. Rights without responsibilities make no sense, and so the two must be understood together. In fact, responsibilities are the hard part of human rights work. It is often easy to agree on the 'existence' or 'ownership' of a right, but the question of whose responsibility it is to ensure that right is met can be much more contentious. Human rights work is mostly, in reality, human responsibilities work: ensuring that the responsibilities that go with rights are met by the appropriate person, group or institution.

Despite the clear and obvious connection between rights and responsibilities, it is common to see a separation between them in political discourse. Those on the political right like to emphasise responsibilities, but are often reluctant to talk about rights because these are seen as dangerously socialist. Similarly those on the political left, while comfortable with the language of rights, are often suspicious about responsibilities because of the discourse of 'mutual obligation' that has been used coercively by more conservative political interests. Hence there has been an ideological divide that has acted to limit the extent to which rights and responsibilities can be considered together as part of a common discourse about how we relate to each other as human beings sharing a finite planet.

For the purposes of this book, understanding the relationship between rights and responsibilities, and seeing them as necessarily connected, is central. Understanding rights and responsibilities together links us with each other in a network of rights and responsibilities: my rights require responsibilities of others; the rights of others impose responsibilities on me. To talk about 'my rights' in isolation, as if they are things that I own and have nothing to do with anyone else, is nonsense. The single person on a desert island has no rights. Rights only exist in community with others (Gewirth 1996), and it is this necessary connection between rights and community that forms the basis of this book. Rights and responsibilities require that we think about human community, and therefore human rights work requires that we think about community development. This will be discussed further in Chapter 5.

Conventional liberal views of human rights, in considering rights and responsibilities, will concentrate on both the rights and the responsibilities of individuals. However, this is a limited and culturally biased view of both rights and responsibilities. As will be discussed below, rights can be understood both individually and collectively, and for the purposes of the present discussion the same applies to duties or responsibilities.

Responsibilities may lie at the individual level – my responsibilities to respect the rights of others – but they can also apply at the family level (for example, the family's obligations to allow children the right to free expression); at the community level (a community's responsibility to be inclusive of others and show them respect); at the institutional level (the responsibility of schools, hospitals, workplaces and the like to respect the rights of those within them and those on whom they have an impact); at the corporate level (a corporation's responsibility to treat its employees, customers, shareholders and the community with honesty and respect); and at the state level (the state's responsibility to provide programs and services that enable people's rights to health, education, income support and so on to be met, as well as the responsibility to ensure that police, military and security personnel respect the rights of citizens and others). In the contemporary globalised world the international, or global, also becomes important as a location for responsibility, as is seen with the perceived role of the UN in preventing human rights violations.

It is important, in considering these various potential locations of responsibility, to understand that it is not necessarily a case of either/or. There is often a tendency, in seeking to assign responsibility, to place responsibility in a single location rather than understanding that, in an interconnected society, responsibility for human rights will inevitably be shared. In Chapter 5 the idea of a culture of human rights will be discussed and this implies that responsibility will be shared and will be seen as both individual and collective. This can help to overcome the inevitable buck-passing of responsibility: the government calling for the community or the private sector to take responsibility; the private sector seeking to have the government accept responsibility; a wish by some for 'the family' to take more responsibility; strenuous advocacy for 'the individual' to be more responsible; and so on.

In recent decades the belief in market forces, and the ability of the market to achieve almost anything, has led to a tendency to 'leave it to the market', resulting in a lack of acceptance of responsibility by other actors. It is clear that human rights cannot simply be left to the market, as markets have proved to be only too ready to encourage human rights violations in the interests of profit (Klein 2007, Shiva 2005), but this does not mean that the private sector has no role in protecting or achieving human rights. Indeed, if the private sector plays such a large role in society it is inevitable that it should be required to take some responsibility for human rights as well as for profit. At the time of writing, the belief in the infallibility of the market is under serious challenge because of the credit crisis and the resulting economic recession, and it is interesting that this is accompanied by a re-emergence of debate around responsibility – for economic activity, certainly, but this may well extend into the arena of human rights as well.

INTERGENERATIONAL RIGHTS

While we are discussing the link between rights and responsibilities, it is important to emphasise that this link can apply across generations (Falk 2000a). There is a common acceptance that human rights violations that occurred in the past can impose responsibilities on people and institutions in the present. Examples include the issue of the repatriation of valuables confiscated from the Jews by the Nazis during World War II and governments in the present apologising, and providing compensation, for the acts of earlier governments in removing indigenous children from their families. Human rights violations in the past can reverberate down the generations and addressing them, decades or even centuries after the event, has become important for governments and for other institutions wishing to implement human rights.

Similarly, responsibilities can extend into the future, and there is acceptance that those alive today bear some responsibility for ensuring the rights of future generations. Nowhere is this more obvious than in the case of the environment. The rights of future generations to live in a world relatively free from pollution, with some level of resources to sustain life and a climate that can support human civilisation and other animal species, impose certain obligations on present generations to address issues of global warming, over-fishing of the oceans, nuclear waste, water conservation and so on.

Thus human rights and responsibilities have to be seen in a historical context, not merely as occurring in a somehow ahistorical present. Human rights, like everything else, are understood at a particular historical moment. There are stories that stretch back into the past, and other stories that extend well into the future, which shape human rights thinking and practice in the present. Knowing and telling those stories is an important aspect of human rights work. This applies both to the historical development of the idea of human rights and to the connection of rights and responsibilities over time.

INDIVIDUAL AND COLLECTIVE RIGHTS

As was mentioned above, the conventional view of human rights has been largely an individual one, and this is consistent with the Western liberal origins of human rights discourse. A focus on the human as an individual, rather than on humanity as a whole, has characterised much human rights thinking and is inscribed in the Universal Declaration of Human Rights and various UN covenants. These spell out the rights of the individual but largely ignore more collective understandings of human rights. This has been the basis of the so-called 'Asian critique' of human rights, in which critics from Asia claimed that human rights, because of their individual bias, were effectively a colonialist attempt by the West to impose its view of humanity on others (Aziz 1999, Bauer & Bell 1999, Meijer 2001). As a response to this, and because of strong advocacy on the part of *groups* that are systemically denied human rights (such as women, people with disabilities, indigenous people and children) in recent decades, there has been more interest in understanding human rights collectively as well as individually (Lyons & Mayall 2003).

The tension between individual and collective understandings of rights has been significant in the human rights field. Some conservative writers (for example Kristol 1989) have claimed that there can only be individual human rights, as any more collective understanding of rights can deny individual freedom by subsuming the individual within the collective. Others, however (for example Lyons & Mayall 2003), have maintained that some collective understanding of human rights is necessary because people can only realise their full humanity in community, not just as isolated individuals. That is the view accepted in this book.

RIGHTS

		Individual	Collective
	Individual	Liberal	Confucian
RESPONSIBILITIES			
	Collective	Socialist	Communist

Individual and collective rights and responsibilities

The tension between individual and collective rights mirrors the tension between individual and collective responsibilities, as discussed above. If we accept that there can be both individual and collective rights and individual and collective responsibilities, we can envisage a simple 2×2 matrix, as shown in the above diagram.

The diagram identifies four potential ideological positions in relation to individual and collective rights and responsibilities. The liberal tradition implies both individual rights and individual responsibilities, as emphasised in conventional Western understandings of rights, but that is only one of the four possibilities. Individual rights and collective responsibilities imply a more socialist or social democratic tradition, in which it is the collective that is seen as being responsible, normally through the welfare state, for individual rights to be realised and needs to be met: there is a collective duty to meet the well-being of the individual. The Confucian tradition, by contrast, emphasises individual duties to contribute to the well-being of the collective and must be understood in any attempt to address the 'Asian critique'. The final possibility is a combination of collective rights and collective responsibilities, best epitomised by a communist ideal where the individual is subordinate to the collective in terms of both duties and rights.

As with all such diagrams, one must be aware of the danger of over-simplification. This diagram represents simple binaries, and it will be argued in Chapter 5 that such binary thinking is incompatible with human rights from below. It must certainly not be taken as implying simple 'either/or' categories. No society could be claimed to lie wholly within one of the four quadrants and the boundaries are inevitably fluid and permeable. However, the diagram does represent a way of incorporating both individual and collective understandings of human rights and human responsibilities that helps us to move beyond the limitations of a single ideological position. It suggests that the traditional liberal view – of individual rights and individual duties – need not be privileged over the others and is only one way of understanding the relationship between rights and responsibilities. It can also provide a basis for dialogue (see Chapter 5) between different cultural and religious traditions regarding what human rights may mean.

HUMAN RIGHTS AND THE STATE

There is an ambivalence about the role of the state in human rights, which goes back to the different views held by two of the most important philosophers in the formation of the Western view of human rights, namely Thomas Hobbes (1588–1679) and John Locke (1632–1704). Hobbes took a negative view of 'man' in 'his' natural state. He argued that, in the absence of any authority or rule of law, we would always be arguing and fighting with each other and seeking a greater share for ourselves through robbery, violence and murder. In the best-known passage of his writing he argued that in the true 'state of nature':

> ... there is no place for industry; because the fruit thereof is uncertain: and consequently no culture of the earth; no navigation, or use of the commodities that may be imported by sea; no commodious buildings; no instruments of moving, and removing, such things as require much force; no knowledge of the face of the earth; no account of time; no arts; no letters; no society; and which is worst of all, continual fear and danger of violent death; and the life of man, solitary, poor, nasty, brutish and short.
>
> From *Leviathan* (1651) quoted in Hayden 2001, p. 60

This bleak view of our natural state led Hobbes to argue the need for a strong 'sovereign' (not necessarily a monarch but a strong ruler, government or state). For Hobbes, the role of the sovereign is to protect the citizens from each other and to establish laws and the necessary mechanisms for their enforcement. Citizens cede to the sovereign the right to use force or violence, which is clearly in their interests as otherwise they would be in constant conflict with each other and could not live in peace. A strong state is necessary, therefore, if we are to have anything that may resemble rights, and to have them protected. For Hobbes, human rights represented our right to pursue our own ends in relative safety from the violence of others.

By contrast, Locke (1967) took a very different view of human nature. For Locke our 'state of nature' is a positive one, as we are placed on

God's earth to enjoy its beauty and abundance. The state, however, threatens to take away this 'natural' freedom, as governments characteristically impose on people's natural rights. Locke argued that the primary duty of the state is to protect people's rights and that governments have a tendency to ignore this and to violate rights instead. In such a case, Locke argued, citizens are justified in overthrowing the state and installing a new government that will better protect their rights. If Hobbes' view is best summarised by the preceding quote, Locke's view is best expressed not in his own words, but in the famous statement (quoted in Chapter 3, page 74) from the US Declaration of Independence, a document that throughout draws heavily on Lockean thinking in justifying the revolution against the British.

While the ideas of both Hobbes and Locke are of course more complex and nuanced than they are presented here, the point for present purposes is that they hold very different views about the relationship of the state to human rights violation and human rights protection. For Hobbes, we need a strong state as a protector of our rights and the only thing that stands between civilisation and barbarism. For Locke, we need to be wary of a strong state, as it is likely to impinge on our freedoms and deny our rights.

This tension about the role of the state continues to the present day. Human rights activists, for example, commonly campaign against the excesses of the state in committing human rights abuse, while at the same time they advocate for the state to take a stronger role in human rights protection. They argue for both a strong state and a state whose powers are circumscribed. The state therefore becomes both the potential hero and the potential villain. Human rights thinking needs to consider the nature of the modern state, and its potential both for human rights violation and for human rights protection/realisation, in a more sophisticated way than is common in many human rights organisations. We still live with the legacies of both Hobbes and Locke and have to deal with the dilemmas they pose between them.

UNIVERSALISM AND CONTEXT

The issue of universalism and context, often framed in terms of universalism and cultural diversity, is one of the most problematic for students and practitioners of human rights and is reflected in an extensive literature (Ackerly 2008, Bauer & Bell 1999, Caney & Jones 2001, Parekh 1999, Schmale 1993, Van Ness 1999). Universalism has been a characteristic of the conventional human rights discourse, which sees human rights as universal in that they belong to all human beings, deriving from their very humanity regardless of background, race, religion, class or culture. Thus the *Universal* Declaration of Human Rights is seen as the cornerstone of the human rights project. People act to stop human rights violations in other cultures because somehow human rights are seen as being above culture, in that they transcend cultural boundaries.

Some notion of universalism has been at the heart of UN human rights work, NGOs such as Amnesty International and Human Rights Watch, and media treatment of human rights. The idea of universalism for many human rights workers gives human rights its power; it enables people to intervene in cases of 'clear' human rights abuses wherever they may occur. Thus any questioning or critique of universalism is seen as potentially reducing the power of human rights and the capacity of human rights activists to achieve their goals.

Despite this potential danger of diluting the power of human rights, such a critique of universalism is necessary. An uncritical universality can readily blind us to cultural difference, and when cultural difference is ignored or denied the dominant culture (for many people the Western cultural tradition) will be uncritically accepted as the 'right', 'legitimate' or 'best' form of culture. It will become the norm against which other traditions will be judged and often found wanting, simply because the dominant tradition itself establishes what criteria should determine the 'best' form of culture.

As discussed in Chapter 3, it is evident that the conventional view of human rights has been shaped by the Western Enlightenment tradition, and that as a result this has come to be seen by many as the norm for human rights. This is inappropriate for people from other cultural contexts and, as has been pointed out by a number of writers, it devalues other traditions and becomes another manifestation of Western colonialism (Angle 2002, Meijer 2001, Nirmal 2000, Pereira 1997). An uncritical universalism can, it might be argued, work against human rights in that it can perpetuate a system that denies or devalues people's right to cultural life other than that of the industrialised West.

This argument has been taken up in the 'Asian critique' of human rights, as indicated above. Although one can argue that these criticisms, and the 'Asian critique' in particular, have been used by political leaders to avoid being held accountable for human rights abuse by arguing that human rights, as a Western concept, does not apply to their countries, this does not fully refute the argument. There is no doubt that universal human rights, as conventionally understood, reflect a particularly Western Enlightenment view of both 'humanity' and 'rights' that is inadequate for a more inclusive world where diversity is valued rather than feared, and where the limitations of the Western world view have become more apparent. Indeed, in a more postmodern world any idea of universalism, with its implied meta-narrative, is suspect.

A naïve and uncritical universalism, therefore, which simply implies one set of human rights for all, is untenable. All our ideas, including those of human rights, emerge in a cultural context and cannot be divorced from it. And cultural contexts vary; what will count as 'human rights' will inevitably be different in different cultural contexts, however strong the urge for universalism may be. The idea of universality remains strong, but it must be a more nuanced and sophisticated universalism (Parekh 1999) if it is to be relevant to the contemporary world.

However, simple relativism is just as untenable. Such a position, denying anything but the contextual, ignores the wider world and the fact that, despite cultural differences, human beings are connected across boundaries. It would mean that a person, group or government seeing what clearly amount to gross human rights violations in another country would be powerless to act. Clearly one cannot simply dismiss events such as the genocide in Rwanda, the Holocaust or other such affronts to humanity as 'cultural' and therefore to be accepted without any sense of moral outrage or attempt to intervene. A naïve and uncritical relativism is at least as dangerous as a naïve and uncritical universalism, and both extreme positions are untenable.

The very idea of 'universal' is problematic and can be understood in different ways. So-called universals can, and do, change over time. What might be understood as universal human rights now is rather different from the understanding in the Universal Declaration, and we can be sure that in another 60 years it will be different again. Universals do not stay constant and will vary with time and place; therefore 'universals' are not truly universal, and never will be.

Similarly, cultures are neither static nor monolithic. They can, and do, change over time, as is reflected in the experience of immigrants who return to their country of origin many years later only to discover that the culture they remember no longer exists. Similarly, cultures are pluralistic. Just because something is a cultural norm or a cultural practice does not mean that everyone in that culture values or practises it. For example, sport is indisputably an important part of 'Australian culture', but there are many Australians who do not play or follow sport, though they do not see themselves as any less 'Australian'. Ideas such as 'universal' and 'culture' are not clear, unambiguous and unchanging.

The issue of universality and context, therefore, needs to be understood in a different way. It is necessary to deconstruct the binary and to stop thinking of universal/contextual as an *either/or* dichotomy. Instead we need to find a way of thinking about them as *both/and*, exploring ways in which the two interact and seeking to understand human rights as inevitably both universal and contextual. There are several ways in which one might approach this task (see also Ife 2007, 2008).

GENERALISED RIGHTS

One way is to think of universals only in a very general sense. From this point of view, the problem with universal human rights is that people have tried to make them too specific, and as soon as this happens they inevitably become contextualised. This perspective accepts that, despite the importance of context, there are nevertheless some universals.

An example might be the right to be treated with dignity and respect. One could argue that this is a universal right – that everyone has a right to be treated with dignity and respect – but that one must then recognise that dignity and respect are themselves cultural constructs, and what counts as dignity and respect in one context does not count as such in a different context. The idea that everyone should be treated with dignity and respect may be a universal value, but it does not imply that everyone should be treated the same way, or that this universal right can be protected through universal laws. In some cultures, for example, to show respect to a woman means to behave in a way that in other cultures might be regarded as demeaning or patriarchal. Context determines what should count as dignity and respect, but despite this there is still, it might be argued, a *universal right* to dignity and respect.

In this way there is still a universalist understanding of some rights, but how those universal rights are worked out will vary with context. Similarly, a universal right to participation in the political process does not automatically imply a 'right to vote'. If people have other ways in which they can participate in politics, such as through processes of deliberative democracy (discussed in Chapter 5), their right to political participation can be met without their necessarily having a right to vote, which can often be symbolic rather than substantive.

This perspective requires that 'universal human rights' be kept at a very general level: the right to political participation rather than the right to vote; the right to education rather than the right to attend school; the right of access to information rather than the right to computer access; the right to be treated with dignity rather than the right to be offered a seat on a bus by a younger person; the right to meaningful work rather than the right to 'a job'; and so on. It is a form of limited universality, specifically leaving open the opportunity (in fact the necessity) of constructing the meaning of that right within a context, recognising that any universal human right would be defined and enacted in context-specific ways.

UNIVERSAL RIGHTS AND CONTEXTUAL NEEDS

Another related way of thinking about universals and context is to draw a distinction between rights and needs. This distinction will be discussed in more detail in Chapter 5 as an important component of human rights from below. Again, the idea is that there are universal human rights only in the most general sense and that universal rights imply specific needs.

An example would be the right to education: a universal *right*, but one that translates to very different educational *needs* in different contexts. In one context the need might be for a school, in another for teachers, in another for simple resources for parents or extended family, in another for books, in another for a library/resource centre, in another for computers. Which combination of these possible 'needs' is required so that a universal 'right' to education can be met will vary and must be determined within the local context. This idea of generalised universal rights and specific needs is the reverse of much conventional writing on needs and rights (for example Doyal & Gough 1991, Max-Neef 1991), and is discussed further in Chapter 5. Here it is presented simply as one possible way through the universal/contextual dilemma.

ASPIRATIONAL UNIVERSALITY

A different way of understanding universalism and context is to understand universals as *aspirational* statements rather than as *empirical* statements. When I make a statement about universal human rights I am making a statement about what principles *I wish* were applied to all of humanity: my own vision of a world where people respect and help realise their own rights and the rights of others. That vision will inevitably be a construct of my own cultural/political/historical context, but it is still a vision of the universal. Another person, in another culture, may also articulate her or his view of universal human rights, and inevitably it will be somewhat different from mine. Both are universal in that they articulate an aspiration of what each of us would wish for all of humanity. The fact that the two differ should not surprise or dismay us; rather it can become the basis for a dialogue between us so that each of us can learn from the other and understand why the other has a somewhat different set of aspirations for humanity.

From this perspective we see any articulation of universal human rights, such as the Universal Declaration or a national bill of rights, not as expressing rights as empirical 'fact' but rather as an aspiration for humanity, made in a specific context. There will inevitably be other statements of aspirational human rights, which will be just as valid, and none can claim universal truth. This represents a different understanding of universalism. There can be many different aspirations and the interplay between them, through dialogue, can only enhance human understanding. Whether there is ever 'agreement' is not the issue. Rather, the diversity of aspirations for humanity represents the diversity of humanity itself and dialogue about human rights, or about what it means to be human in different contexts and what people would wish for their fellow human beings, can only enrich the humanity of all and strengthen our respect for, and understanding of, 'human rights'.

UNIVERSALS AND CONTEXT COEXISTING

Another line of argument around universalism and context is to see each as dependent on the other: all universals are contextual, and all context statements have elements of universalism. This is a more nuanced position than those described above, but also a more powerful one.

Any statement of universals, however it is worded, takes place in a context: historical, political, cultural and social. The Universal Declaration, for example, is not context-free. It was drawn up at a particular historical moment, in the political context of the late 1940s, within the culture of international diplomacy at the time. The meanings ascribed to the words were those of that context. Reading the Universal Declaration sixty years later, in a different cultural context, gives its words different meanings for the reader(s).

There can be no such thing as a context-free statement of universality. The context provides the meaning for the constructions of 'universality' in any statement, declaration, bill of rights or convention. Words, especially the words of a human rights declaration, are imprecise and only partially capture the intended meaning, as argued both by Wittgenstein (1974) and, more prosaically, by Humpty Dumpty in *Through the Looking Glass*, declaring that words mean 'what I choose them to mean'. Words only have meaning in a context. However much a legal construction of human rights may seek to use universalising context-free language, there is no escaping the inevitability of context in giving meaning to any universal statement.

Not only does universalism require a context, but context also requires some more universalist understanding to give it meaning. Any statement about a context (cultural, political or historical) implies a comparison with some wider norm. For example, to state that 'US culture is materialist' implies that the person making the statement has some sort of understanding of other cultures as well and is able to compare the materialism of 'US culture' to others. Similarly, a statement that 'the Cold War was a time of heightened tensions' implies a knowledge of other historical periods and an implication that most of them were less tense than the 'Cold War' era. Any statement about context thus requires some wider frame of reference, which might be understood as some kind of quasi-universal: a world beyond the narrowly contextual.

Just as no universal statement can exist without a context, so no contextual statement can exist without some wider form of quasi-universality. In this sense, universal and contextual are no longer binary opposites, where each excludes the other in a simple matter of 'either/or'. Rather, each needs the other in order to make sense, and the universal and the contextual are inevitably linked. From this perspective, any statement of human rights carries with it both universal and contextual meanings. One may be emphasised to the apparent exclusion of the other, but the other is in fact implied by the very existence of the primary statement. Human rights are therefore always about both universalism and context, and each is needed to give meaning and substance to the other. A human rights perspective cannot be just universal or just contextual, but will inevitably be both. When we understand human rights in this way, the 'dilemma' of universalism and context disappears and we need to think through how any human rights question, issue or statement relates both to universal ideals and to specific contexts, recognising the problematics of each.

This section has suggested a number of different lines of thinking around the issue of universality and context. All of them seek to break down the simplistic dichotomy and to find 'both/and' ways forward. There can be no simple solution to this dilemma, no magic formula that simply 'resolves' the issue to everyone's satisfaction. But there are certainly ways in which we can think about the issue that will dissolve the simple binary opposite of universal/context. This is a good example of how human rights is a field that involves more than simple moral certainty and zealous activism. It is important to think through the complexity of 'human rights', to be critical and analytical and to recognise that the complexity of the issues is a source of enrichment rather than frustration.

Before leaving the issue of universalism and context, it is worth revisiting the three traditions of human rights outlined in Chapter 3: the natural rights tradition, the states obligations tradition and the constructed rights tradition. As indicated in Chapter 3, each has a different view of the universal/contextual debate. The natural rights tradition is most consistent with universalism: all people are born with rights because of their very humanity, and hence rights are the same for all, namely universal. In fact, from a natural rights perspective all human rights are universal. The states obligations tradition, with its emphasis on law and regulation, implies universality only when laws or regulations can apply universally; for example as part of international law or through the UN human rights regime. Otherwise it acknowledges context to the extent that different jurisdictions may be different, though it seeks uniformity within any particular jurisdiction. The constructed rights tradition, on the other hand, fully recognises context and has some difficulty with any notion of universality, beyond the idea of aspirational universality or the form of universality that requires context and that in turn gives significance to any contextual statement.

HUMAN RIGHTS AND THE HERITAGE OF THE WESTERN WORLD VIEW

As has been mentioned elsewhere, the dominant construction of human rights has been very much within the Western world view. Here we will concentrate on what this legacy has meant for human rights, and the issues and dilemmas that result.

INDIVIDUALISM

The individualist bias in human rights has already been discussed above. It is simply worth noting here that the liberal individualism, on which conventional human rights has been largely based, has served to devalue collective or group rights and has made the very idea of collective rights a 'problem' or 'issue'. As will be discussed later in this chapter, we can understand *all* human rights as having both individual and collective aspects and, as with universalism and context, it is important to stop thinking about individual *or* collective rights, but instead to see human rights as incorporating both.

GENDER

One of the important aspects of conventional human rights is that its construction has reflected dominant patriarchy. Historically, the view of 'the human' has been a male one and women have not been included in understandings of matters such as democracy, rights, political participation and education. In Western cultures women were, until recent decades, largely seen to be for the convenience of men rather than as fully 'human' in their own right.

If women were excluded from the category of 'human' it is hardly surprising that they were excluded from human rights. This is not particularly remarkable; in a patriarchal world structures and discourses of patriarchy will affect everything, and human rights is no exception. It can be seen in the language of human rights – the 'rights of man' – and in the gendered language of the Universal Declaration, reflecting the time in which it was written. There have, of course, been dissenting voices, the most significant being that of Mary Wollstonecraft (1759–1797), an early feminist writer who reacted against the 'rights of man' rhetoric of Tom Paine (1994) and others by writing about the rights of women, arguing that women were being left out of consideration as human beings with rights (Wollstonecraft 1975).

Wollstonecraft was not alone, and there have been other dissenting voices from advocates of women's rights (Brems 2003, French 1992, Howland 1999, Peterson & Parisi 1998, Rendel 1997). Feminist writers have argued that patriarchy in human rights goes deeper than simply the omission of women from the human rights discourse. A concentration on 'the rights of man' has devalued the rights of women and allowed women's rights to be violated while men's rights are championed.

This is particularly so when we consider human rights across the public/private divide. The 'human rights movement', especially in relation to civil and political rights, has concentrated on human rights in the public domain: the right of free expression, the right to freedom of assembly, the right to freedom of association, the right to a fair trial, and so on. This is traditionally the male domain; the human rights of women tend to be realised, or violated, in the domestic or private sphere, examples of the latter being domestic violence, rape and not being afforded dignity and respect. The human rights movement, it can be argued, by concentrating on violations in the public domain, has been more concerned with the human rights of men than the human rights of women.

This criticism has led to a broadening of understanding of human rights and deliberate attempts by organisations such as Amnesty International to extend their mandate to include those human rights violations that most affect women. However, it is clear that patriarchal discourses have strongly affected the construction of human rights in the past and, despite the influence of a strong feminist critique, it would be naïve to suggest that contemporary human rights are no longer influenced by gender. This still results in systematic denial of the human rights of women in many different cultural settings, including the West.

It is important to remember that the boundary between the public and the private is itself problematic, that it is another example of a simple binary within the world view of modernity, and that it parallels the boundary between the personal and the political. The feminist analysis that the personal is political and the political is personal means that also the public is private and the private is public. Our 'private lives' spill over into the public, just as our 'public lives' spill over into the private, and to draw a sharp distinction between the two is false. Any understanding of human rights that is to be meaningful for people's lived experience must not only incorporate both the public and the private aspects of our humanity, but must also accept that the two cannot be separated.

THE SECULAR

As mentioned in Chapter 3, human rights in the Western tradition have been understood from essentially a secular position. This is consistent with the Enlightenment heritage. It must not be thought that the Enlightenment was atheistic – many of the key Enlightenment thinkers held strong religious beliefs – but they sought to limit religion to matters of personal faith and spirituality. This was in response to the religious conflict that engulfed Europe in the sixteenth and seventeenth centuries in the wake of the Reformation (MacCulloch 2003). If such violence and brutality could be unleashed in the name of religion, it was argued, surely it was time to develop ideas of morality, ethics and justice on the basis of human reason rather than on competing interpretations of religious texts and the conflicting teachings of different traditions of Christianity (Hunt 2007).

As a result, Western philosophy was able to develop free from the apparent constraints of religion. Philosophers such as Hobbes, Locke, Rousseau, Kant, Mill and others, who advanced thinking about human rights even if they did not all use the term, developed their arguments largely without any reliance on the 'will of God' or the interpretation of scripture (even though Locke, in particular, talked about rights as God-given). This secular tradition is characteristic of Enlightenment thinking, but very much at odds with Western philosophy from earlier periods and philosophical traditions from the non-Western world.

This has led to a contemporary human rights regime that is inherently secular. Other than freedom of religious expression, there is very little acknowledgement of religious ideas in the Universal Declaration, UN covenants or other human rights charters. This puts Western human rights very much at odds with human rights as they may be understood within the non-Western world, where religion in one form or another is central to one's world view. Within the Muslim tradition, for example, it would be unthinkable to talk about human rights in a secular sense with no reference to the Qur'an, the teachings of the Prophet or other teachings of religious leaders (Dalacoura 2003, Moussalli 2001). Nor would it be possible to think about the realisation or the protection of human rights without the engagement of the Mosque. For this reason, the dominance of the Western Enlightenment tradition of human rights presents an obstacle to inter-faith dialogue about human rights, which is a challenge for those who consider such dialogue essential for the sharing of our understandings of humanity and the development of a genuinely multicultural human rights tradition.

UTILITARIANISM, BENTHAM AND KANT

One of the characteristics of Enlightenment thinking was the importance given to the study of the 'real world' through scientific observation and classification. This emphasis on the material world resulted in a valuing of utilitarian knowledge, knowledge that would be 'useful' in adapting to and shaping the world and the harnessing of that knowledge to create a 'better' world. It is therefore no accident that the Enlightenment was rapidly followed by the Industrial Revolution, when ideas of technological advance, large-scale production, efficiency and effectiveness became more significant.

In this climate, the philosophy of utilitarianism, promoted most notably by Bentham (Hayden 2001), became influential. Utilitarianism is often summarised as the principle of 'the greatest good for the greatest number', implying what was termed 'the calculus of happiness'. In summary, an action was good if it could be shown that net human happiness would increase as a consequence (Goodin 1995). This suggests, of course, that some people might have to make sacrifices for the greater good and that these sacrifices could be justified. The principle of utilitarianism thus allows for urban planning to disrupt neighbourhoods, for 'collateral damage' in times of war, and for people's interests to be compromised in the name of 'the economy' (some must lose their jobs for the 'greater benefit'). It is a principle that is all too readily appealing to politicians, for whom people's votes may be seen as an indicator of their happiness or unhappiness, and it is a principle that can readily lead to the disadvantaging, marginalising or exploitation of minorities who are required to suffer so that the majority can be apparently advantaged.

Standing against utilitarianism is the philosophy of Kant, specifically his 'categorical imperative' (Appelbaum 1995). Kant argued that human beings must have ultimate value, not instrumental value, and that they must be only seen as ends, never as means. Thus humans should not be sacrificed for some 'greater good' – there is no greater good than the human. The other aspect of Kant's categorical imperative is the idea that we should 'act only in accordance with that maxim by which you can at the same time will that it should become a universal law'. By this, Kant means that we cannot apply a different morality to our own actions from that we would wish to be applied to the actions of all others. In this way he is anticipating the idea of universality that is so important for human rights.

Because of Kant's primary valuing of the human, and his invoking of some idea of constructing universal laws of morality, he is very much at the heart of modern ideas of human rights. It is a view that clearly rejects the utilitarianism of Bentham. Most human rights advocates would be much more comfortable in a Kantian world than a Benthamite world. Indeed, Bentham was scathing about the very idea of human rights (Bentham 2001), seeing human rights as confusing and as 'rhetorical nonsense' with no place in his system of calculating and maximising human happiness.

One example of the conflict between a Kantian and Benthamite view, of relevance to contemporary debates about human rights, is the issue of torture. Torture is often justified on utilitarian principles: the physical suffering of one person may be justified if, as a result, many lives can be saved, and so some use of torture on terrorism suspects may be acceptable if it increases net human happiness. For a Kantian, however, torture is unacceptable in any circumstances; a human being must never be seen as a means only. Contemporary debates about torture, for example between spokespersons for the Bush Administration in the United States and human rights advocates, are clearly a case of Kantian principles being opposed to utilitarian justifications.

There is no doubt that utilitarianism has a strong appeal. People seem to accept, for example, that some people must suffer for the good of 'the economy', or that the 'honourable' death of a soldier in war is justified in the national interest. However, it does conflict with a Kantian approach to human rights, and the latter raises some awkward questions that often cannot be adequately answered in a utilitarian world.

Of course human rights need not be constructed from within a Kantian world view. Kant can indeed be critiqued, and it is doubtful that his attachment to universal laws of morality can be fully justified in a postmodern world where universality comes under question, as we have seen above. However, the 'Kant versus Bentham' debates are a contentious and problematic legacy of Enlightenment thinking and must be understood by any student or advocate of human rights.

PROGRESS

The belief in progress is a strong legacy of the Enlightenment (Carroll 2004). The aim is to become 'more' enlightened, to acquire knowledge and to use that knowledge to improve the human condition. This is so ingrained in Western thinking that it is hard to imagine that there could be societies that are not committed to the idea, and the inevitability, of human progress; though in Buddhist or Hindu societies one finds a very different tradition in which 'progress' is often seen as illusory and the regular cycles of human life are the dominant theme (Macy 2007, Shiva 2005). Progress very much permeates Western ideas of human rights; they are seen as the culmination of historical progress, sometimes in celebratory or even triumphalist terms (Laber 2002, Lauren 1998). The story of the rise of human rights is seen in the context of creating a better world and as part of the progress of civilisation. It is part of the Enlightenment legacy of human rights.

The ecological crisis has posed a significant challenge to the idea of the inevitability of progress. Human 'progress' is now seen by some as making the world less liveable rather than more liveable, and as likely to contribute to increased human misery as it is to increased human happiness (Shiva 2005). Nevertheless, the response to the ecological crisis is typically one that advocates increased or new technology, developed as a result of new research and human ingenuity: a classic Enlightenment approach (Postman 1993). More critical questions that cast doubt on the very idea of the value of progress and 'achievement' are seldom asked, and those that do ask them are marginalised and labelled as 'fringe' or 'extreme' (Macy 2007). This demonstrates the power of the belief in human progress and achievement, but despite this it appears that this belief will continue to be challenged as the ecological crisis inevitably worsens.

In the context of human rights, it is important not to tie the human rights story too uncritically to stories of human progress because, if the belief in progress is challenged, then human rights may be as well. Rather, there is a role for more reflective and nuanced histories of human rights (for example Hunt 2007, Sellars 2002) and ways of seeing human rights not just as part of some grand narrative of human improvement but rather as reflecting the diverse ways in which people are always striving to assert, express and realise their humanity and that of others.

RACISM AND COLONIALISM

The colonialist agenda of human rights has already been mentioned several times. It is important to mention it again here, as this is undoubtedly a consequence of the Enlightenment tradition. As we become more 'enlightened' we start to compare ourselves to others who are, by definition, less 'enlightened' than we are. This leads, naturally, to ideas of superiority over others, and racism is the inevitable result. Along with the Enlightenment came a strengthening of ideas of Western superiority and a consequent devaluing of other cultural traditions as being more 'primitive' and as being somewhat behind in the inevitable march of human progress.

Not only did this reinforce racism, but it also gave a moral justification to colonialism. If others are less 'enlightened' and more 'primitive' than we are, then we readily assume an obligation to 'enlighten' them by helping them to replace their inferior cultural traditions with our more developed ones. Hence the Western colonialist project of the eighteenth, nineteenth and twentieth centuries had a moral justification that earlier colonial escapades had not. No longer was colonialism simply about resources, power and greed. It could now be justified by more 'noble' aims of enlightenment in the form of education (in Western knowledge), religious evangelism, imposition of Western traditions of law and governance and so on. And if these were not accepted there was clearly a justification for the use of force, as it was obviously 'for their own good'. Of course Western colonialism was also always about resources, power and greed, but an army of teachers, missionaries, doctors, nurses, agricultural scientists and, in more recent decades, development experts, gave it significant legitimacy, at least in the eyes of those from the colonising culture if not always from the perspective of the colonised (Larsen 2000, Said 1993, 1995, Young 2001).

This colonialist legacy has also affected human rights. Human rights have been criticised as a Western imperialist project, part of the imposition of Western cultural values on the rest of the world, even if this was done apparently from the noblest of motives (Aziz 1999, Pereira 1997). This creates a real problem for human rights: how to extricate ideas of human rights from the Western colonial project and enable people from other cultural backgrounds to develop a sense of ownership of human rights. This is a major aim of human rights from below, through concentrating on the idea of a *culture of human rights*, and will be discussed in more detail in later chapters.

RIGHTS, FREEDOMS AND SELFISHNESS

One of the problems of human rights is that it has become loosely equated with the idea of human freedoms. This is very much the legacy of writers such as John Stuart Mill (1906), who wrote strongly in defence of individual liberty, to pursue one's ends as one wishes, provided only that this does not impinge on the rights of others. This led to the perception of rights as being freedoms: the right to self-determination, to live one's life as one wishes unhindered by others or by the state. The role of the state, for Mill, is to safeguard our individual liberties and not to interfere with them any more than is necessary.

This linking of rights and freedoms has had an important consequence: the possession of a right allows one to exercise that right as much as one wishes; anything less is considered an infringement of individual liberty. This has proved problematic: the right to own property, for example, becomes understood as the right to own as much property as one may wish and can afford. This can mean the concentration of property in the hands of a wealthy minority, who have been simply 'exercising their rights' while others have been unable to afford to own property.

This is potentially the case with the right to anything that is a finite resource. The right to health care can be interpreted as the right to whatever unnecessary medical treatment one may wish – repeated cosmetic surgery, endless psychotherapy, expensive pharmaceuticals – even though this means that hospital and other health facilities are thereby denied to those who may need more urgent or necessary treatment but cannot afford private medical services. In each case – property and health care – any attempt to limit the right in the interests of others would be immediately criticised as an infringement of rights. Equating rights with freedoms can easily lead to the justification of excess as simply the exercising of human rights.

There is thus a need to uncouple rights from freedoms and to understand that having a right does not imply permission to exercise that right to excess. Alternatively, we may want to be more prescriptive about just what is involved in a right. The right to health care, for example, could be redefined as the right to *a basic standard* of health care, not as the right to unlimited access to medical treatments. Similarly, a right to housing does not imply the right to live in a mansion but rather the right of access to a basic level of shelter, comfort and security.

The use of rights language to justify excess is therefore an issue that needs to be considered in thinking about human rights. It is linked not only to the idea of freedoms but also to selfishness. Many claims of rights, it may be argued, are selfish: *my* rights, with an implication that others have the responsibility to meet them. This is discussed further in Chapter 5 so need not concern us here, beyond noting that the construction of rights in a society that values individual achievement and acquisitiveness can reflect the dominant selfish 'look after number one' ideology. Such a view of rights is the negation of human rights as understood in this book, and is one of the reasons why a 'human rights from below' approach is so important.

HUMAN RIGHTS AND THE LAW

The dominance of human rights discourse by the law and the legal profession is a theme throughout this book. At this point it is important simply to note the consequences for the way in which human rights have been understood and enacted. One consequence has been the privileging of civil and political rights over other human rights, as these tend to be the rights that are the most readily justiciable and the most readily dealt with through legal structures and processes.

Another consequence has been the marginalisation of other professions and occupations in human rights work. When considering the right to education, for example, one would think that it would be teachers who were the human rights experts; with the right to health care it would be the various health professionals; with the right to water it would be engineers; with the right to be treated with respect and dignity it might be community development or community education workers. However, this broad, multi-professional approach to human rights work is not well accepted and most teachers, health professionals, engineers and community development workers do not see themselves as human rights workers. While lawyers clearly have an important role to play in human rights work, they can hardly claim exclusive dominance of the field.

A further consequence of the legal domination of human rights is that human rights are seen as a field for rational, positivist inquiry, as that is characteristically the way the law works (Meckled-García & Çali 2006). Human rights abuse is 'understood' through documentation, empirical investigation and the like. However, there are other ways of 'understanding' human rights and human rights abuse. The dominance of the law marginalises other ways of understanding, such as the psychological, the sociological or the philosophical. It also marginalises the work of artists, poets, performers, writers and musicians in exploring the human condition and 'understanding' human rights and what they mean. This requires very different epistemologies from the positivist, empirical world of the law.

The law, and the workings of the law, are rather remote from people's everyday experience beyond the occasional need to use the services of a lawyer or the watching of police and legal dramas on large or small screens. As discussed in Chapter 3, most of the things we do, the ways in which we treat others and the ways in which we expect to be treated have nothing to do with laws or regulations. These aspects of our lives are grounded in lived experience, in cultural context, in family dynamics, in socialisation and in media messages. They have little to do with the law or with lawyers. If human rights are to become more grounded in lived experience, they will need a much broader grounding than the purely legal.

Further, legal processes are not readily accessible to ordinary people; hence the need to have a lawyer represent them. If human rights remain understood largely within the law, they will exclude most of the population from any sense of ownership of human rights and of the responsibilities that go with them. Defining and enacting legislation is, by its very nature, a top-down process and more is required if the idea of human rights from below is to have substance.

CONCLUSION

This section has identified many of the issues raised by the idea of human rights. Although in some cases it has sought to show possible ways forward, for example in the important case of universality and context, its aim has primarily been to raise issues rather than to provide 'answers'. Many of these issues will be taken up again in the following chapters, where community development and human rights are brought together and the idea of 'human rights from below' is further explored.

DIMENSIONS

Human rights are commonly divided into two or three categories. The division into two categories – civil/political rights and economic/social/cultural rights – follows the usage of the UN. While there is a single Universal Declaration, in developing more specific covenants that could be defined in accordance with international law the UN split rights into these two categories with a separate covenant for each. This reflected the political climate of the time, strongly affected by the Cold War. Civil and political rights were readily accepted by the Western tradition with its emphasis on 'freedom' and 'democracy', while the West was rather more circumspect about economic, social and cultural rights, as these suggested an element of socialism. On the other hand, the communist bloc would readily assent to economic, social and cultural rights, but was rather more reluctant about civil and political rights. Establishing the two covenants was therefore an effective way to involve both the major power blocs of the time in the UN human rights regime. These two categories of rights therefore became part of the conventional human rights discourse (Lauren 1998, Sellars 2002).

Later in the twentieth century, the so-called 'Asian critique' of human rights became prominent (Bauer & Bell 1999). As discussed above, this accused the West of dominating the human rights discourse and imposing its view of human rights on the rest of the world as part of a colonialist agenda (Pereira 1997). In particular, the Asian critique concentrated on what it perceived as an individualist bias in Western views of human rights, which it saw as inappropriate for Asian cultures with a more collectivist, Confucian tradition (Davis 1995, Meijer 2001). Despite the way in which some Asian leaders used this critique simply as an excuse to validate their own human rights violations, and to attempt to avoid international scrutiny of their practices, there were many in the 'developed' West who nevertheless saw the critique as making a valid point, requiring a more inclusive human rights regime. The Universal Declaration and major UN covenants are predominantly about the rights of individuals rather than the rights of collectives, and more collectivist understandings of 'the human' are not included.

To deal with this critique, and in an attempt to include Asian nations within the human rights discourse, a number of writers (such as Galtung 1994) started to talk about a 'third generation' of human rights, understood as 'collective rights' – namely those rights that only make sense when understood collectively and that can apply to communities, societies or nations rather than to individuals. These include, commonly, environmental rights, rights to benefit from economic development and at least some aspects of cultural rights.

As a result, it became common to understand human rights as having three dimensions or 'generations':

- civil and political rights: for example rights to freedom of speech, freedom of assembly, justice before the law, freedom of religion, political participation (such as the right to vote), freedom from discrimination
- economic social and cultural rights: for example the rights to education, health, employment, housing, income security, choice of marriage partner, cultural expression
- collective rights: for example environmental rights, the right to benefit from economic development, the right to community cohesion and harmony.

PROBLEMS WITH THE THREE GENERATIONS

The three 'generations' of rights summarised above have had strong intuitive appeal. They loosely correspond with the tripartite slogan of the French Revolution: 'Liberty, Equality, Fraternity'. However, on closer examination it is an unsatisfactory classification, derived from historical accident and the necessity to react to the politics of the time. The Cold War is now long gone, the postcolonial critique is being reformulated in the context of globalisation, and a human rights classification based on the geopolitics of the years 1948 to 1990 no longer makes sense.

The first problem is with the very idea of three 'generations'. Using the term 'generation' suggests a historical lineage, with the first emerging initially, followed by the second and then the third. However, this only makes sense from the perspective of modern *Western* thought. In Western thought it is true that the first generation 'emerged' with eighteenth-century ideals of liberalism, the second with nineteenth-century ideals of socialism and the third with twentieth-century ideals of solidarity. However, in other traditions the order of emergence of these ideas is different, and the use of the term 'generation' betrays the very Western bias that proponents of the 'third generation' were seeking to avoid.

In addition, using the terms 'first', 'second' and 'third' can suggest a prioritising of rights, with first-generation rights being seen as somehow more important and taking precedence over the second generation, and the second generation in turn being seen as more important than the third. This is clearly inappropriate. For many people, some second-generation rights would have priority (who bothers about freedom of association when they are starving?), though this is not true for others (for example 'better dead than red' and 'give me liberty or give me death'). Again, it might be argued that third-generation rights are the most important: what is the point of other human rights if environmental rights are violated to such a degree that life itself is threatened? Any attempt to pose one 'generation' as more important, or fundamental, is doomed to failure and we need to maintain that all categories of rights are important. For some people, in some places, some rights will be more significant than others, while for other people, in other places, the priorities will be very different.

While we may come up with different names for the three groups to avoid the problem of perceived priority, as for example was done by Galtung (1994) who proposed the terms 'blue', 'red' and 'green' human rights respectively (suggesting a parallel with associated political ideologies), there is still a problem of classification, which makes the three 'generations' an inconsistent framework for understanding human rights.

The first problem is the issue of the third generation being understood as *collective* rights. This implies that the other two generations comprise individual rights, which is clearly not true. The individual bias of the Western view of human rights has led to first- and second-generation rights being understood largely in individual terms; but this is not necessarily so, as these rights are also experienced collectively.

For example, the first-generation right to freedom of expression can readily be applied to the rights of groups (such as indigenous people or people with disabilities) to have their views heard, as well as to the rights of individuals (Garkawe, Kelly & Fisher 2001, Lyons & Mayall 2003). We can understand second-generation rights collectively when we talk about the rights of women to education, the right to meaningful employment for people with disabilities and the right of indigenous people to adequate and culturally appropriate health care. Indeed, it is possible to understand all rights that are commonly listed in the first two generations as having both individual and collective aspects, and as being able to be expressed, realised, protected or denied at either the individual or group level. To establish a separate category for collective rights therefore makes little sense. Indeed it only serves to reinforce the predominantly individualist approach to human rights that the advocates of the third generation were seeking to challenge.

Similarly, the rights commonly claimed for the third generation can also be understood individually; for example, individuals as well as communities can be said to have a right to benefit from economic development, or from a clean environment. It is surely much more inclusive, and much more holistic, to understand all human rights as being both individual and collective, and hence to do away with the separate 'third generation' of collective rights.

There are further problems with the traditional 'three generations' approach. While civil and political rights belong naturally together, both being concerned with citizenship rights of participation in civil society, the political process and the public domain, the second 'generation' of economic, social and cultural rights is a much less coherent classification. It might be thought of as including all those rights that were not clearly 'civil and political' at the time of the Universal Declaration, rather than having any classificatory coherence. Economic, social and cultural rights have little in common and do not belong easily together.

Also included in this category are what we might call 'survival rights', the rights to those basic things needed for simple human survival: food, water, shelter, clothing and health services. These are perhaps the most basic of all rights, as our very survival depends on them, but there is nothing about them that is particularly economic, social or cultural, and it is unclear why they are included within this particular category. Again, the category seems more like a grab-bag for whatever rights were left over after listing civil and political rights, rather than a coherent and consistent grouping.

Economic rights are a conceptually different category from other rights. Money itself has no intrinsic value and does nothing to enhance our humanity in the way that, for example, education, health, cultural expression and freedom of association can. The importance of money is its exchange value. In modern society we cannot live without money, as we use it to buy the things we need as well as the things we want. However, it is possible to imagine a society without money, where all other human rights are realised, where people lead full, enriched lives and where their humanity is realised. Many would claim that indigenous societies, or hunter-gatherer communities, achieved this without having to bother about money and 'economic rights'. While we may argue that social, cultural, civil and political rights are all necessary at some level, if we are to realise our humanity, the same is only true of economic rights within a society where there is a currency and where this is used for the exchange of goods and services.

In modern society, economic rights are important only because we need money to realise some of our other rights: to pay for food, housing, transport, property, cultural participation, health care, education and so on. Economic rights are instrumental rights; they are important only because they allow us to achieve other human rights, rather than being ends in themselves. For this reason, economic rights are conceptually different from other rights, and to include them in a grab-bag of rights along with social rights, cultural rights and survival rights is inappropriate. They deserve a category of their own.

It can also be questioned whether it is appropriate for social and cultural rights to be grouped in the same category. While there is some justification for this, in that both are primarily about relationships, there are important differences between the two. Most important, if the two are grouped together there is a tendency for the 'social' to dominate the 'cultural'. The area of culture is critically important in human rights and, as discussed earlier in this chapter, it is essential for giving human rights their context.

Yet culture is also contentious; advocates of universality find the idea of cultural difference to be awkward in the articulation of human rights. To advocate the right to cultural difference is at the same time to undermine the universality of human rights, unless one takes a more nuanced approach to universalism as discussed earlier in this chapter. Linking cultural rights with social rights enables this awkward category of rights to be linked with rights where universality is, at first glance, easier, as social rights (such as the right to marry, the right to have children or the right to education) can more readily be articulated in a universalist framework. The importance of culture in any articulation of human rights, and especially in an understanding of human rights from below, requires that cultural rights, too, have a category to themselves and not be conceptually diluted by association with other rights.

There is a case, then, for the disaggregation of the 'grab-bag' category of economic, social and cultural rights into four different categories: survival rights, economic rights, cultural rights and social rights. We can add to these the traditional category of civil and political rights (which does seem to be a conceptually coherent category), but we also need to ask whether this list is exhaustive. Are there other rights that are important which might be missed out by this categorisation? We have abandoned the conventional 'third generation' on the grounds that all rights can be individual or collective. However, there is one set of rights, traditionally included in the third generation, that is not included in any of these other categories, and that is environmental rights. In a world facing ecological crises of almost unimaginable proportions, which will cause profound changes in all human societies in the next 100 years or so, environmental rights assume major significance. For a human rights regime to fail to account adequately for environmental rights is to doom it to insignificance and irrelevance by the end, or even the middle, of the twenty-first century. For this reason alone, environmental rights need a category of their own.

A further category of rights, which reflects an important aspect of humanity that is often ignored in the secular West, is spiritual rights. While it may be argued that these could be included under the category of cultural rights, for many people the spiritual transcends the cultural because it involves a different dimension of humanity, one that is often devalued in the West but which nevertheless is widely embraced. Although spirituality is experienced and expressed within a cultural context, the same goes for all other aspects of human experience, and this is no reason to relegate spiritual rights to a subcategory of 'cultural rights'.

As discussed in more detail in Chapter 2, the idea of spirituality is broader than simply the expression of institutionalised religion. Many in the West, while disavowing any serious connection to organised religion, will still claim that some form of spirituality is important for them. It may be experienced through the natural world, through meditation, through music and dance or through deep emotional experiences that are otherwise inexplicable. Some form of spirituality seems to exist in all cultural contexts and in all historical eras, as far as we can gather from the attempts of history and prehistory to tell the human story (or, more properly, human stories). Such a powerful and pervasive dimension of the human experience demands to be included in a consideration of human rights. Spiritual rights are the rights that have been least discussed and considered within the conventional Western discourse of human rights, and their further exploration is long overdue. (There will be a further discussion of spiritual rights, and what they may mean, in Chapter 6.)

From the above discussion, an alternative classification system to the traditional 'three generations' emerges (see also Ife 2006). This identifies seven groups of rights:

- civil and political rights
- survival rights
- economic rights
- social rights
- cultural rights
- environmental rights
- spiritual rights.

Of course any attempt at rigid classification is doomed to failure, and such classifications are characteristic of modernity, a world view that this book seeks to move beyond. The boundaries between such categories are inevitably blurred, shifting and permeable. This is presented here not as a definitive classification system for human rights, but rather as a way of thinking about human rights that is conceptually more coherent than the conventional 'three generations'. Rather than rigid categories, they might be considered as dimensions of human rights, which represent a framework for thinking and analysis. It is, of course, like all such categorisations, a construction that makes some sense at this historical moment but should not be read as being a categorisation for all times and for all contexts.

It will be recalled from Chapter 2 that, in discussing community development, a similar list of 'dimensions' was derived. The similarity between the two sets of dimensions is not really remarkable. Both human community and human rights are ways in which we seek to define and enact our own humanity, and so the list represents different dimensions of defining and experiencing 'the human'. This simply underlines the parallels between human rights and community development and provides a powerful framework for bringing the two together within the idea of 'human rights from below', which will be the task of the remaining chapters.

Part 3
Bringing human rights and community development together

Hope has never trickled down. It has always sprung up.
Studs Terkel 2004, opening words, *Hope Dies Last*

5

Principles of human rights from below

CONTRIBUTIONS OF EACH TO THE OTHER

IN THIS SECTION, we will examine the potential contributions that community development and human rights can make to each other, both theoretically and in terms of practice.

Both human rights and community development are powerful ideals and, in the forms developed in previous chapters, each has the potential to make significant contributions to progressive politics and to movements for social change. However, this does not necessarily happen. Both community development and human rights can be constructed in ways that are more conservative and indeed reactionary. Community development can readily become a discourse of exclusion, of border protection, used to pursue racist, sexist or homophobic ends. Similarly, approaches to human rights can be developed in ways that reinforce an individual's right to dominate others, including the right to manage, the right to bear arms, the right to own media and manipulate public opinion, the right to express views that insult the dignity of others or the right to earn excessive salaries while others remain poor.

It must therefore be emphasised that, in the discussion that follows in this and later chapters, the terms *human rights* and *community development* are used specifically in the ways outlined in previous chapters and not in other ways that may be adopted by various media and other commentators. Each is a complex and contested idea requiring nuanced understanding, and each contains political/ideological implications that need to be identified and articulated. With this caveat, we will now examine ways in which each can enrich the other.

A HUMAN RIGHTS FRAMEWORK FOR
COMMUNITY DEVELOPMENT

The need for some form of social justice or human rights approach to community development is clear. Trusting the process alone and valuing 'wisdom from below' above other voices can lead to exclusion and discrimination. Examples include the community group that wishes to exclude those of different racial or cultural backgrounds; the community based on a particular cultural identity that devalues other cultures; the community wishing to use more water from a river for irrigation and thereby denying that resource to communities further downstream; the community in which the very idea of 'community' is defined in narrow religious terms, thereby excluding those of other faiths; the community that is based on employment in a highly polluting industry (such as a coal-fired power station) and that fights for the retention of that industry despite the damage it causes to others. Sometimes, in the name of community solidarity and prosperity, a community may act to protect a paedophile, to cover up corrupt practices by community leaders or to accept poor employment practices in local industries that are otherwise threatened with closure.

These are all examples of why some kind of social justice or human rights framework is necessary in community development, and indeed is needed by community development workers as a way to define ethical practice. A close parallel can be drawn between ethics and human rights, and human rights can thus provide a basis for making ethical decisions (Ife 2008). Communities cannot operate in an ethical vacuum. An approach to community development that denies this in the name of community autonomy and self-direction is dangerous. In times of perceived threat, whether from cultural 'invasion', immigration, economic collapse or ecological crisis, this danger can be exacerbated and the powerful potential of community development can readily be used for exclusionary and oppressive purposes.

In this sense community development, rather than supporting human rights, can actually work against human rights ideals and become a tool of human rights abuse or denial. It therefore becomes essential for community development to be grounded in and informed by human rights so that it becomes a process for the furthering, rather than the restricting, of rights.

A human rights framework thus effectively places some limits on community self-direction by requiring that human rights (that is, the rights of *all* people, whether community members or not) be respected in whatever that community does. Here the legal tradition of human rights can have some advantages: when human rights are seen as defined in conventions, charters or declarations, they have an evident and external validity and can provide a context for community development. Community development that operates within an explicit human rights framework will make use of such human rights charters as are relevant in the local context, and these charters will provide a useful reference point for discussions about what might or might not be appropriately ethical courses of action. Without such reference points, decision-making in communities can be more problematic; a community group can become more inward-looking and take less account of the world around it, and of the community's responsibility both to people within that community and to other communities or individuals.

Human rights can also contribute to community development at a more theoretical level. The issue of universalism and context, as discussed in the previous chapter, is of concern not only to human rights but also to community development. This is reflected in dilemmas over the extent to which communities can or should be decentralised and autonomous. Principles of autonomy, change from below and self-direction come up against the need for communities to be able to relate to the larger society in which they are located. The actions of one community, while fully justifiable within the parameters of that community's own world, may have significant negative impacts on other communities or groups. A community's economic development may detract from the economic development of other groups or regions; a community's actions may impact on the environment in ways that affect others (for example by polluting streams or rivers), or a community's success in gaining funds for local initiatives may deny those resources to others.

To what extent should a community's local needs be allowed to impact on the wider society without some form of control or monitoring, and how much should higher-level authorities be able to intervene in community processes or decisions? This is the perpetual dilemma of local government and its relationship to central government, but the tension is not limited simply to matters of formal governance. The tension also applies in more informal relations, in media and in cultural expression.

This tension is analogous to the tension in human rights between the universal and the contextual. Just as human rights has had to deal with this tension in ways described in the previous chapter, so community development work is also faced with the dilemmas such tension throws up. In fact it is probably true to say that, at a theoretical or conceptual level, the human rights field has wrestled with this and thought it through more thoroughly than has been the case in community development.

The kind of analysis presented in the previous chapter, suggesting that in human rights neither an uncritical universalism nor an uncritical relativism can be sustainable, also applies to community development. Similarly, it is necessary for community development to incorporate a *both/and* approach rather than an *either/or* perspective in thinking about the local and the wider societies. Community development has addressed this issue to some extent in relation to the global and the local through ideas of globalisation from below and the 'think/act/global/local' concept, but has not applied such analysis as much to the more intermediate level of community/society. Here it is instructive for community development to borrow from human rights thinking, perhaps using the discussion of rights and needs as outlined in the previous chapter, to incorporate a view that the local and the societal are necessarily related and that each operates as a context for the other.

A COMMUNITY DEVELOPMENT FRAMEWORK FOR HUMAN RIGHTS

While the contribution that human rights can make to community development is both necessary and important, the contribution that community development can make to human rights is perhaps more significant, though it has been given less consideration in the literature. This discussion will become the basis for the idea of human rights from below, which will be developed later in this and subsequent chapters.

The dominance of the state obligations, or legal, approach to human rights has resulted in human rights being commonly accepted as defined in legal documents and agreements. These are, inevitably, drafted and agreed to by small groups of people in positions of privilege. They are politicians, diplomats, academics, opinion leaders and a few prominent human rights activists. Until relatively recently, the criticism was that it was predominantly privileged white men who were defining human rights. In more recent times the voices of women and the voices of people from non-Western backgrounds have been prominent in human rights discourse and have had an impact on human rights documents.

However, these are still voices of privilege; they are still politicians, academics and opinion leaders. Even if gender and cultural barriers have been breached in human rights discourse, class barriers have not. Human rights remain largely *a discourse of the powerful about the powerless*, and this is itself a human rights abuse: a denial of the right to define one's rights. From a community development perspective this is unacceptable, and it becomes necessary to examine ways in which the definition of human rights can become a much more democratic and participatory process.

A community development approach to human rights would focus on participation. This has long been a central focus of community development. The task for human rights therefore would be to apply community development principles to the definition of human rights. This would produce a very different idea of what constitute human rights. There would inevitably be different and overlapping views of human rights in different contexts, with different emphases depending on the world view of the definer. Conventional human rights have accepted the validity of the definers' world – the United Nations, international diplomacy, the 'corridors of power', law schools and the courts – and these are far removed from the lived reality and constructed worlds of the overwhelming majority of the human population.

There is a further reason why participation is an important part of a community development approach to human rights. This is to do with the exercise of rights. There is not much point to 'having' human rights, whether at an individual or a collective level, if those rights are not exercised. The right to freedom of expression, for example, becomes irrelevant if nobody bothers to claim and exercise that right and people just keep quiet. Similarly, what is the point of the right to education if only a few people actually take advantage of that right?

Many of our 'rights' were the hard-won result of significant campaigning and sacrifice by previous generations. To ignore such rights, or to not bother to exercise them, can be seen as a betrayal of those who have gone before and have fought hard for those rights. A society that embraces human rights is one in which those rights are not only guaranteed but are also exercised. It is therefore an active participatory society where people take their citizenship obligations (which are derived from their rights) seriously. Community development is very much about the promotion of such a society: one in which citizenship rights are accompanied by citizenship obligations to play an active role.

This link between rights and responsibilities emphasises the inherently communal tradition of human rights. As already discussed in Chapter 4, an individual in isolation (the metaphorical 'man on a desert island') has no rights, as there is nobody to meet the responsibilities that go with any claim of rights. To say that the desert island dweller has a right to free expression, a right to democratic participation, a right to health care or anything else, makes no sense. Our 'rights', however we construct them, require somebody else – whether family members, fellow citizens or the state – to recognise those claims and to help to meet them. Similarly, I cannot really claim that I have a right without also recognising my responsibility to respect the rights of others and to meet my responsibilities towards them.

Rights, therefore, require human interaction. We hold rights not individually, but collectively. In this sense, rights only have meaning within some notion of human community, a community of rights and responsibilities (Gewirth 1996). Seen in this way, any understanding of human rights requires some sort of assumption of human community in which those rights can be realised, and community is therefore at the core of the experience of human rights. If it is only in human community that we can fully define, discover and realise our humanity, it is only in human community that we can achieve human rights.

In this sense human rights are inherently about community, and community development becomes effectively human rights development. One could therefore argue that it is impossible to have human rights without human community, and hence community development becomes not merely a location for human rights education (as is commonly thought) but a prerequisite for human rights themselves.

Human rights and community development therefore have significant commonalities. Each, indeed, needs the other if it is to achieve its goals, and the two also have common goals: to help people define and achieve their full humanity in community with others.

HUMAN RIGHTS FROM BELOW: SOME THEORETICAL CONSIDERATIONS

In this section, we will revisit some of the issues discussed in earlier sections with a view to building an understanding of *human rights from below*, as incorporating both community development and human rights. The thrust of the discussion up to now has been that neither community development nor human rights can be complete, or can operate effectively, without incorporating the perspective of the other. Yet the two have traditionally been conceptualised separately. Human rights has largely been understood within a legal/political tradition, while community development has largely been understood within a paradigm of human services or of economics. Later in the chapter it will be argued that a further paradigm, the ecological, has largely been missing from both discourses, though it represents a strong imperative for both human rights and community development in the contemporary world, and any understanding of human rights from below must incorporate an ecological perspective.

HUMAN COMMUNITY AND COMMON HUMANITY

The commonality between human rights and community development can be seen in the similarity of the two terms *human community* and *common humanity*. Human community is commonly seen as the goal of community development, recognising that stronger and healthier communities are necessary for the achievement of full human potential and can significantly improve people's quality of life. A common humanity, on the other hand, is seen as the goal of human rights. Human rights arise out of a recognition of that common humanity, and statements of human rights are seen as definitions of that humanity that transcend difference and see human rights as universal. Such a view of universality makes human rights only valid if there is such a thing as a 'common humanity' to which we all belong, and from which we can derive our *human* rights as opposed to our rights as citizens of a particular state.

The similarity between the two terms *human community* and *common humanity* is obvious. Both hold ideas of humanness and of holding-in-common. If these are the two goals of community development and of human rights respectively, then the two are engaged in a common project, or at least in heavily overlapping projects. Such a view goes beyond the argument thus far – that human rights has a lot to contribute to community development and community development has a lot to contribute to human rights – as this would be treating them as separate projects. Rather, it suggests that they are common projects and that the two need to be understood together: this view is characterised in this book by the phrase *human rights from below*. As we explore the idea of human rights from below, it will become clear that this approach addresses many of the problems and critiques that have been levelled at both community development and human rights.

SHARED HUMANITY

First, however, it is important to look more closely at the idea of a 'common humanity', so often accepted as the basis for human rights. It is a term that has many positive connotations, as it encourages people to transcend boundaries of race, gender, culture, ethnicity, age, ability and sexuality. We can see this as perhaps a necessary correction to the tendency of much social science to concentrate on difference. An exclusive concentration on discourses of difference – gender, race, class and the like – can serve to emphasise the things that divide us and ignore the things that unite us. There is a strong case that discourses of difference, while important, need to be balanced with discourses of unity and that we should concern ourselves with what unites us, or brings us together, rather than only what separates us. From this perspective, a discourse of 'common humanity' can be appealing and powerful.

There are, however, problems with the idea of a 'common humanity'. In terms of the human rights traditions discussed in Chapter 3, it brings us back to the natural rights tradition, seeking some essentialised, fundamental humanity. Beyond the purely biological, it is hard to make a case that there is such a thing as a common humanity, and it can lead to the danger of imposing a single view of 'humanity' (most likely a Western one) on the entire human race. This has been a significant problem with the Enlightenment view of the 'human' and with the Western project of seeking to define the 'human' so that the humanist project could be pursued. The pursuit of the 'ideal human', in the name of the 'human ideal', became thoroughly discredited in the twentieth century when it led to the Eugenics movement and to the Nazi idealisation of the 'pure Aryan'. It is hardly an adequate basis for human rights in the way we would now understand that term. Yet the very idea of a 'common humanity' keeps alive the potential for that exclusive, and excluding, construction of 'the human race'.

This problem can be overcome by replacing the idea of a 'common humanity' with that of a 'shared humanity'. This suggests that there are indeed commonalities between people, which can be explored and affirmed at the level of lived experience, but without the necessity to identify the single 'common' form of the human condition applying to everyone. It allows for overlapping commonalities discovered in encounters with others, but does not necessarily mean the universal sharing of a single commonality.

Further, the idea of sharing one's humanity is an active one. When we share, we give what we can and we take what we need, in accordance with our perceptions of our own needs and the needs of others. Sharing our humanity is thus a much more active idea than holding our humanity in common. It gives people more agency in contributing to a dynamic shared ideal, and it allows humanity to be seen as being constantly reconstructed as part of a multitude of dynamic processes, rather than being held as a static, monolithic, empirical truth.

Hence, for an understanding of human rights from below we need to move from seeking and affirming a 'common humanity' to seeking and affirming a shared humanity. This approach also recasts our understanding of 'human community'. Replacing 'common' with 'shared' suggests that the idea of community needs to be rethought so that it too does not fall into the trap of seeking the 'common' ideal. It reasserts the idea, discussed in Chapter 1, of community as built on difference rather than sameness, and gives a more active role for encounters with others as the arena in which humanity and community are constructed.

RIGHTS FROM ABOVE AND COMMUNITY FROM BELOW

The two discourses have different traditions in terms of 'top-down/bottom-up'. Human rights has traditionally been seen as a top-down discourse and has had difficulty dealing with the contextual, and with ideas of difference and diversity, within its more conventional frameworks. Community development, on the other hand, is naturally contextual and does not deal well with universals beyond such nebulous ideas as 'the human community' or ambitious and flawed attempts to derive detailed principles and practices of community development that have universal validity. Human rights from below, by bringing together these two discourses, seeks to engage with the interplay of the top-down and the bottom-up. It sees the two as not necessarily a clear-cut binary, but enables the experience and affirmation of humanity to be influenced by both. However, the perspective developed here, of human rights from below, places particular emphasis on how a bottom-up community perspective can influence ideas of human rights and of human rights practice.

NEEDS AND RIGHTS

The next element to contribute to an understanding of human rights from below is a consideration of the relationship between needs and rights. This is a problematic relationship, which has significant implications for the way human rights are constructed.

Writers such as Doyal and Gough (1991) have sought to develop a universal theory of needs from which rights can be derived. This is similar to the approach of Max-Neef (1991), who attempts to categorise human needs in a quasi-scientific framework as a basis for derived human rights. We all have, for example, a biological 'need' for food; this is common to all human beings and can be used to infer a universal 'right' to food. The list of human needs can be extended, perhaps using Maslow's well-known hierarchy of needs, and a list of rights is thus derived. This is analogous to the tradition of 'natural rights' and needs, like rights, are seen as somehow inherent in one's humanity.

Needs of course are often viewed as contextual rather than universal: the needs of a community or a family, for example, may not be common human needs held by everyone. Whether the usage of the word 'need' is universal or contextual, the discourse of needs is essentially positivist, the tradition of needs somehow 'existing' in a quasi-objective sense. This is clearly seen in the language commonly used to describe needs: needs are 'identified', 'assessed' and 'measured'; there are attempts to develop need indices, and the task of understanding needs is regarded as a technical matter for empirical research methodology.

This view might be characterised as natural needs implying constructed rights. An alternative perspective is that of natural rights implying constructed needs. This was referred to in Chapter 4 as one way to move beyond the universal/contextual binary. Universal rights can be transformed into contextualised needs. (For example, there is a universal right to education and so this community needs a good school with competent teachers.) If rights and needs are respectively the universal and contextual side of human rights, then by linking rights and needs we are linking the universal and the contextual.

However, the problem remains the same. Whether human needs imply human rights, or human rights imply human needs, there is an implicit positivism in the view that either a need or a right 'exists' in some kind of quasi-objective and measurable (or at least empirically verifiable) way in order somehow to justify the other. Such positivism is of course problematic, regardless of whether we are talking about human rights or human needs. It represents an attempt to find a quasi-scientific justification for either rights or needs when in reality both are constructions located in particular social, cultural and political contexts. Any attempt to justify either a theory of needs or a theory of rights on the basis of positivism will result in an approach to needs and rights that privileges the expert and works against the kind of participatory project implied by human rights from below; this will be taken up in more detail later in this chapter. Positivism moves social issues out of the realm of ordinary people and redefines them in such a way that they become the domain of the technical expert, rather than a matter for democratic participation. (Economics represents perhaps the extreme example of this; see Bronk 2009.) Hence a theory either of human rights or of human needs grounded in such a paradigm is hardly conducive to the idea of human rights from below.

It is important when thinking about human rights from below to understand both needs and rights as constructions. Neither can be regarded as existing in a positivist sense, but rather each is the result of human definition in political, social, cultural and historical contexts. While a case can be made for a small number of human 'needs', such as the need for food, to be objectively demonstrable, they are limited to the most basic 'needs' for survival. When we move beyond that to the needs to belong, to be respected and affirmed, to be loved and, in Maslow's terms, for 'self-actualisation', we are talking about concepts that are clearly social/cultural/political constructions that will vary significantly in different contexts. This does not mean they lose their power, or their significance, except to those who wish to inhabit a purely mechanistic, uniform, positivist world. Rather, it draws attention to the act of construction, or definition, of the right or need, instead of seeking to give that right or need an independent validity.

The important point to note about a statement of need is that it implies the idea of a necessary condition. To say something is needed suggests that it is needed *for* something. It is therefore possible, for any statement of need, to ask why something is needed, since a 'need' is never an end in itself but is always instrumental. A statement of need can be either empirical or normative. It is empirical if it simply states that A is needed for B, with no necessary implication that B ought to be provided. The normative use of a need statement, however, implies that the need should also be met.

Put simply, does a 'need' imply an 'ought'? A statement of the first type might be 'I need a pen in order to write': a simple statement of 'fact' that does not imply a claim that I should be given a pen. Indeed the statement 'A murderer needs a weapon in order to commit the crime' most certainly does not imply that the murderer should therefore be provided with a weapon. On the other hand, statements of need that might be classified as 'human needs' or 'community needs' tend to be normative. When we say 'This community needs a child care centre' or 'This family needs emergency accommodation' or 'This person needs language tuition' we are not only saying that these things are needed for something, we are also implying that they should somehow be provided. These are clearly normative statements of need, as distinct from the empirical statements about pens and murderers.

One of the interesting features about such normative statements of need, however, is that they usually omit all mention of *why* the particular provision is needed. It is assumed, rather than stated. Why, for example, does the community need a child care centre? What is it needed for? These are important questions, because it is in answering them that the ideas of rights that are embedded within such statements of need become apparent. In this example, the community needs a child care centre so that parents can be employed, and so that their children can receive adequate care while their parents are absent. The right of parents to work, and the right of children to adequate care, are therefore what provide the imperative for the need to be met; the implicit rights give the need statement its power.

Identifying the rights implicit in a statement of need is important, especially where the grounds for the claim of need may be unclear. For example, I may claim to 'need' a new office chair, but there may be different grounds for such a claim. It may be that I need it because I feel I have a certain status that warrants a more prestigious chair, or I may need it because the colour of my current chair clashes with the office décor, or I may need it because I have chronic back pain and require more ergonomic support. Obviously these claims differ in how they will be evaluated by others, as they involve different rights.

Need, then, is as problematic a concept as right, and to seek to base a theory of rights on a theory of needs is no recipe for simplicity or clarity. The language of needs, used in the normative sense, implies some notion of rights, and similarly the language of rights can be used to imply specific needs. Human rights from below would reject any notion of either needs or rights as being determined, *a priori*, from above, whether as universal human rights or as common human needs. Each leads to the trap of positivism, giving the concept an independent and quasi-objective validity, and each also leads inevitably to top-down practice in which generalised truths are used to determine how to act in specific contexts.

Human rights from below rather sees both needs and rights as constructions. They are defined by human beings in social, political and cultural contexts, and it is the act of definition that should be of primary concern. The critical questions thus become: Who is doing the defining of the need or the right? (and, by implication, who is excluded from the act of definition?) On what information do they base this definition? What process do they use? In what context(s) does the definition take place?

DISCURSIVE AND REFLEXIVE DEFINITIONS OF RIGHTS

The definition of human rights can be understood as occurring either discursively or reflexively or, more commonly, some combination of the two. The discursive definition occurs when ideas of human rights are embedded in dominant discourses, whether these are spelled out in formal documents such as a bill of rights, or whether they are taken-for-granted definitions implicit in the way journalists, commentators, politicians or other opinion leaders use the term 'human rights'. The reflexive definition of human rights occurs when people address the idea themselves and, rather than accept the dominant discursive construction uncritically, think about and define what human rights mean in their own context.

The difference, simplistically understood, is essentially one of how much we allow 'reality' to be defined for us and how much we define it for ourselves. While there will inevitably be some interplay between the two, the perspective of human rights from below seeks to emphasise the reflexive, making people active participants in the definition of what should count as 'human rights' and what those rights may entail in terms of duties and responsibilities.

In this sense, human rights are constantly being defined and redefined, constructed and reconstructed, in people's daily lives and their interactions with others, and also in their conscious reflection of what 'human rights' mean in context.

DEMOCRACY

Some notion of participatory democracy is therefore inherent in human rights from below. This requires active participation by the citizen, not only in exercising her/his rights and respecting the rights of others, but also in the definition and affirmation of what are to count as human rights. Participation has long been a central concern of community development, as was discussed in Chapter 2, and hence the approaches to encouraging and maximising participation, well-known to community workers, become an essential tool for human rights workers. It is not enough simply to assert the existence and importance of rights and to work to have those rights respected; it is also necessary to find ways in which people's democratic participation can be maximised.

Democracy, of course, is itself a complex and contested idea. Without going into the details of theories of democracy (see Beetham 1999, Held 2006), three forms of democracy will serve to ground the present discussion. *Representative* democracy, arguably the most familiar understanding of democracy in the modern world, requires people to vote for their leaders in regular elections. It is recognised that the task of government is varied and complex, and too much for all citizens to be actively engaged in deciding every issue. Therefore democratic participation becomes simply a process of democratically selecting those who will then govern. This limits a citizen's democratic right to a single act of voting every few years, and often that is rendered irrelevant through media manipulation or through the person happening to live in a 'safe' constituency where their vote will have little value.

Apart from that single act of voting, the citizen is relatively powerless in the formal political process, and it might seem extraordinary that such a limited level of citizen participation in decision-making has been so readily accepted as the ideal and perhaps only form of 'government of the people, by the people, for the people'. Certainly it is the regime that is imposed on the rest of the world in the name of 'democracy' by the leaders of the 'free' world.

By contrast, *participatory* democracy requires that citizen involvement in decision-making extend beyond elections, and that citizens have some form of direct say in decisions that affect them. This may take the form of referendums, or it may involve citizens meeting in smaller community-based groups to debate issues and make decisions. This was the original idea of democracy in the Athenian city-state (Sinclair 1988, Watson 2005), though it needs to be added that it only included free adult male 'citizens'. In more modern societies it is difficult to extend this system to the more complex and varied policy matters that need to be decided. However, there are some ways in which this can be at least partially achieved; for example through the Swiss system of referendums or in locally based issues where it is possible to bring all the affected people together. It also applies in a number of community-based organisations and community groups, which seek to work on the basis of consensus decision-making (Gastil 1993, Williamson 2003).

The third form of democracy of interest to us here is *deliberative* democracy. Here citizens are involved not simply in decision-making, but in a deliberative process of research, analysis, discussion and consideration of various policy options. The roles of policy expert and analyst are democratised, rather than merely the role of the decision-maker. This requires the citizen to take on more of the responsibility that goes with decision-making, and seeks to draw on the wisdom of 'the people' in the processes that lead up to decision-making as well as in decision-making itself. It is a form of democracy that aims to maximise the informed contribution of the citizens, not merely in reacting to policy proposals, but in generating policy itself (Roemer 1999, Saward 1998, Uhr 1998, 2000).

It is this deliberative approach to democracy that is most relevant to human rights from below. The idea of human rights from below requires that citizens have a role in the definition of human rights and the way in which those rights will be constructed (see Chapter 7 for a further discussion). It requires, on the part of the human rights worker, the capacity to encourage participation in community activities generally, but particularly in the engagement with the idea of rights and responsibilities and the way in which those are linked in human community. Community workers have developed a number of strategies to encourage participation, and to deal with the dilemmas that participation throws up, and these were discussed earlier in Chapter 2 (see also Ife 2002).

In summary, human rights from below requires an active, participatory community. It was noted in Chapter 4 that this is a necessity for human rights to be realised – human rights must be exercised, not merely recognised – but here the emphasis is more on the necessity of strong, active participation in order not just to exercise rights but to generate or construct them as well.

DIALOGUE AND THE ENCOUNTER WITH THE OTHER

To engage with the kind of deliberative participation and building of a community of rights and responsibilities, dialogue is essential. Contemporary Western society is not well skilled in dialogue; rather, *debate* is the more common word used for talking about issues. Debate and dialogue are different. In debate, the aim is to muster as many arguments as possible to support one side, to attack the arguments of the other side and to 'win' the encounter by having your point of view prevail. It is adversarial, and one listens to the 'other side' only in as far as is necessary to pick holes in the arguments. There is a winner and a loser, and the aim is to win.

By contrast, in dialogue the aim is to learn from each other. Listening to the other is as important as putting forward one's own views, and each party enters the dialogue with a willingness to listen to the other's point of view. This requires that the other's views be understood and respected rather than attacked. Each party seeks to learn from the other so that both can move forward in a way that neither would be able to otherwise. In dialogue, neither side claims to know the whole truth or the one true way, but there is an element of humility or of recognising that, while one may have some ideas that are worth the consideration of others, there will also be other ideas from which one can learn. The aim is to share and to learn from an equal, rather than to defeat an opponent (Yankelovich 1999).

The power of dialogue lies in its capacity to empower both parties, rather than leaving one triumphant and the other defeated, or both dissatisfied from a 'draw'. Successful dialogue affirms both participants. It allows each of them to grow from the experience and to move on, in a form of practice famously developed by Paulo Freire (Freire 1972, 1985, 1996, McLaren & Lankshear 1994, McLaren & Leonard 1993). In a Gandhian sense (Gandhi 1964) dialogue is inherently non-violent, while debate is inherently violent. Hence dialogue has more potential for building strong communities and for developing a powerful form of human rights from below. It might be argued that debate, by its very nature, does not respect human rights (specifically the right to be treated with respect and dignity) while dialogue, by contrast, encompasses human rights.

Also, an important principle of community development is that means and ends cannot be separated (see Chapter 2). Means that respect human rights must be used if the aim is to achieve human rights as an 'end'. Unfortunately, not all organisations that claim human rights as their mandate follow these principles.

This importance of inclusive and respectful means is reflected in language. Often community organisations committed to human rights will use language more appropriate to the military than to human rights: words such as 'strategic', 'tactics', 'campaign', 'battle', 'offensive' and 'rearguard action'. These words betray a mind-set that is hardly conducive to dialogue, non-violence, valuing of process and other important principles of both human rights and community development.

At the heart of dialogue is the idea of reaching out to the other with respect and humility, recognising the other's humanity and seeking to share one's humanity with the other. It is the working out of the idea of shared humanity. As noted above, sharing one's humanity is an active process, involving both giving and taking, and genuine dialogue enables this to occur. The recognition of the ultimate worth of another human being in an encounter between two people has been seen by both Buber (2002) and Levinas (1998, 2006) as being at the heart of ethics and responsibility for the other. It represents a powerful human response, since the other makes an ultimate claim on us and requires us to respond with our full humanity.

For present purposes, rather than seeing this human encounter as the basis of ethics and responsibility, we are particularly concerned with this encounter with the other as central to ideas of human *rights*. It is in our response to the humanity of the other that we recognise their rights, not as legal or quasi-legal claims but as the expression of their humanity, in relationship. Human rights from below is built on relationship – dialogical relationship – and the way in which this then becomes the basis for our connection to the other through mutual rights and responsibilities.

However, human rights from below requires more than the interaction between two people. It is built not simply on dyadic relationships but on *community*, where more than two people are in interaction with each other. For the principles of dialogue, as discussed above, to be applied at this broader community level, we are required to respond to *others* rather than just to 'the other', and the principles of approaching an interaction with humility, respect and a willingness to learn as well as to teach are extended to a group or communal context. This of course creates additional layers of dynamics and relationships, but it is still the basis of much of the literature dealing with consensus and non-violent decision-making in community groups (Gastil 1993). Striving for such community interaction therefore represents a key component of human rights from below. There are a number of ways this can be facilitated, in different contexts, and this will be discussed in Chapter 6.

A CULTURE OF HUMAN RIGHTS

The idea of a community of rights and responsibilities, core to the notion of human rights from below, requires that human rights will be defined, negotiated and enacted within different contexts. This means that human rights are located primarily in culture rather than in law. The limitations of a purely legal understanding of human rights have been mentioned at various points in this and previous chapters. A focus on a culture of human rights, rather than on the law of human rights, helps to overcome these problems. Understanding human rights as located in culture underlines the importance of relationship in human rights. If indeed human rights are about the achievement of our humanity, this occurs in relationships rather than in courtrooms, and the focus of human rights work needs to be on culture and relationships. This of course includes relationships within community as well as within families, households, workplaces and public spaces.

The centrality of culture to the achievement of human rights points towards a significant component of human rights from below, namely working towards the development of a strong and viable community-based culture that defines, respects, achieves and defends human rights. Community cultural development thus becomes a major focus of human rights work, and this will be discussed in more detail in Chapter 6. Cultural work has often been seen as marginal to the main human rights agenda: important for expressing human rights ideals or highlighting human rights abuses through art, music, drama and literature, but taking second place to law and political activism as the 'main game' of human rights. However, the idea of human rights from below requires a more central place for cultural development and cultural expression. Creating a culture of human rights requires that much more attention be paid to matters of culture than has often been the case in the human rights literature and in human rights work, at least within the Western context. It means that culture is a starting point, rather than an 'add-on', in understanding human rights and developing a viable human rights practice.

Any understanding of human rights cannot be divorced from its cultural context. This has been seen as something of a 'problem' for those concerned with a universalising understanding of human rights, and has been understood as the 'problem' of universalism and relativism. The integration of universalism and relativism, as discussed in Chapter 4, goes some way to resolving this, but a human rights from below approach goes even further: it sees the contextualising of human rights as a strength rather than a problem, as indeed culture provides the only viable context within which human rights can be experienced in daily life.

Rather than try to adapt contexts to fit a universal ideal, as happens in traditional human rights work, this perspective requires that any ideas of universality must be able to be grounded in day-to-day lived experience and defined in those terms. It also suggests that, in education for human rights work, the core should be provided by disciplines such as anthropology, cultural studies, philosophy and sociology rather than by law and politics, as the conventional view of human rights would suggest. This is not to say that there is no room for law and politics – they have an obvious relevance to human rights study – but they are not necessarily the most important disciplines for study or areas of expertise for the human rights worker.

Developing a culture of human rights is at the same time both easier and harder than the legal approach. It is easier in that it does not require the specialised and often arcane knowledge of the law, and is less open to monopoly control by one profession. On the other hand it is harder in that cultures are complex, contested, dynamic and pluralist. To establish 'a culture' of anything is a major challenge, and because of differences between cultural contexts there can be no single 'right' way to do this. Establishing a culture of human rights is very much more a case of trial and error, of feeling one's way and of engaging in an organic process where there are few 'clear guidelines' or specific 'models of practice'. Nor can one necessarily learn from the specific experience and the achievements of others, as what works in one community will not necessarily work in another.

However, all is not lost for the cultural development worker concerned to establish a culture of human rights. Drawing on the considerable experience of community development, and in particular community cultural development workers, there are some generalised principles that can be drawn upon, and here the reader is referred to the earlier discussion in Chapter 2 of the principles of community development. Community cultural development will be explored further in Chapter 6.

BEYOND POSITIVISM

The limitations of positivism were discussed briefly above in relation to needs and rights. However, for the purposes of human rights from below it is important to extend this argument in a broader sense to apply generally to the knowledge base of human rights from below. Positivism seeks verifiable, objective truths and seeks to measure phenomena accurately so that their precise interrelationships can be determined. This then forms the basis of a series of causal laws, enabling the social 'scientist' to predict, and hence control, future behaviour, whether of individuals or of larger groups.

Such knowledge is inevitably knowledge that is in the hands of elites, those who understand the 'science'. This leads to a practice of technocratic control, or control by managers, researchers, psychologists, sociologists, economists and others schooled in the methodologies and the vocabularies of various disciplines. These are the 'experts': those who know what is best for us and whose expertise the citizen is asked both to respect and to trust. Such an approach to knowledge and practice is the antithesis of community development, which values the knowledge and wisdom of the people most involved, and hence is also the antithesis of human rights from below.

The critique of positivism has featured in debates within many disciplines over several decades, and this critique is neither new nor unfamiliar (Fay 1975). However positivism, despite the challenges to it, remains strong in a number of disciplines, including human rights.

This is largely because of the dominance of legal discourses in human rights. The law by its very nature is understood from within a positivist paradigm: it seeks to apply a single regime to all people within a jurisdiction, regardless of cultural and other differences, and seeks to 'impose' a legal system whose validity cannot be questioned (Meckled-García & Çali 2006). It provides a framework for the resolution of disputes that admits only verified 'facts' and unchallenged 'evidence' in support of a particular case.

In this world of certainty there is no room for ambiguity, for intuition, for ambivalence or for variation. It is a case of striving to define a single system and impose it equally upon all. This is classical positivism, and indeed the law might be seen as almost a caricature of positivism. This is what makes the law so easy to satirise and parody, as it is often in the operation of the law and the legal system that the limitations and contradictions of positivism and the positivist world view become evident.

Human rights from below, therefore, needs to draw on other paradigms and to move beyond the limitations of positivist knowledge. To simplify what is a complex and contested field, we can identify two broad categories of knowledge that move beyond the positivist, namely the interpretive and the critical (Crotty 1998, Fay 1975, Sarantakos 1998).

Interpretive social science seeks not to identify universal laws of behaviour but to understand meanings, symbols and the 'laws' that make sense to people in the way they live their lives. These 'laws' are not universal, but are grounded in the cultural experience (for example the laws of queuing, the laws of politeness and respect, the laws of gift giving and receiving, the laws governing interpersonal communication, the laws of welcoming the stranger, the laws governing romance and intimacy and laws about family obligations).

These laws are important for all people in all cultures, but they are not written in statute books or regulated by police and security forces, except perhaps in extreme cases of repressive regimes that seek to control private lives and interactions, such as the Taliban in Afghanistan. These rules are located in cultural understandings; they are specific to particular contexts. The aim of interpretive social science is to uncover these laws for the purpose of understanding, rather than of control.

As well as these culture-bound laws, interpretive social science is concerned with understanding symbols, meanings and ways of understanding, and relating to, other people and the natural world. Such understanding opens up the possibility of interpersonal communication and of increased understanding between people and between groups. It is this increased understanding that is the ultimate aim of interpretive social science, and the relevance of such a perspective for human rights from below is obvious.

The other tradition of inquiry that represents an alternative to positivism is the critical tradition. A critical perspective, drawing on a range of work loosely described as 'critical theory' including, but not confined to, the Frankfurt School (Calhoun 1995, Fay 1987, Ray 1993), is concerned not merely with understanding but with change. It seeks to develop a social science that understands the world in such a way that it takes account of various forms of social, cultural and personal experience, but does so in such a way that it enables people to take action to achieve change and address structures and discourses of inequality and oppression.

Such a perspective, while incompatible with a strict positivism and its implied 'objectivity', is consistent with an interpretive perspective in that it values the shared meanings, cultural productions and constructed realities of people's lived experience, but also requires an orientation towards achieving some form of change in the direction of a more just and equitable world, however that may be defined. As with the interpretive paradigm, the relevance of a critical paradigm for human rights from below is obvious. A discourse of human rights implies that those rights must not just be understood within any particular context, but that they should also be achieved or realised, and hence a world view that seeks to identify possibilities for social change is not only desirable but necessary.

Moving beyond positivism requires that other forms of knowledge than narrowly scientific, evidence-based laws be seen as legitimate, and indeed important, knowledge for the achievement of human rights. This allows forms of knowledge such as intuition, literary or artistic expression, group consensus, religious or spiritual insights and historical traditions to become important in understanding what it means to be human, and what that means for our 'rights' in any given context.

However, it does not necessarily negate the significance of empirical research into human rights issues. While it is true that positivism privileges empirical research over other methodologies, it does not follow that a rejection of positivism requires a rejection of empirical methods or empirical knowledge. To document the frequency of, for example, Aboriginal deaths in custody, sexual assaults, unlawful detentions, denial of access to education, claims of torture or abuse, wrongful denial of social security benefits, abuses in nursing homes or psychiatric institutions, or refusal of medical treatment on the grounds of inability to pay, is clearly important and useful. It is also useful to be able to perform statistical analyses on these numbers to see, for example, whether there is a significant correlation between denial of benefits and the race, age or gender of the person concerned, or a correlation between educational access and social class. Moving beyond a positivist paradigm does not negate the importance of such research. It means simply that these numbers do not have an objective significance in their own right and do not imply a value-neutral 'truth', but that they can be interpreted and used as part of a political process – to help articulate important human rights issues and to achieve rights that may be denied.

POSTMODERNISM AND POSTMODERNITY

As was discussed in Chapters 3 and 4, the discourse of human rights has been defined largely within the context of modernity, and as a result post-modernism poses a particular challenge for human rights. This emphasises the usefulness of insights gained from postmodern theorists in understanding human rights from below. The postmodern turn in the social sciences (Seidman 1994) takes the argument in relation to positivism one stage further. It argues against meta-narratives such as the meta-narrative of human rights, and perceives 'reality' as undergoing a constant process of construction and reconstruction.

Using the analogy of the text and the reader, postmodernism sees 'reality' not as the text itself, nor as the intention of the author of the text, but rather as the meanings given to that text by the reader, which will vary with different readers or with the same reader at different times. This idea of 'text' extends beyond a written book or document to all aspects of life. For example, a building may have been understood in a particular way by the architect and the builder, but the most important meanings it has are those of the people who use the building, who work or live in it, who visit it, or who walk past it. For these people the building takes on a whole range of meanings and associations unanticipated by the architect, some of which will be shared with others. These meanings, which will vary from person to person and from time to time, represent the 'reality' of the building in a far more meaningful way than the physical bricks and mortar (or concrete and glass) or the architect's plans.

One could make a similar argument seeing, for example, a family, a court case, a death, a football game, a terrorist attack, an economic crisis, a demonstration or a bill of rights as 'texts' that are read in multiple and varying ways. There is thus more than one 'reality' and these realities will often be contradictory. From this perspective there can be no one 'right' answer, no single 'right' way to understand or to do something, no 'best practice', but rather a diversity of understandings and realities is inevitable. Hence the over-arching meta-narrative is rejected in favour of a diversity and a multiplicity of perspectives, and this gives both individuals and groups more agency in defining realities, rather than simply accepting a unitary reality as defined by an expert, a manager or a politician.

Postmodernism is, of course, more complex and contested than has been presented here, but this account is sufficient for present purposes. It will be clear that postmodernism does not sit comfortably with conventional legalistic ideas of human rights, or human rights from above, as this is reliant on a meta-narrative of human rights and the codification of that meta-narrative in legislation, international covenants, charters and conventions.

It is, however, fully consistent with the idea of human rights from below, which allows for multiple understandings of human rights that are contextualised and arise from people's own lived experience. For this reason, human rights from below is better suited to the world of postmodernity, when the search for certainty and for universal truths that so characterises modernity is no longer of such primary importance. Postmodernism, therefore, represents an important theoretical source for human rights from below, and the often difficult theorising of postmodernism has a good deal to offer the student or practitioner of human rights from below. It leads to an emphasis on different discourses of human rights and different understandings of 'my rights', 'my duties', 'your rights' and 'your duties'.

One of the misconceptions commonly held about postmodernism is that it amounts simply to 'anything goes'. While it is true that postmodernism seeks to break the restrictive bounds of the modernist world view, it does not therefore lead to a moral vacuum. Writers such as Bauman have sought to articulate postmodern ethics. There are still ethics and morality in a postmodern world, but these are worked out not through reference to universal standards or charters, but rather are negotiated in the day-to-day existence of the actors concerned.

For a postmodernist this has always been so, and codes of ethics or charters of rights have never been a substitute for the negotiated understandings of ethics and morality established between people within their own cultural traditions (Bauman 1993, 1995). They may have important symbolic significance, and legislation can be used to enforce certain standards (though inevitably this is selective), but they represent merely one construction of human rights. On the ground, people will interpret and use these conventions and codes in ways that make sense to them, emphasising some things and downplaying or ignoring others, and investing their own meanings and understandings into the words of the document.

This means that we should not necessarily discard conventions, documents and treaties such as the Universal Declaration of Human Rights, the UN conventions, charters or bills of rights. These have important symbolic significance and can be used as powerful tools for pursuing human rights goals. However, these documents will lose their status as infallible and immutable statements of rights that apply to all people, at all times and in all places. Instead, they will become particular constructions of human rights that are themselves the product of particular human interactions in a certain cultural and historical context. They can still thus contain wisdom – indeed inspiration – and be useful to people in thinking through the ideas of rights and duties in their particular location, but they will be by no means a final authority and should be open to question and to scrutiny like any other construction of human rights.

In this regard, documents such as the Universal Declaration or a national bill of rights can become the focus of community-level consideration of human rights. It can be useful to discuss, for example, what the Universal Declaration does *not* cover, what items might be added to it, what might be redrafted and so on, to make it a relevant document for the community concerned. Rewriting the Universal Declaration from a community perspective can be an important component of consciousness-raising and can be part of the reorientation of the idea of 'human rights' that is required for human rights from below. This will be taken up further in Chapter 7.

BEYOND DUALISMS

One of the important limitations of modernity is its reliance on binary logic, which locates the binary dualism at the centre of reasoning. It is impossible to eliminate binaries from our thinking. For example, a review of this chapter alone will identify many binaries: from above/from below, needs/rights, discursive/reflexive, debate/dialogue, legal/cultural and modernity/postmodernity.

The last of these is a good example of the problems of such dualistic thinking. It is common to juxtapose modernity and postmodernity as opposites, the latter implying a negation of the former and thereby implying that postmodernism requires us to discard all ideas and insights from the world of modernity. However, it must be remembered that the prefix 'post-' does not imply an opposite. It implies an idea of moving 'beyond', of adding to or replacing, rather than necessarily of negating. Nevertheless, the dualistic thinking implied in modernity leads us to pose the two as an opposing binary.

Moving beyond binary, dualistic thinking is one of the greatest challenges of postmodernism, at least for those from the Western intellectual tradition, given the dominance of such dualisms in Western thought. Conventional human rights discourse is, unsurprisingly, riddled with binaries: perpetrator/victim, rights/duties, positive/negative, compliance/noncompliance, universal/relative, individual/collective, and so on. The view of human rights advocated here requires that each of these binaries be questioned rather than uncritically accepted, and it is when this questioning/critique occurs that one can enter some interesting fields.

For example, questioning the simple binary of perpetrator/victim can suggest that perpetrators can also be victims of the system that creates the abuse and sometimes – more controversially – victims may themselves be part of the system that has led to the human rights abuse. Breaking down the sharp distinction between perpetrator and victim is just one way in which questioning binaries can lead to interesting, and controversial, questions. A further example is the breaking down of the universal/relative binary, as was discussed in some detail in Chapter 4. A similar questioning of the other binaries mentioned above can result in similarly important and 'left-field' theorising. Some of the categories created by binaries can, of course, be useful, but a postmodern approach of human rights from below requires that at least they be questioned rather than taken for granted.

GLOBALISATION AND LOCALISATION

Globalisation, discussed in Chapter 2 in relation to community development, is an important component of all contexts of human rights in the early twenty-first century. Global interconnection applies not only to business and the economy, which is the conventional context for discussion of globalisation, but to all aspects of human activity, thanks to the power and pervasiveness of communications technology. There has been not only the globalisation of trade and the economy, but increased interconnection across cultural, social, political and environmental activity.

This raises significant issues for human rights from below: local context is never only local, as it will always contain an element of the global. Thus, whenever we discuss a local community or a local context for human rights, there will always be global issues to be taken into account. The impact of global media, of communication through the internet, of global marketing, global power and increased mobility has negated any notion of 'the local' being purely local, with no connection to the rest of the world.

Similarly, there can be no such thing as a purely globalised world. When globalisation becomes too threatening for people, they retreat into a form of localisation (Bello 2002, Hines 2000, Hopkins 2008, Mander & Goldsmith 1996) where local community becomes more important as a basis for identity, or where there is a reassertion of alternative identities, as is the case with resurgent nationalism or religious fundamentalism (Sim 2004). These movements have subverted a straightforward globalisation, just as globalisation has subverted the purely local. Hence the binary global/local is being dismantled, and any understanding of human rights cannot afford to ignore either the local or the global.

This is particularly important for human rights from below. The arguments presented thus far in support of human rights from below may be seen to be advocating a return to clearly identified local contexts as the basis for human rights, whereas such demarcated local contexts no longer exist (if they ever did). The context of human rights is not purely local, with no impact from a wider world. Rather, the context within which human rights from below are constructed, respected and realised is a complex interplay of both local and global forces and forces that emerge somewhere between these two extremes (such as national or regional identities).

Some of the earlier critics of globalisation (Brecher & Costello 1994, Falk 1993) have argued for an idea of 'globalisation from below', where globalisation is pursued in the interests of people and communities rather than in the interests of corporate profit. The argument for human rights from below is somewhat similar, in that it seeks to insert the lived experience of people in different community and cultural contexts into our understanding of human rights.

However, the idea of globalisation from below was established very much as a binary, and a more sophisticated analysis suggests that to draw a sharp distinction between the global and the local, implying that one must have one or the other, is too simplistic. Rather, the global affects and defines the local, and the local reflects and defines the global, so that they are interrelated rather than mutually exclusive. In the same way that feminist writers insisted that the personal *is* political and the political *is* personal, we can similarly see the global as local and the local as global. Thus it is necessary to move away from the idea of the context of human rights as being either local or global, but rather to realise that it is inevitably both. Human rights from below is thus not simply a reflection of localism. It insists that context is essential for understanding human rights, but that context itself is problematic and requires further deconstruction. How this is worked out will, of course, vary, but such an analysis suggests significant lines of questioning in the establishment of human rights from below, which will be taken up further in Chapter 6.

THE ECOLOGICAL IMPERATIVE

Just as globalisation is an inevitable part of the context of human rights, similarly the ecological crisis cannot be ignored in any attempt to develop an approach of human rights from below.

The unsustainable nature of the global social, economic and political system which has been a theme in green writing since the late 1980s, has now become clear to a much wider audience. Global warming is perhaps the most significant aspect of the ecological crisis, as its likely impacts are becoming increasingly documented, and as the limited capacity of governments to deal with this threat becomes more apparent. At the time of writing, global temperature rises of at least two degrees Celsius seem inevitable, regardless of the effectiveness of policies aimed at countering global warming, and rises of three or even four degrees by the end of the century seem highly likely. Even a rise of two degrees will result in significant ecological changes that will create major crises in the lives of most of the world's population (Spratt & Sutton 2008).

To the threat of global warming must be added other environmental and resource issues: the inevitability of peak oil (Roberts 2004, Hopkins 2008) with its dramatic consequences for the global economy; the impending world food crisis, resulting from increasing desertification caused by climate change, from the use of land for bio-fuels and from increased competition for limited food stocks; the over-fishing of the oceans, which seems likely to lead to a major shortage of seafood by the middle of the century (Mitchell 2008); increasing scarcity of water, whether for drinking or for agriculture (Barlow 2007); the dangers of serious pandemics caused by the mutation of viruses in an overpopulated and highly mobile world; and the effect of continuing use of chemicals and pesticides.

These ecological crises have serious implications for human rights. Increased competition for scarce resources of food, water and energy seem likely to fuel significant conflicts, and the twenty-first century could become the century of resource wars (Dyer 2008). Similarly, there will be more forced migration as environmental refugees seek new homes when their existing locations become uninhabitable through lack of water, lack of food, flooding or severe storms. The plight of these refugees will be serious, given that nearly all countries will be suffering from resource scarcity and there is likely to be increased 'border protection'. We know from the history of the twentieth century that wars and mass movement of refugees are both triggers for major human rights violations, and therefore human rights is likely to remain a major area of concern as the world seeks to come to terms with problems of a nature and magnitude never before seriously contemplated.

The human rights implications of ecological problems have begun to be addressed in the literature, specifically in relation to global warming (Adger et al. 2006, Northcott 2007). This has been concerned with both the human problems associated with climate change and the ways in which climate change policies themselves may be implemented so as to enshrine human rights values.

However, the thrust of government policies has tended to take account first of the needs of the national economy in shaping climate change policy rather than the needs of people and communities, let alone the needs of the planet, in a sad replication of much twentieth-century public policy. The economic crisis of 2008–09 may have the potential for a major re-evaluation of the social aims of economic policy, but the strength of economic rationalist arguments may still ensure that the needs of 'the economy' are given priority over the needs of people. This will inevitably exacerbate human rights concerns.

Nevertheless human rights, especially human rights from below, has the capacity to make a more significant contribution than simply influencing the reaction and consequences of ecological change. The important need that emerges from the ecological crisis is the need for humans to re-evaluate their relationship to the natural, 'non-human' world. The idea that the rest of the world exists as nothing more than a resource for human enjoyment is now being questioned, and it has become clear that policies and practices must no longer envisage the non-human world in purely instrumental terms, but rather as having value in its own right.

There is a clear interdependence between the human and non-human worlds, and while this interdependence has been acknowledged in indigenous communities throughout the world, in some non-Western religions and more recently by various green thinkers (Lovelock 2006, 2009, Macy 2007, Shiva 2005), the dominant view of the Western world, and of the global economic and political system, has not recognised this interdependence but has seen the non-human world purely in instrumental terms. This is clearly evidenced in conventional economics, which assigns no value to nature unless it becomes used as a 'resource' for human ends.

This view of economics has been challenged by green economists since the late 1980s (Diesendorf & Hamilton 1997, Ekins & Max-Neef 1992, Henderson 2006, Mander & Goldsmith 1996), but such economic views have been treated as marginal, if not deviant, by the mainstream. It is only in the early years of the twenty-first century that such views are, tentatively, becoming more accepted as the ecological crises facing the world become all too apparent.

There is, then, a need to establish a new understanding of the relationship of human beings with the non-human world: a new contract with nature. This goes to the heart of our understanding of the human, the 'nature of humanity', and what distinguishes the human from the non-human world. As was discussed earlier in Chapter 3, the idea of the human is problematic as a product of Western modernity. The need to rethink 'the human', both in the context of postmodernity and in the context of the ecological crisis, becomes one of the significant challenges of the coming decades. Human rights, and especially human rights from below, is very much concerned with the construction and reconstruction of 'humanity'. Ideas of what makes us human are central to ideas of human rights, and so human rights from below can play an important role in the process of redefining humanity and its relationship to the non-human world.

This raises the important question of animal rights, and indeed the 'rights' not only of animals but of all the non-human world. As discussed in Chapter 3, there is a difference between human and animal rights, in that we cannot expect animals to engage in the same moral reasoning about rights and duties that we can as humans. Animal rights are really concerned with humans' duties towards non-humans, rather than non-humans articulating their rights and duties to each other. This does not, however, render them any less important. As a process of human rights from below seeks to articulate what it means to be human and what that means in terms of our rights and responsibilities to each other, it must also include our responsibilities to other species as part of building a more sustainable and ecologically aware world.

To refer to Lovelock's (1987, 2006, 2009) important work on what is known as the 'Gaia hypothesis', we must ask: what are the rights of Gaia, and how do the rights of humans, the rights of non-humans and the rights of Gaia interact? Human rights need to be understood from a Gaia perspective if they are to be a viable idea in a future world of sustainability and ecological awareness. This is a new field for human rights. Traditionally human rights has not extended into the environmental area beyond seeking to ensure that responses to ecological change will not have adverse human rights consequences. Linking human rights with Gaia, and recognising that our understanding of human rights reflects what it means to be human in a world where humanity is causing gross ecological damage, locates human rights at the centre rather than on the periphery of the response to the multiple ecological crises that will dominate the twenty-first century.

This requires an ecological approach to human rights. This may mean that some rights that have been largely taken for granted will need to be circumscribed, for example when the exercise of that right is resource-intensive or creates pollution or waste. Examples may include the right to mobility when this entails the extensive use of air travel; the right to land ownership when that 'ownership' implies permission to pollute or degrade that land; or the right to fish in waters where fish stocks are already depleted. These examples are where the rights of Gaia, of non-human species, of nature, are brought into moral considerations of what counts as human rights and what duties we owe to non-human species and the natural world. Seen in this way, human rights from below must be understood not only in its cultural context and in its globalised context, but also in its ecological context.

This is an instance where human rights has something to learn from the experience of community development. For some time now community development has been concerned with the ecological crisis. There is a firm belief among many environmental writers and activists that strong communities, with as much as possible happening at the community level rather than being more centralised, represent potentially the most sustainable form of social organisation and the most likely to achieve some level of ecological balance (Hopkins 2008). Concern for the environment has been one of the imperatives for community development (as discussed in Chapter 1), and for some time ecological concerns have figured strongly in the community development literature. The tradition of linking the environment with local community action is strong, and the incorporation of ecology and environmental concerns into human rights work can thus only strengthen human rights from below.

RECONSIDERING CONTEXT

If human rights from below requires that the context of people's lived experience is to be taken into account in articulating, realising and protecting human rights, then the above sections suggest that the very idea of 'context' is itself problematic. Asking the question 'what is the context?' requires a consideration not only of the cultural, but of other factors such as the global and the ecological. To say that human rights only makes sense when understood in context requires us to consider much more carefully the nature of that context. Much of the understanding of context has been located in the cultural, and while of course cultural context is critically important for human rights, it is not the only aspect of context that must be taken into account. Human rights from below might be renamed 'contextualised human rights', with context itself a matter for careful consideration and analysis in any situation.

Technological progress, increased personal mobility, cyberspace, new media, globalisation and the ecological crisis make the 'context' of any human activity almost unrecognisable from the context of 100, or even 50, years ago. Context is no less important for the definition and realisation of our humanity – it is indeed a necessity – but the nature of that context has changed, and the project of contextualising human rights must take account of the newly emerging contexts of human activity.

CONCLUSION

This chapter has developed a number of ideas in relation to human rights from below. It would be wrong to label this a coherent 'theory' or, worse, 'model'. Rather its goal has been more modest: to identify a number of important questions in relation to human rights from below, suggesting the kind of analysis and understandings that are necessary if we are to approach human rights from this perspective.

The chapter has not attempted to deal with the more practical questions of how one might institute a human rights regime based on human rights from below. This is partly because it is impossible to delineate specific practice principles in community development; as I have argued elsewhere (Ife 2002, Ife & Tesoriero 2006) and in Chapter 2, community development relies on community processes determining what needs to be done and how it should be done, rather than imposing 'how to do it' solutions. This does not mean that there is no point in discussing the reality of practice. Exploring potential worthwhile directions for practice, without being too specific or didactic, is important if we are to move from the considerations of this chapter to the practice of human rights from below. Here, again, human rights can draw on the experience of community development, and that will be the theme of the remaining chapters.

Part 4
Enacting human rights from below

Defenceless under the night
Our world in stupor lies.
Yet, dotted everywhere,
Ironic points of light
Flash out wherever the just
Exchange their messages.

W.H. Auden, 'September 1, 1939'

6

Seven arenas of human rights from below

IT WILL BE RECALLED that in previous chapters seven dimensions of community development and of human rights were identified: social, economic, political, cultural, environmental, spiritual and survival. When we discuss these seven in relation to enacting human rights from below, we must remember that a holistic approach to human rights from below implies that all seven are important: none should necessarily have primacy over the others in a general sense, though in any particular community setting one or two may be seen as more important in responding to local circumstances.

While different human rights workers will have strengths in different areas, and will choose to concentrate on perhaps one or two areas in particular, they should never lose sight of a more overall, holistic view of human rights from below. Just as all seven are necessary for effective community development, so all seven are necessary for human rights from below, as without all seven some important aspects of humanity, and of community, will be missed.

SOCIAL RIGHTS AND SOCIAL DEVELOPMENT

Social rights are particularly appropriate for a perspective of human rights from below. Our social rights to things such as education, housing, health care (though this can also be included under 'survival rights'), recreation, choice of marriage partner and family lifestyle, work and meaningful relationships cannot readily be articulated in a universalist, context-free sense. What these social rights mean, and how they are defined and enacted, will vary significantly according to context.

At one level, it is almost trite to say that a strong community will enhance people's social rights if we think in terms of the strength of people's relationships, social solidarity, the opportunity to form relationships and so on. If we take into account the social dimension in human rights, it becomes clear that some form of community is necessary if those rights are to be realised. As stated on a number of occasions through this book, human rights cannot be realised in isolation. They need to be embedded in a community, and this is particularly true of social rights.

Social rights also need to be understood to have a broader compass than simply relationships, important though these are. Social rights include a whole range of rights that may be met either through the free market or through some kind of public provision: education, health, housing, employment and income security. The adequate protection and realisation of these rights has been the task of social policy; and social policy, like human rights, has often been conceptualised as a 'from above' rather than a 'from below' activity. For human rights from below to address social rights adequately, it is necessary for the key questions of social policy to become part of a community agenda rather than to be seen as the sole prerogative of bureaucrats, politicians and academics.

Many of the key questions for social policy revolve around the issue of the proper role for the three sectors – the state, the market and the community (or non-profit) sectors – in the meeting of social need (Bryson 1992), and this is largely an ideological issue (George & Wilding 1994). Social democrats, especially in Europe and Scandinavia, favour the welfare state with a major role for the state in the provision of social services. Neoliberals and neoconservatives tend to favour an expanded role for the market and a reduced role for the state; therefore they tend to favour privatisation and reliance on market mechanisms, allowing people to purchase the services they feel they need. Others favour the non-profit sector, the community sector or the 'third' sector, with social services planned and provided through a strong civil society.

Few people would argue exclusively for any one sector at the total expense of the other two. Rather, there is a broad consensus that it is appropriate to have some mix of the three; typically, there is strong disagreement about what that mix should be. Should the state be a provider of services, or should the state simply fund and support the community sector which is, supposedly, closer to the people? Or should the state contract out services to either the private sector or the community sector through a process of competitive tendering? Should the community sector determine the agenda and make submissions to government for funding for services they regard as needed? Should the state only provide services for those who cannot afford to purchase in the private market (such as housing)? Or should state provision be for everybody? Or for everybody except those who wish to opt out and purchase an alternative in the private market (for instance, education)? If we have a mix of public and private, how do we then avoid the problems of two classes of provision, one for the rich and one for the poor? Or is such a division acceptable?

These questions are sufficiently complex that they cannot be dealt with adequately here. To address them properly requires some level of expert social policy knowledge in terms of 'what works and what doesn't'. More importantly, these questions are also ideological. There is no one 'best way' to organise social policy because it depends very much on what kind of society we want and how we balance the competing claims of equity, efficiency, freedom, public ownership, accountability and other considerations (George & Wilding 1994). However, regardless of their complexity, these questions are very significant for the practice of human rights from below.

In recent years, in Western democracies (especially the English-speaking ones) there has been an increasing reliance on the market for the provision of human services, given a strong impetus by the Thatcher–Reagan policies of the 1980s. Belief in the market has received something of a reality check with the economic crisis that is still being experienced as this book goes to press, and this raises the question about what happens to community services when there is market failure.

We cannot simply rely on the market for the provision of services that meet the requirements of human rights unless we assume that the market will never fail to deliver. This is clearly not the case. In Australia in late 2008 a large private provider of child care, ABC Learning Centres, failed, leaving many working parents without assured child care for the next year. There was a strong move from various community groups to have the child care centres taken over by the community sector rather than by other private providers. This met with only limited success, and those centres that did go to the community sector were taken over by large-scale NGOs with relatively little local community engagement.

The future security of services operated by the private sector at times of market failure is in question, and from the point of view of this book this is a human rights issue. Moreover, from a community development perspective it can be argued that, wherever possible, services should be run in a way that maximises the involvement of the people of the community itself, rather than the involvement of distant entrepreneurs, distant NGO managers or distant bureaucrats.

This question of what happens to market-based services when the market fails is likely to become more urgent at a time of increasing economic uncertainty, especially as the welfare state is also facing limited resources and increasing demand and its capacity to rescue such services will be limited. What might be the consequences, for example, of health insurance funds or retirement savings funds failing in the market environment through poor investment decisions or through fraud on the part of fund managers? At a time when the resources of the state have been eroded through the ideology of lower taxation, it would be impossible for states to step in and fully ensure people's social rights. This will be an important issue in the future for those concerned about ensuring social rights.

It is important to note that the three domains of social policy actors mentioned above – the state, the market and the community sectors – can all operate either in a top-down or a bottom-up way, and hence can either hinder or reinforce human rights from below. The state – or government – need not be a remote, unapproachable machine. Local government is, at least in theory, a level of government that is accessible to the people in a day-to-day fashion, and hence can be completely compatible with human rights from below. In relation specifically to social rights, local government can provide a range of services that help people to realise these rights, including health, recreation and education (both formal and informal, including through libraries and other facilities), and there is the potential for significant involvement of the community in determining the nature of these services and programs.

Similarly, the market can operate at a large scale – national or global – well out of the reach of people in communities who can feel powerless to do anything about 'market forces'. However, like government, markets can also operate at a local level, and indeed it was at this level that markets first developed, and they remained predominantly at that level until relatively recent times. When markets operate locally, they can be embedded in the community and serve community interests rather than asking the community to serve 'market' demands.

The idea of local markets will be taken up in the next section, but as far as social rights are concerned it is significant to note that social provision can indeed be traded in the marketplace, and this can be done at a local level with much less likelihood of an inequitable result. For example, a teacher or local health professional may 'trade' his or her services in a local market system and people can pay for their services 'in kind'. Also, like the state and the market, the community sector can operate in a remote, top-down way or use a locally based bottom-up approach. Examples of the former are the large national or international charities or NGOs that operate many social programs. Even though the rhetoric is that they are 'closer to the community' this is often not reflected in reality. There is little difference between a government bureaucrat in a capital city managing a national program and the manager of a large national charity, with an office in the same capital city, also managing a national program. Indeed, the two are in all probability working in 'partnership', and the boundary between government and non-government programs has become very blurred.

The point of the above discussion is to emphasise that, from the perspective of human rights from below, the traditional social policy question of 'private, public or community sector' is less important than the issue of whether the community is actively and meaningfully engaged in defining needs and determining the kinds of services that are appropriate and the way they will be delivered. Each of the three sectors can operate in a way that is consistent with human rights from below and, equally, each can operate in a way that denies such an approach. Indeed, much of the literature on 'social development' assumes very much a top-down perspective (Midgley 1997). This literature emerged as a reaction against purely economic models of 'development' being implemented in 'developing' countries, and insisted that social aspects of development were just as important and needed to be addressed as part of the development process. However, this view of development is still large-scale and written from the perspective of international NGOs and the United Nations, rather than from a perspective of *community* development, as is the purpose of this book. The traditional view of social development may be important in achieving social rights, but is not really consistent with the idea of human rights from below.

The important question for social rights from below is how much people are able to articulate their needs and the needs of their community, and whether they are then able to transfer that articulation of need into a definition of right. This requires some form of community-level consultation.

Let us take, as an example, the right to education. It is easy to declare that everyone has a right to education, but what does this mean in a community context? First, it is important to think about education beyond the idea of schools or other formal education structures, such as colleges. People's right to education can be realised in a number of other ways and must never be confused with a right to a qualification; one can have education without a qualification and, sadly all too often, one can have a qualification without education. As well as schools and colleges, resources through which the right to education can be realised include:

- local libraries
- courses at a community centre
- television and radio programs
- newspapers and magazines
- the internet
- workers' education programs
- resources for families to educate at home
- education 'on the job' as part of employment
- informal learning circles or study groups
- education components of other services, for example health education as part of a fitness program or consumer education as part of a community legal service.

These activities can be initiated as part of a community development process. Even radio and television programs can be initiated using community access channels or local radio stations; articles can be submitted to local newspapers; or people can be helped with internet access. The result can be a community where education is not just something that happens in schools, but rather something that is embedded in community life.

Similar points could be made about other social rights. However, there is a more important aspect to social rights from below than simply initiating such a range of activities. There is also a need to establish some form of community control over the service and how it is delivered. The common practice of a community management committee, which may operate either as a formal board of management or in an advisory capacity, is a way to achieve this. Community management committees can consider, for example, the hours a service might operate, the qualities required of staff (such as knowledge of community languages in a multicultural community), physical location and so on.

There can be tensions when a service employs professionals (for instance lawyers, teachers or doctors) who may be uncomfortable about being accountable to unqualified people, but this is a narrow view of 'qualifications'. Community members are also qualified, though in different ways, and the community development principles discussed in Chapter 2 suggest that this expertise and local wisdom be valued and recognised. This may require some re-education on the part of professionals, or careful selection processes to ensure that people will be employed who respect and value not just a level of community involvement but also community ownership.

Community ownership and community management committees can pose problems, particularly when community members have little experience in such roles, or understanding of the responsibilities involved. Legal requirements of boards and committees can be intimidating and it can be important to include an element of expertise in the area of legal obligations, for example in keeping proper financial records or dealing with suspected criminal behaviour. For example, if a committee of a community-based child care centre becomes aware that one of the staff may be a paedophile, it is important to take immediate action and not put it off because the person concerned is a friend or colleague (the experience of churches with child abuse is a salutary example in this regard), and management committees need to be aware of these obligations.

For this reason it can be tempting to have a management committee that consists of experienced professionals with relevant expertise who are aware of such issues and are able to deal with them. However, this can defeat the purpose of the community management committee, especially if it is a community where most people do not possess such qualifications and experience. While it may be necessary to include some of this kind of expertise on a committee, it must always be remembered that the committee is there to represent the interests of the whole community, not of the narrow, sectional professional interests of those who 'know best'.

Much of the above discussion is familiar territory for community workers, though it is perhaps less familiar for human rights workers. The important point for present purposes is to understand it as a way for people to be able to define their social rights themselves and to establish processes to have those rights established. For this reason, those familiar with community development processes need to be seen in the light of human rights, especially the right of people to articulate their social needs and to control the ways those needs are met. It is not merely an infusion of community development principles into human rights work; it is also the infusion of human rights principles into community work.

Of course this does not imply that there is no role for the state, or indeed for the market or the third sector, at a more centralised level. Social rights from below may only be possible if there is some support from the centre in the provision of resources (both financial and expert) and in allowing space for local initiatives to develop and thrive. Unfortunately, all too often the state cannot resist the temptation to control the agenda on the assumption that the politicians and bureaucrats, with their overview and expertise, know 'better' than the local communities with their limitations and parochialism. Therefore there has been a tendency for governments to work on a 'purchase of service' model, where they determine what is needed and then contract it out to the private or community sectors that are asked to tender for the work. Sometimes such arrangements are dressed up in the rhetoric of decentralisation or of 'partnerships', but they remain essentially a state-controlled agenda, and the implication is that governments are in the best position not only to define people's social rights, but also to decide how they should be realised. This is hardly compatible with social rights from below, as it allows little voice to the people most concerned.

One way in which social rights from below are often implemented is in the form of charters of rights relating to particular services. Hospitals, for example, commonly have charters of patients' rights, as do many other social agencies. They are often displayed prominently on notice boards and this can be a useful way of setting a human rights framework for the service concerned and helping people to use rights language.

However, they can also be tokenistic, making it appear that something is being achieved when in fact it is not. The sight of a charter of residents' rights displayed on the wall of a nursing home, where most of the residents are suffering from dementia and seldom wear their glasses, does not suggest of itself a strong commitment to human rights, though there is some value for visiting family members who may see and read such a charter. Placing a charter on a wall or notice board may be a good idea, but there is then the temptation to think that this is all that needs to be done to incorporate human rights. For human rights to be more than tokenistic, people must have the opportunity to talk about them, to maintain dialogue (see Chapter 5) and to have human rights as an ongoing project rather than a statement.

One important aspect of the idea of social rights from below is that it means that community-based human service workers – such as health workers, teachers, social workers, community development workers, recreation workers and youth workers – are effectively human rights workers. This provides workers with a different frame of reference for thinking about their work and their relationship with the people and communities with which they are working. A rights-based approach to human service practice incorporates an understanding of the rights of service recipients, the rights of community members, the rights of colleagues, supervisors and students, and the corresponding responsibilities that go with those rights (see Ife 2008 for a fuller analysis). Human service workers, their 'clients' and their colleagues are seen as linked together in a community of rights and responsibilities, and this leads to a form of practice that emphasises dialogue and action, as discussed in Chapter 5.

A final point to be made about implementing social rights from below is that, consistent with the discussion in earlier chapters, it is important to incorporate diversity and to have community-based services that both welcome and encourage diversity and draw on the richness of a diverse community. This means resisting the temptation to pursue 'best practice' or to implement a 'model' that has been developed elsewhere, as this will have a tendency to generalise, to treat everybody more or less the same way (on the false assumption that equality of treatment can be equated with equity), and not to allow for cultural difference. Social rights from below must be based on the idea of 'community-in-difference' as discussed in Chapter 1.

ECONOMIC RIGHTS AND ECONOMIC DEVELOPMENT

As discussed in Chapter 4, economic rights are unlike the other categories of rights in that they are instrumental. It is common to declare that you cannot eat or drink money. Economic rights are really only important in that they enable us to purchase goods and services with which other rights can be realised, as money is not an end in itself but merely the means to many other ends. Our economic rights are therefore important in terms of their relationship to other rights. And economic rights, like other rights, will vary with context: the economic system that operates in a particular society will determine how economic rights are defined and achieved. Economic rights will take very different forms, for example in a modern free-market capitalist society, in a subsistence-level peasant society, in a centrally planned communist society and in a Scandinavian welfare state.

Because of the dominance of economic rationalist thinking, which assumes that 'if the economy is all right the rest will follow', community economic development can be particularly vulnerable to the kind of fundamentalist community development thinking mentioned in Chapter 2. There it was pointed out that any attempt at community development that emphasises only one dimension of community is unlikely to be very successful, in that it fails to take account of the holistic and multidimensional nature of human community. Such a narrow approach is probably more likely with community economic development, and economic rights from below, than is the case with any of the other dimensions of human rights from below considered in this section. Therefore, it is important in any program of community economic development that links be clearly made to other dimensions of community – the social, political, cultural, environmental and spiritual – and that economic issues not be seen as separate from, or more important than, the others.

Community economic development aims to develop strong, viable and sustainable economies at the local community level. It thus aims to meet people's economic rights, and can do this in ways that are not assured by larger-scale macroeconomic development. The conventional top-down model of economics has not always been very successful at meeting needs at a community level or ensuring people's economic rights (Diesendorf & Hamilton 1997, Mander & Goldsmith 1996, Shragge 2000). In so-called 'developed' countries there are often large areas where the apparently healthy economy has resulted in economic deprivation at the community level: these can include marginal rural communities with significant levels of poverty or decaying 'rust-belt' areas where industry has been closed and jobs lost in the name of economic development.

Many people feel disconnected from, and betrayed by, the global economy, and many others feel vulnerable, given the tenuous nature of their community's economic base, potential job losses and factory closures. In developing nations, even those in the process of 'economic miracles', the gains can very easily be reversed and the poor and unskilled are usually those most at risk. It is little wonder, then, that the idea of community economic development has been so attractive to many communities and for those seeking more sustainable alternatives to the existing order. If human rights from below is to have meaning, the protection and realisation of economic rights at the community level is essential.

As mentioned in Chapter 2, community economic development can be broadly divided into two approaches. One seeks to help a community to operate more effectively within the existing economic order. It accepts the economic order as given, and seeks ways that a local community may better be able to benefit from it. The other, more radical, approach sees the dominant economic order as part of the problem, so it cannot be part of the solution. This approach, instead, seeks ways in which alternative community-based economic systems may develop at a local level despite the dominant order, rather than because of it.

The former, more conservative, form of community economic development is characterised by seeking to make the community more competitive. This includes trying to attract new industry to the community – though this often involves a community in making sacrifices to a point where the industry may be of doubtful value – through various incentives such as making land available, or forgoing local taxes, or ignoring potential environmental problems.

When an industry is attracted from outside the community its presence is never really permanent; an industry that is attracted by one community can always potentially be attracted by another community and decide to move again. The mobility of capital has meant that economic activity that is connected to the global market is unlikely to become embedded in any community but will always be potentially transient, and once a community has attracted such industry it will probably have to struggle and make further concessions in order to keep it. At times of economic downturn, such communities are particularly vulnerable to plant closures and job losses. This has been an ongoing issue for communities reliant on the motor vehicle manufacturing industry, though it is common with many other industries as well, and is hardly a secure guarantee of economic rights for the members of the community.

Potentially more sustainable is the attempt to develop local industries, drawing on the resources and natural advantages that a local community may have. Here at least the decisions affecting the future of that industry can be made in the community and can take account of the interests of the community as well as the owners of the business. This of course is no guarantee of permanence or sustainability either, but it does mean the economic rights of community members are less vulnerable to outside influences and more under local control, in line with community development principles as discussed in Chapter 2.

Of course some communities are better placed than others to develop locally based industry because of access to transport routes, suitable physical environment and so on. There is sometimes a tendency among community economic developers to implicitly 'blame' some communities for not having a sufficiently 'can-do' attitude, when the reality is that the more successful 'can-do' communities have natural advantages such as historical monuments or spectacular scenery to attract tourists, accessibility to main travel routes or fertile soils.

Although such economic development projects may be more sustainable, there are still potential problems, especially in the case of the tourism industry. The tourism industry is particularly sensitive to overall economic conditions, and a community relying on tourism for its economic base is naturally vulnerable to economic downturn. Tourism can also be problematic in that the nature of the relationship between community and tourist is inevitably exploitative, as the economic benefit to the community depends on the community persuading tourists to part with their money.

Tourism can also have negative effects on community life. Tourists typically want to see something that is different and unique, yet when it comes to meals and accommodation they tend to want the familiar and the comfortable. Hence there is a split within the community between the part that the tourists want to see – preserved often in the artificiality of the pioneer museum or the heritage building – which has to be as different from the familiar as possible, and the part that provides them with services, which has to be as similar as possible to the comforts of home. Often the pressure on, and price of, accommodation in a tourist town can be such that the people who work there cannot afford to live there and have to commute; there are plenty of facilities for the tourists, but few for the locals. This is hardly conducive to a healthy and thriving community, or to enhancing the rights of the local people.

There is some place for tourism in many communities, and it can play a part in strengthening the local economy, but there are clear dangers in an over-reliance on tourism as the basis of a sustainable local economy. It is, at best, a problematic way to secure community economic rights in a sustainable way.

Problems such as these do not mean that some of these more conservative approaches to community economic development are not worth implementing. They can in some circumstances be very beneficial for a community, but it would be a mistake to rely on them exclusively. More genuinely community-based approaches, which seek to establish a viable local economy in spite of, rather than because of, the dominant economic order, are also important for community-based economic rights.

The other main approach to community economic development is to establish local community-based economic systems that are, to some degree at least, independent of the mainstream economy. If the global economic system has not met the needs of a community or of a section of a community, then it makes sense for that community to seek to establish some kind of alternative that does meet their needs. Communities have more ability to establish such alternative economies than do governments. If a government tries to stand up to global capital, it is likely to face severe threats in the form of the withdrawal of investment and a major economic crisis. Governments have to do more or less what global market forces require, even if they do not want to.

However, the same does not hold for local communities. It is harder for global capital to bully a local community if that community decides it wants to go its own way. For this reason, many opponents of global capital have emphasised the importance of alternative action at the local level (Mander & Goldsmith 1996, Shiva 2005), rather than trying to persuade governments to change their ways. If the global economic system denies many people their economic rights, which is clearly the case, then an important aspect of human rights from below is to develop alternative ways in which those rights can be better protected and realised.

Local trade and local currency systems have become known as LETS systems, though there is some disagreement about the actual term for which LETS is an acronym (see Chapter 2). LETS has become increasingly popular in areas where there is a shortage of jobs or where there are a number of people who are unable to compete in the local labour market. LETS is simply an extension of the informal system of local barter or exchange that has always existed, especially in smaller, more self-contained communities (Kennedy & Kennedy 1995, Meeker-Lowry 1996).

Commonly such schemes involve establishing a local currency, which can be used in exchange for goods and services produced and consumed locally. This has the advantage of ensuring that the 'profits' made from the production of local goods and services remain in the community, rather than being appropriated by distant shareholders. It gives the local community control over the local economy and enables people who do not have access to 'normal jobs', for whatever reason, to earn funds in an alternative currency. LETS also strengthens local community by providing a way of bringing people together and by emphasising their interdependence.

In times of economic downturn, when many people lose their jobs, LETS becomes a viable alternative for more people. The fact that there are many LETS schemes already established means that, if the global economic system reaches a major crisis (as seems increasingly likely), there is a community-based alternative readily available that could quickly become mainstream.

The form that LETS takes will vary somewhat from one community to another, in accordance with community development principles. Although LETS schemes learn from each other's experiences, it would be wrong to assume that there is one 'right' or 'best' way to run a LETS scheme. Indeed LETS, because of its local base, allows for a diversity of approaches. However, it remains an important way in which economic rights 'from below' can be realised.

Whatever form a community economy takes, it is important that it reflect some notion of an equitable distribution of wealth and resources. Economic rights are denied when the few become wealthy at the expense of the many, and this can also happen at the community level. Doing something at the community level does not necessarily imply that it is equitable, though it is true that mechanisms to ensure equity are more likely to be set up when the structures and processes are local, because they are more accessible to people.

The need for a consideration of equity – what is just and fair – must always be a feature of local community economic development. A human rights framework allows this to be addressed through asking such questions as whose rights may be protected or realised, whose rights may be under threat, what corresponding community-level duties go with economic rights, and so on. A human rights perspective also insists that basic economic rights be guaranteed for all, rather than only for some, of the community.

Any consideration of community economic development and economic rights 'from below' must take account of the idea of the market. The market has become a reified concept in the era of global capitalism. It is seen as the preferable mechanism for determining everything, from health care and economic development through to education and environmental protection. Further, the market is seen as having a logic of its own and as demanding respect. Governments are loath to entertain any policy that may not 'meet with the market's approval', as if 'the market' were a person of such authority that they are not to be questioned.

The ideology of the market has caused considerable problems in relation to human rights and social justice (Shiva 2005). Blind faith in markets has not resulted in equity in the distribution of resources, opportunities or rights. Markets have not proved to be effective in the equitable provision of education, health or housing, as in each case a section of the population has proved to be unable to 'compete' in the market and to afford adequate social provision. This has resulted in the need for public provision of health, education and housing alongside the market as a 'second best' option for those who are 'disadvantaged'. This dual system, or one system for the rich and one for the poor, is hardly conducive to stronger communities in which people celebrate their interdependence.

However, markets have their uses and we could not live without them. Indeed, LETS schemes as discussed above are a form of market. For many centuries markets have served communities and have proved to be good mechanisms for the exchange of goods and services where there is a reasonable equality of access and of need. Hence market distribution of food, so long as everybody has an adequate minimum income, works quite effectively, as food is something for which we all have a roughly equal need (unlike, for example, health care), and which local markets can price within reach of everybody.

Distributing food by market mechanisms, however, does not work when some people do not have an adequate minimum income, when the overall supply of food is inadequate (at times of famine, for example) or where large players, such as national or international corporations, take over and can manipulate the market for their own profits. In those cases, people will go hungry. Markets cannot be relied upon in all circumstances.

However, the important point to note is that, when they are embedded within communities, when communities can control markets and not *vice versa* and when profits can be retained at a local level and not exported to distant shareholders, markets can play a vital and positive role in communities and in the protection and realisation of economic rights. Healthy local markets, where both traders and customers are local people, are a sign of a strong and economically viable community. How this is worked out will vary with context. In some places a system such as LETS can help this process, while in others it is simply unnecessary because the right conditions exist without it. Consistent with community development principles there is no single right way, but the idea of healthy local markets is an important agenda for community development, and for the achievement of economic rights.

CIVIL/POLITICAL RIGHTS AND CIVIL/POLITICAL DEVELOPMENT

Civil and political rights represent an important way in which human rights from below can be different from human rights from above. The traditional 'from above' view of civil and political rights regards these rights largely in a negative sense (see Chapter 4) according to which the role of the state is to prevent abuse of those rights. The emphasis is on the *abuse* or *violation* of those rights. The response of the state is to intervene when those rights appear threatened and to provide mechanisms for their *protection*.

At the level of human rights from below, however, these rights take on a different connotation. As suggested in Chapter 5, there is no point in having rights if they are not exercised, and civil and political rights in particular only make sense if people are willing to exercise them. At a community level, these rights can move from being negative to positive. Instead of merely being protected, they can also be encouraged and developed. Like other rights, working out what civil and political rights mean can vary with context. The right of freedom of expression, for example, can mean different things in different contexts and does not necessarily mean simply the right to make public statements, write letters to a newspaper, or take part in a public demonstration. At a community level it can overlap with other categories of rights, such as story-telling (cultural rights) or teaching (social rights).

Civil rights – the rights to be respected and treated with dignity – and political rights – the rights to participation in the political process – can only be guaranteed if they are well entrenched at the community level. If they are entrenched in that way there is little need for heavy-handed 'enforcement' at a more centralised level. Indeed, civil and political rights can only be fully realised and protected if there are appropriate measures at a community level for their implementation. There is only limited use for laws and conventions at the national level to protect, for example, the right to be treated with dignity or the right to freedom of expression if these are not actually experienced in people's daily lives.

These rights are recognised differently at a community level. They require the establishment of community structures and processes to ensure that everyone is able to participate fully in community life and that everyone is treated with dignity and equity, that basic personal security is ensured, and that nobody is subject to discrimination or exclusion.

A wide range of community activities can be used to achieve this. Effective local citizen participation is essential if these rights are to be achieved, and is synonymous with local political rights. For this to occur, it is important to look at the various ways in which people can participate in decision-making and local community processes.

Participation was discussed in Chapter 2, where it was emphasised that participation is more than simply attending a community meeting and speaking out. There are many different ways of achieving participation and these will vary with cultural context and personal circumstances. As well as public meetings there are the possibilities of community surveys, discussion groups, writing groups, community theatre, story-telling and so on, all of which can be mechanisms for people's active participation and hence the realisation of their political rights.

However, these processes can also exclude. A rights-based community worker will seek to ensure that these processes are inclusive by, for example, making sure they occur at convenient times for people, that child care is available, that transport is arranged, that there is access for people with disabilities, that interpreters are provided, or whatever else may be appropriate in the particular context.

Another way in which participation, and hence the realisation of political rights, can be maximised is by ensuring that there is a diversity of ways in which that participation can take place. If there are only one or two forums for participation some people will inevitably be excluded, but a greater variety of possibilities for participation will clearly increase the likelihood that political rights will be maximised.

Political rights at the community level require the implementation of local democracy. As discussed in Chapter 5, the idea of democracy is more complex than the simple idea of 'the right to vote'. In that discussion the ideas of participatory and deliberative democracy were introduced, and they represent important components of human rights from below. These ways of thinking about democracy do away with the notion of democracy being simply equated with voting, and instead look at other ways in which people can play a role in the decisions that affect them.

Participatory democracy requires that citizens be able to participate in decision-making, rather than simply having input into decisions or reacting to them after the event. This is problematic in complex modern societies, where many decisions need to be taken which require special expertise. However, it is usually possible to increase the extent of local participatory democracy. Community meetings represent one way and another is precinct meetings: smaller meetings at very local levels, where people have a chance to discuss issues and reach decisions together.

Participatory democracy requires some form of consensus decision-making where decisions are not taken by a simple majority, but rather where people talk among themselves until a consensus is reached, which everyone agrees either to support or at least not to oppose. There are a number of techniques available for building consensus and reaching consensus decisions, and this is a powerful way in which political rights at a community level can be strengthened (Gastil 1993).

Deliberative democracy has a somewhat different orientation, in that it seeks participation not simply in making a decision, but in the earlier phases of research, discussion and the development of different options. It concentrates on helping people to equip themselves with the necessary background not just to make a decision, but to make an *informed* decision. Thus there is an element of education involved and the recognition that a decision will be better made if people have taken the effort to understand the issue in some depth. This also strengthens political rights at a community level; deliberative democracy is therefore an important aspect of human rights from below.

Civil rights, in contrast to political rights, are more about people's right to be treated with dignity and respect and to personal security. They tend to become legislated in more complex ways, such as the right to a fair trial, the right not to be detained without trial, the right to legal representation, the right to be free from harassment and intimidation and the right to be free from discrimination on the basis of race, nationality, gender, age, beliefs, religion, sexuality or disability.

However, these are simply ways to ensure that all people are treated with respect and dignity, and enjoy a level of security. In seeking to enact these rights at a community level the notion of respect and dignity, and what they mean, becomes important. This consideration can be couched in terms of a question such as 'How should members of this community be treated?', or 'How can we show respect to each other in this community and make sure nobody is left out or devalued?' Questions like these can become a focus for community workshops and for dialogue within and between different groups in the community.

A different aspect of the development of political rights is the political right of the community itself to have its voice heard and recognised in wider political forums. Some communities are better able to do this than others because of the connections, lobbying capacity and media skills of community members. Helping a community to have its voice heard in the wider arena is an important aspect of community political development, and a community-based human rights worker may spend some time assisting a community to develop its lobbying and communication skills so that the articulation of human rights can be made in a larger arena than the community itself.

In doing this, it is important for a community-based human rights worker not to take the role of advocate/lobbyist if possible, but rather to support and assist community members to do this as part of a program of skill-sharing. It is all too easy for a community worker to assume an advocacy role and thereby inhibit the realisation of the rights of community members to speak for themselves. The problem with advocacy, and its potential for disempowerment, will be discussed further in Chapter 7. It may well be that initially a worker has to assume such roles, but it is important always to remember the aim of education and skill-sharing. Ultimately a community will be more powerful, and be better able to define and assert its rights, if its members are able to speak for themselves rather than have somebody do it for them.

In community work, the political aspect of the role is often seen as the 'radical' arm of community development, as it is identified with the need for radical change and political activism. This has been the legacy of the community organising of Saul Alinsky, who drew on his experience with the labour movement to organise Black and/or low-income communities in the United States, especially in Chicago, in the 1960s and 1970s, using essentially a conflict approach. Although Alinsky used some novel and effective techniques of community organising, much of his work was aimed at helping disadvantaged communities compete more effectively within the existing political order. He did not really question the political order, but accepted it and simply helped communities to operate more effectively within it.

This approach, while often effective, could hardly be called 'radical', despite the titles of Alinsky's best-known books *Reveille for Radicals* (1969) and *Rules for Radicals* (1971). Alinsky's *methods* may have been radical, in the sense that they were different and unusual and had the ability to shock, but his political aim was certainly not radical, in that it did not question the dominant order or suggest that there was a need for the system itself to change. This had led the word 'radical' to be loosely identified with 'activist', whereas what passes for radicalism is often actually conservative in its uncritical acceptance of the pluralist nature of the political process.

It may well be that other aspects of human rights from below can be more radical, in that they have the potential to ask more fundamental questions and to suggest some directions for more radical change to the social, economic and political order. For example, alternative community-based economic systems such as LETS, discussed above, have more potential to challenge the economic status quo than a group of demonstrators outside a meeting of bankers.

At this point it is worth mentioning specifically the work of Amnesty International, as it has built its effectiveness by campaigning for civil and political rights while using local community groups as its main means of activism. Of course such a statement is an over-simplification. Amnesty International now includes other rights than civil and political in its mandate, though it was specifically in the area of civil and political rights that Amnesty historically built its reputation.

Amnesty uses more than local community groups for its campaigning and often runs sophisticated media campaigns and employs professional lobbyists, although again it was the mobilisation of 'people power' that made Amnesty initially so successful. The combination of civil and political rights and grassroots community activism means that Amnesty represents a particular example of community-based civil and political rights, and its example has been followed by other NGOs such as Oxfam.

However, these NGOs can readily be distracted by the pull of modernity and can find themselves engaged in debate about 'top-down' legal definitions of what constitutes human rights abuse. In this sense, Amnesty has defined human rights quite conventionally, at a centralised level, and used local communities to further the cause of these centrally defined human rights rather than allowing local groups to articulate their own understandings of human rights. The energy and activism of the local groups have been harnessed, often to very good effect in terms of human rights outcomes.

Amnesty is in many ways a community-based organisation, but it has also been quite centrally coordinated and has been at times perhaps too preoccupied with strategic and operational plans, performance indicators, business plans and the other trappings of managerialist modernity.

This discussion should not be taken to be too critical of Amnesty International (with which the author has had a long association) and similar organisations. Such NGOs have made a major contribution to human rights and the world is undoubtedly a better place because of their existence and their work. The significance of Amnesty International's human rights campaigning is widely acknowledged and greatly appreciated in many countries. The point for present purposes is simply that it does not really represent human rights from below in the way this idea has been described in this book, even though it does combine aspects of both a human rights and a community-based approach.

CULTURAL RIGHTS AND CULTURAL DEVELOPMENT

As was discussed in previous chapters, a community development approach to human rights is concerned with establishing a *culture of human rights*, where human rights and responsibilities are embedded in a cultural context so that they become part of the daily lived experience. In many instances this is already the case, as ideas of rights and responsibilities are part of most if not all cultures, even if they are not named as such. This suggests that community cultural development is a particularly important component of community-based human rights. Culture provides the context within which people work out their mutual rights and responsibilities and how they should be enacted. Therefore community cultural development extends beyond what might normally be understood as 'cultural rights' to incorporate a broader range of human rights and responsibilities.

Although globalisation has taken a predominantly economic form, implying the globalisation of trade and financial markets, it has also spawned a form of cultural globalisation. The creation of a single 'mass culture', largely based on US consumer culture and its imposition on much of the rest of the world, has been in the interests of economic globalisation, as it is easier and more profitable to sell to a single global market than to different markets characterised by different cultural traditions and consumer preferences. Thus people in many different parts of the world increasingly wear the same or similar clothes, listen to the same music, watch the same movies and television, eat the same or similar food and speak, or at least understand, the same language, namely English. The corresponding erosion of diversity is to the detriment of local communities and local cultures, but very much in the interests of global capital.

This has proved to be one of the more powerful motivations behind community cultural development – an attempt to reassert local cultural traditions and the importance of cultural diversity – as there is a perception that the imposition of a global culture results in significant loss of meaning for many people and a less varied and rich experience of humanity. In this way there is a very clear link with human rights, not only in terms of the right to cultural expression and the maintenance of cultural heritage, but also in terms of the context within which human rights can be defined and enacted. The enhancement of cultural diversity and cultural expression is a powerful way to question the imposition of global culture and the consequent homogenisation of the human experience. Questioning globalisation and the assumptions behind it is important for human rights – for example, many anti-globalisation protesters point out that globalisation can violate human rights for many people and communities – and so community cultural development, in articulating the importance of local cultural traditions and of cultural diversity, can be important in promoting human rights in a more general sense.

Many community cultural development programs are aimed at the preservation and valuing of local cultural traditions. This can take the form of researching and writing local history, establishing a local museum, mounting displays in a local library or community centre, keeping newspaper and photographic archives, erecting monuments, naming roads or localities after significant figures, and so on. However, while such activity can be important in helping people to identify with a community's heritage, and can emphasise the significance of history in creating the present, there are some problems with the celebration of heritage. Any history or museum display will be the construction of one or several people, who will have made decisions about what is worth recording and what is not, which voices should be included and which should not and which stories should be told and which should not.

A 'heritage' can easily exclude and marginalise, and present an idealised picture of a community that may not coincide with the 'reality' as experienced by many people. Typically, such programs can omit or devalue the voices of women, the poor, children, people with disabilities, indigenous people, people from ethnic/cultural minorities, gays and lesbians and others. Even if efforts are made to include such groups, it must always be remembered that such historical 'heritage' projects are always constructions and must be understood as having been undertaken within a particular political and cultural context for particular purposes. Because of this, the way those histories are constructed is critical from a human rights perspective. Histories can perpetuate a tradition of the denial of human rights, or can be presented in such a way that human rights violations of the past are opened to scrutiny. A community's heritage is not necessarily positive and may include, for example, a heritage of racism, sexism, intolerance, violence, exploitation and the displacement of indigenous people. However, the idea of 'heritage' is that it is something to be celebrated. An uncritical acceptance and celebration of 'heritage' may do more harm than good to the ideals of human rights.

The celebration of heritage can exclude because it is based on the idea of community based on common experience rather than on community-in-difference as discussed in Chapter 1. Personal mobility is a feature of life in almost every country of the world, with unprecedented travel, immigration and people moving to seek employment or other opportunities. Economic uncertainty, political instability and climate change will only increase the numbers of refugees and every community will be faced with 'strangers' seeking acceptance. If a community constructs its identity primarily in terms of its heritage, the acceptance and inclusion of anyone who is seen as different – not 'one of us' – becomes problematic, and this is even more of a problem if that community feels threatened in some way. Political and economic uncertainty can fuel xenophobia and there will always be the temptation for some politicians to exploit this for political ends. Developing community strength around a constructed ideal 'heritage' is hardly helpful in such an environment. For this reason it is important for any consideration of a community's heritage to be undertaken critically, with a willingness to explore and embrace diversity.

Of course this is easier said than done, especially with communities that perceive themselves as under threat. Most especially indigenous communities, which have a long history of dispossession and of 'the outsider' coming to exploit and dispossess, can find it hard to be open to new arrivals and to diversity. Indigenous communities are rightly suspicious of the motives of any 'stranger', and have used their cultural heritage as a key organising point for their community identity and for their claims of human rights. To expect such a community suddenly to adopt a position of liberal tolerance when they themselves have been the victims of 'liberal tolerance' in the past is simply unrealistic.

This applies not only to indigenous communities, but also to any community that feels that it is under threat and needs to band together for its very survival. In such instances a way forward requires dialogue and a spirit of open learning from each other, as described in Chapter 5. This can only happen if there is an acceptance that mutual learning is beneficial. Too often relationships between indigenous and non-indigenous communities were based on the ideology of colonialism, which assumed that the learning would be all one way and that one of the two cultural traditions was self-evidently superior to the other. One tragedy of an ideology of colonialism is that it can be held by the colonised as well as the coloniser, so that the colonised can be persuaded that their own culture is 'inferior'. Whether this view is conveyed or not, an ideology of colonialism is incompatible with ideas of human rights, and one of the important agendas of community cultural development is to allow different cultural traditions to be articulated and recognised.

The embracing of cultural diversity, therefore, becomes a key component of community cultural development from a human rights perspective. It is necessary both for the development of strong communities and for the protection of human rights. Cultural diversity is now an inevitable fact of life in almost every part of the world. The old world of self-contained cultural groups has passed and some form of multicultural diversity is now the norm. The capacity of communities to develop and embrace such diversity is crucial, and this becomes a key component of community-based cultural development.

There are many ways in which such diversity can be encouraged and embraced. The making available of facilities that are clearly multicultural – for example, books in a library in a number of different languages, bilingual or multilingual signs and multilingual newsletters – not only can make different groups feel included and welcomed, but also makes a statement to everyone in the community and to the wider society. Multicultural festivals, where people can enjoy music, dance, art, food and crafts from different traditions are important, again both substantively and symbolically. The idea is not only to help make a community multicultural and inclusive, but also to help that community to be proud of its diversity and to see diversity as part of its self-identity.

However, such symbolic activities, though important, do not go far enough. It is also important to encourage people from different backgrounds to interact, to get to know each other and to learn from each other's experiences. This can often be achieved through the use of common facilities such as a school, library or community centre. Children at school making friends across cultural boundaries can be a first step towards the parents forming friendships. Support for a common sporting team, working together as volunteers on a community project and other such activities are all ways in which these next steps can be taken. The workplace is also important. People will often form friendships with people they meet at work, and if local employers are inclusive in their hiring policies this will also have an ongoing impact.

A different aspect of community cultural development is the enhancement of participatory culture. As discussed in Chapters 1 and 2, much of our experience of culture is as passive consumers rather than as active participants. Rather than make music ourselves we go to a concert, buy a CD or download music to an iPod; rather than take part in a play we watch TV or a DVD. Rather than play sport we watch others do it; rather than paint a picture we buy a painting. Such cultural activity is something to be done only by the talented elite (whom most of us will never be able to emulate) and to be purchased and consumed by everybody else. Cultural 'products' thus become commodified. Culture then fits easily within capitalist society and the internationalisation of this culture fits easily within globalised capitalism.

However, culture does not have to be like that. For most of human history people have made their own cultural entertainment and have not been mere passive consumers. One need only think of the popularity in Western societies, until recent decades, of amateur dramatics, music-making at home and mass participation in amateur community-based sport to realise that commodified passive consumerist culture is a relatively recent phenomenon and not part of the natural state of being human. For this reason, one of the most important aspects of community cultural development has been to encourage community-based participatory culture as a way of helping people to express themselves, to feel part of their community and to 'own' their local culture. This is a way of realising cultural rights, but there are three other ways in which participatory culture can contribute to community-based human rights.

One way in which community participatory culture contributes to human rights is as a form of human rights education. Theatre, art, music, dance and story-telling can all be used to convey a human rights message and to help people articulate their human rights in their own terms. This idea was behind the 'theatre of the oppressed' of Augusto Boal (1979), as well as the consciousness-raising literacy education of Paulo Freire (1972, 1985, 1996). Both these pioneers have been profoundly influential in consciousness-raising and in helping people to articulate their rights, and there have been many other instances of people using cultural activity as part of human rights education. In most cases it is far more effective than organising classes about the Universal Declaration of Human Rights, bills of rights or the instruments of the UN. This is especially true in cultures where there is a strong tradition of performance and especially of music and dance – sadly lacking in most English-speaking cultures, but central in Africa and Latin America, for example. To attempt human rights education in Africa or Latin America without some component of performance, dance, poetry, fiesta, theatre or music would be to invite irrelevance.

Another way in which community participatory culture contributes to human rights is through its ability to involve the marginalised or excluded. One example among many is the Choir of Hard Knocks, the initiative of a musician in Melbourne who recruited homeless people and people with mental health problems to form a choir. The choir practised, performed to much enthusiastic support and has now released a CD and appeared on television. This was a way of supplying a voice to the voiceless, but it also gave the people concerned a sense of belonging and self-worth that society had previously denied them. It asserted their human rights in a visible and audible way and undoubtedly enhanced their humanity as well as their acceptance in the wider community. There have been many similar projects involving people with disabilities, both physical and intellectual – people with mental health problems and people from low-income areas, for instance. Participatory culture can be a very powerful force in working towards improved self-esteem, confidence and human well-being, and this is surely important in human rights terms.

The third area in which participatory culture has been used to further human rights is in the area of trauma recovery. People, especially children, who have experienced trauma can often tell their stories and come to terms with what has happened to them through drama, painting, music and dance. It is an area where art therapy and music therapy have been found to be useful, as often what is too painful to be put into words can be more readily expressed in these ways. This applies not only at an individual level, but also at a community level. Trauma recovery can take place for a community, not just for an individual, and this is especially important for trauma recovery programs in cultures with a more collective tradition than the conventional Anglo-Saxon West.

The potential for community-based cultural development to contribute to human rights is almost endless. Music festivals, film festivals, poetry readings, street theatre and community arts can all have a human rights theme, either stated or implicit. Working with communities to produce their own documentary films has a long tradition in community development, and this can readily be harnessed for human rights. It is often more in the making of the documentary than in its showing that the important developmental human rights work can occur, and such documentaries can be a way in which people can come together and think about their community and its needs and about ways human rights may be articulated within it.

Music and film can also be used to help make a community aware of human rights issues beyond its own locality. One of the important things about human rights is that it has the potential to link people across nations and cultures in the understanding and construction of their shared humanity. Hence it is important for people to be able to explore human rights issues in other parts of the world, whether in Afghanistan, Sudan, Tibet, the Palestinian territories (to mention four places in the news at the time of writing) or in places with less media exposure. Film, poetry and music can be used to expose people to the suffering and human rights abuses that are experienced and also to the complexities, the different cultural contexts and the ambiguous politics in which these human rights issues are being constructed. In all the above four cases, for example, there are very different and conflicting accounts of 'what is really happening', who is suffering, at whose hands, and why.

Community radio and television can also have a major human rights impact. As an example, a small community-based human rights organisation in Cambodia has for some years been operating a radio station, in the face of considerable opposition and threats from powerful interests, for poor people and communities to help educate them about their formal rights, about what they can do if they feel they have been discriminated against or denied services and provisions that are rightfully theirs, what they have to do in order to vote and how they can contact their political representatives. This is human rights education at a grassroots level, using radio as a means of informing and educating, and it undoubtedly makes a difference to the achievement of community-level human rights.

Two of the most important foci for rights-based community cultural development in recent years have been indigenous communities and refugees and asylum seekers. Indigenous people and communities in Western countries are at last beginning to achieve the recognition that is their cultural right, and they are also at last being seen not just as 'a problem' or 'an issue' that needs to be addressed, but rather as people who have long traditions of wisdom from which more recent occupiers of the land may have much to learn. The human rights violations that have been committed against indigenous people and communities are one of the worst indictments of the Enlightenment tradition of the West and represent one of the most significant human rights concerns of contemporary society. This can only begin to be addressed if indigenous cultures are respected, if indigenous people are treated with dignity and respect, and if the full range of human rights are addressed. For this to be done there needs to be cultural recognition at a community level and the adoption of the principles of human rights-based community cultural development.

The other group – refugees and asylum seekers – represent another serious category of human rights abuse. Many countries, both Western and non-Western, are now experiencing a perceived 'refugee crisis' with the associated threat of racism and xenophobia, made worse by economic uncertainty and political instability. It is a major human rights 'challenge', and it is clearly an area where community cultural development as discussed above is critical. Refugees and asylum seekers are almost always from a different cultural group from that of the host country and the capacity of communities to be inclusive, to celebrate diversity and to welcome the stranger will be essential if this contemporary human rights issue, which can only become more serious, is to be adequately addressed and if human rights are to be genuinely respected and realised.

ENVIRONMENTAL RIGHTS AND ENVIRONMENTAL DEVELOPMENT

The environmental crisis has raised challenges for humanity that we are simply not accustomed to. It questions some assumptions that have assumed fundamental status, and it has become clear that more of the same is simply not an option if there is to be an environment in the future that is able to sustain some form of human civilisation. The strands of the environmental crisis have been identified in previous chapters and

need not be repeated here. These various crises are the inevitable consequence of the lifestyles that the affluent West has chosen to lead, and that
most of the rest of the world seeks to emulate. There is an increasing awareness that, if the planet is to remain a congenial place for human existence,
radical change is necessary.

> The world is too much with us. Late and soon
> Getting and spending we lay waste our powers.
> Little we see in nature that is ours
> We have given our hearts away, a sordid boon.
>
> Wordsworth, sonnet: 'The world is too much with us'

There is an urgent need to move away from seeing growth as the answer
to everything (as is the case with economic growth) or as inevitable (for
example in the growth of large cities or the growth of population) and to
recognise that continual growth is harmful rather than beneficial and that
the term 'sustainable growth' is an oxymoron. Similarly, there is an equally
urgent need to stop seeing the non-human world (and indeed much of the
human world as well) as 'resources' to be exploited as needed, and instead
to develop a more ecocentric view that sees humanity as linked with the
non-human world, as discussed in Chapters 4 and 5.

This sort of thinking has, by and large, been too difficult for policy-
makers, politicians and the elites who control (or try to control) the global
economy. Their solutions to the problems of climate change, for example,
simply involve finding technological and market solutions so that 'business
as usual' can be retained. Under their direction there will still be growth
and the resources of the earth will continue to be plundered for short-
term human benefit. In the long term, this will do little to resolve the
crises facing the world and to develop a truly sustainable and ecocentric
future.

If there is to be the kind of radical change that leads to such a major
rethinking, the impetus will come from the community, from grassroots
action to build a different world and to pressure national and international
leaders to follow suit. As mentioned in Chapter 2, Jared Diamond's study
of societies facing ecological collapse (2005) found that the societies that
were able to face such challenges did so either because of strong political
leadership from above, or because of strong pressure from below at a grassroots level. In the present global ecological predicament the former seems
unlikely, and so it is in the potential of the latter that the possibility of a
sustainable future lies. Community environmental development, therefore,
is of critical importance for the future.

The community is the context within which such radical rethinking can best be undertaken. Away from the world of profits, votes, budgets, stakeholders, shareholders, lobbyists and all the other reasons politicians have for inaction, at the community level people can understand their connection to the natural world, and reconstruct their relationship with it, in a real and immediate way. That world directly impacts on their daily lives. In many communities – especially indigenous communities but also in many non-indigenous rural communities – there remains wisdom about how to understand and care for the natural world that has been ignored by the researchers and policy-makers.

There is also a real understanding of some of the negative effects of pollution and the degradation of the natural world, especially if people are exposed to waste dumps, air pollution, noise pollution and the destruction of natural bushland. Making the environment a local issue is important for the environmental movement. One of the reasons why we often treat the environment so badly is that modern consumers are generally unaware of where their consumer products came from before they bought them in a shop. They don't know of the reality of mines in poor countries, the depletion of natural resources or sweatshop factory conditions. They don't know where their waste goes after their bins are collected – to create toxic landfill or ocean pollution or, in the case of plastics, to remain in the environment for centuries.

A community-based approach to the environment seeks to draw a direct connection with the environment. If possible it does this by encouraging local production and local waste disposal, but otherwise through education: understanding our purchase and consumption of a product as interconnected with a series of other events, many of which damage the earth and affect future generations.

There are many environmental programs that can be undertaken at a community level, including community solar or wind farms; local conservation groups for bushland, creeks, wetlands, coastal management and so on; local clean-up campaigns; car-pooling; lobbying for better public transport or cycle paths; group purchase of household wind or solar generation; community gardens; recycling schemes; community compost; or advocating climate-sensitive design in new public buildings (Hopkins 2008).

Different communities will have different needs and different possibilities, but whatever form the action takes the environment has to become a major focus for local community action. In response to concern about climate change and government inaction, there has been a proliferation of spontaneous climate action groups in local communities, determined to take the lead where their national leaders singularly fail to do so.

'Project Twin Streams' in Waitakere City, Auckland, Aotearoa (New Zealand) is an inspiring example of how an environmentally based community development program can move well beyond simple environmental concerns. The two streams, in an outer-suburban low-income area, had been in a state of environmental degradation. Local initiative developed a community program that not only involved people in activities such as cleaning up the streams and their environs and planting trees, but also linked it to increasing their understanding of the history of the area, its native flora and fauna and its importance for indigenous people. It also encouraged local schools, community groups and recreation clubs to take responsibility for a section of a stream.

This in turn led to community events, festivals, art, music, poetry, exploration of spiritual issues and gaining an understanding of wider environmental issues, all with the 'twin streams' as the underlying focus. It thus served other community development goals: bringing people of different ages and cultures together, encouraging local participation and giving people a sense of both pride in and ownership of their local environment. From a human rights perspective it allowed people to exercise their rights of cultural expression, free association, education and broader social rights of community membership. And all from a couple of degraded, muddy streams.

Such locally based initiatives are not confined to the developing world, and it is wrong to suppose that concern for the environment is only a first-world problem, a 'luxury' not important to people in poor countries whose first concern is survival. At a community level there is a high degree of environmental awareness in the developing world, especially in communities whose environment is directly affected by the profligate consumption of the West (Shiva 2005, Zarsky 2002). This may be from toxic waste, pollution from factories, clearing of forests, pollution of water supplies, forced relocation to make way for dams or other undesirable manifestations. There are many local environmental initiatives in developing countries that show not only a frustration with the way people's environments have been destroyed, but also an understanding of the connection with larger economic and political forces and a level of personal commitment, born of desperation, to activism.

In the history of community work, it is clear that environmental issues of one kind or another are often the easiest issues around which a community can be mobilised. This has been especially true of reactions to the destruction of neighbourhoods and communities by urban 'development' such as the building of freeways, when people have felt the need to come together to do something about the physical conditions of their neighbourhood. With environmental awareness more recently reaching much higher levels and an increasing sense of urgency about issues such as global warming, it has become easier than ever to mobilise communities around environmental issues. People feel a sense of threat, a sense of urgency and a sense of being let down by their leaders, and these are ideal conditions for community organising.

For this reason, environmental issues represent a powerful entry point for a program of community-based human rights, but this requires that the link between the environment and human rights be clearly articulated. This can be achieved in four ways, each of which can be the subject of community processes. First, there is the importance of human rights considerations in environmental issues and in the way in which governments respond to them. There is now a literature on climate change and social justice, which seeks to ensure that programs and policies designed to address climate change do not adversely impact on the disadvantaged but are used to promote social justice rather than to exacerbate injustice (Adger et al. 2006, Northcott 2007).

Climate change will have particularly adverse effects on many poor and disadvantaged communities, and there is a fear that policies addressing climate change will similarly favour the most advantaged. For example, many of the proposed policies to address climate change are designed primarily to preserve affluent lifestyles in the developed world as much as possible, rather than to address the needs of the most vulnerable populations. Those who claim that the environmental crisis represents an 'investment opportunity' are similarly seeking to justify climate change programs as benefiting the entrepreneur and the shareholders, rather than the community.

It has become important to subject environmental policies to careful screening to ensure that they promote, or at least respect, human rights rather than denying human rights to the disadvantaged. At a more extreme level, there is a danger of eco-fascism, which uses the environmental crisis as a justification for draconian legislation that effectively denies or violates human rights, for example by forced migration, invasion of privacy to make sure people don't use too much water, forced relocation to 'sustainable' housing and the like. Shearman & Smith (2007) have argued, ominously, that 'democracy', as it has been understood and practised, has proved to be incapable of dealing effectively with the challenge of climate change and that either an authoritarian regime or a radically changed democratic program will be required. The threat of terrorism produced, in the Western world, a raft of 'anti-terrorist' measures that significantly eroded human rights, and there is a danger that the ecological crisis may similarly provide a justification for the denial or erosion of some civil and political rights.

The second way in which a link can be made between human rights and the environment is by an understanding of environmental rights as human rights (Zarsky 2002). This suggests that a clean and safe environment is a human right, and therefore work towards a better environment at a community level is itself a form of human rights work, as it seeks to realise environmental rights.

To argue this requires a move from the environment as something we enjoy – an amenity – to something we require to realise our humanity – a human right – and means that local environmental activism is seen as working towards important human rights. For this to occur, the environment can be treated in the same way as other rights. The community can be asked to articulate what environmental rights mean in their context, and what needs to be done so that they can be protected and realised. This of course will be different in each community context, since local environments will differ, and what is required to meet environmental rights will need to be determined in a local context.

The third way a connection can be made between the environment and human rights is to see the environment as essential to the realisation of other human rights. There is an obvious link that can be made to the right to health, as the environment can be responsible for many diseases and disabilities. Similarly links can be made to the right to safety and security, the right to cultural expression and spiritual rights (that is, the importance of the natural world for many people's spiritual experience).

Lastly, and most profoundly, a link can be made between human rights and the environment by articulating the need for a new relationship with the natural world, defining our humanity in terms of its connection to nature rather than as separate from nature (Macy 2007). This represents perhaps the greatest challenge for community environmental development from a human rights perspective and may be a step for which some communities are not ready. However, it is still possible to ask questions that help people to reformulate their understanding of the relationship between humans and the rest of the world, and to understand our rights as part of a broader understanding of the rights of the whole world, including animals, plants, and Gaia itself. It was argued in Chapters 2 and 5 that such a rethinking is necessary if we are to move towards ecological sanity, and it is through community environmental development that this can be initiated.

By making these important links, community development around environmental issues can become central to the idea of community-based human rights. Environmental development programs are important in ensuring that environmental rights are realised locally, in the community context where people live their daily lives. However, this is not to deny the importance of the 'big' environmental issues, as these too have their local consequences. Part of the reality of the globalised world, where the global is the local and the local is the global (see Chapter 5), is that the big issues also affect local communities. Part of community-based environmental development is public education around environmental issues that affect not just the local community but also communities on the other side of the world, and indeed the potential future of human civilisations.

In the longer term, one of the most important aspects of community-based environmental development is the importance of learning from indigenous wisdom in relation to the needs of the earth and the relationship of humans to the rest of the biosphere (Knudtson & Suzuki 1992). As has already been noted, a fundamental reformulation of our understanding of 'the human' is necessary, and from this will inevitably flow a profound reconstruction of the very idea of 'human' rights.

Indigenous people and communities, in terms of human rights, have for a long time been cast as victims, the objects of human rights violations and human rights denial across the full range of human rights. Indigenous people themselves have suffered by being omitted from the category of 'human' in the age of colonialism. The struggle has been to articulate the rights of indigenous people and to have them realised and protected. There is now a growing awareness that, far from being 'part of the problem' and being cast in the role of 'victim', indigenous people represent an important part of the solution in that they possess wisdom about the land and about how to care for it, over a very long period of time, which has been lost to Enlightenment 'civilisation', and which is essential if there is to be a way forward from the present crisis towards a truly ecologically sustainable future.

SPIRITUAL RIGHTS AND SPIRITUAL DEVELOPMENT

Discussing spirituality in relation to either human rights or community development presents special difficulties. The Enlightenment tradition, which has so affected ideas of both community and human rights, does not deal well with spirituality. Indeed, the Enlightenment arose in part as a reaction to the European religious wars of the sixteenth and seventeenth centuries, and sought to remove religion and superstition from our understanding of the world and from our moral reasoning. Accordingly, spirituality does not occupy a central place in Enlightenment thinking. It is accepted as essentially a personal matter, not open to 'rational' inquiry and not of great importance.

Of course there have always been people, including theologians, within the Enlightenment tradition who have been profoundly religious, who have maintained a strong spiritual side to their being, or who have sought to apply rational analysis to matters of religion and the spirit, but the overall narrative of the Enlightenment has relegated spirituality to a marginal position. Hence it tends to be omitted from the discussion of subjects such as human rights and community.

Yet spirituality has for centuries been a central part of the experience of humanity, and it remains so for the vast majority of the global population today. To discuss human rights – what it means to be human – without including the spiritual is to deny the reality (however constructed) of most of the world. The same applies to community; ideas of community are, for many people, so intensely connected to the spiritual that to discuss community without spirituality would be meaningless.

However, the traditions of Western Enlightenment thought remain sufficiently strong that treating spirituality as a part of human rights and community still presents major difficulties. The very idea of writing in traditional academic prose about spirituality is to miss the whole point. To explore spirituality we need other media than this: media such as poetry, music, theatre, film, story-telling and experiencing nature, because spirituality extends beyond the normal understanding of 'rational', 'analytical' or 'logical' to those important areas of the human experience not readily acknowledged by Enlightenment rationality or reached by rigorous scientific inquiry.

For these reasons, the spiritual dimension of human rights and of community can be a challenge for hard-headed activists and community workers. The legal construction of human rights does not help in this regard. The law, as understood in Western societies, is perhaps the ultimate manifestation of Enlightenment rationality, while other traditions of law – such as 'tribal law', 'Islamic law' or 'the law of Moses' – tend to be devalued or seen as not really counting when it comes to defining and protecting human rights. There is little room for the spiritual in the Western secular legal tradition, on which much of our conventional understanding of human rights rests. The other dimensions of human rights as discussed in this section can fit comfortably enough within the Enlightenment world view, but spiritual rights is an area of discomfort; it requires the involvement of poets and writers, clergy and theologians, singers and actors, and it certainly cannot be encapsulated neatly in legislation or bills of rights.

Human rights workers and community workers are not alone in this. Human service professionals such as health professionals, social workers and psychologists have also begun to include the spiritual within their professional discourses. This has not been easy, and in Western contexts such a move is still in its early stages, but it has also proved to be very rewarding (Gale, Bolzan & McRae-McMahon 2007). The same applies to human rights, and this has been given impetus by the interest in inter-faith dialogue, which will be discussed further below.

Another obstacle to the incorporation of the spiritual into human rights and community development work has been the poor reputation of much that passes for 'spiritual'. Some of the more bizarre manifestations of New Age philosophy have not helped the cause, as they have been so readily held up to ridicule and have been used by those peddling useless or fraudulent answers to a whole range of problems. This is not to condemn the entire New Age movement, which has undoubtedly proved to be important for a number of people, but rather to question some of the more extreme and dubious forms it has taken.

Another trend that has given the spiritual dimension a poor reputation has been the practices of fundamentalist forms of the major religions, which have acted to exclude, marginalise and condemn those who are not 'true believers' (Armstrong 2000, Howland 1999, Sim 2004). Fundamentalism of any sort – religious or otherwise – is the negation of the approach to human rights and community outlined in this book. The certainty of the fundamentalist and the imperative for fundamentalists to convert others to 'the one truth' is the antithesis of the dialogical approach discussed in Chapter 5, and it has certainly helped to make many people wary of anything that is related to religion or spirituality.

However, spirituality does not have to be like this, and fundamentalism only represents a small group among those who value the spiritual. Spirituality, and some forms of institutional religion, can pose questions rather than impose answers, can accept uncertainty and ambiguity as opening up possibilities, can relish the prospect of dialogue and can welcome diversity. This has much to contribute to our understanding of human rights, of community, and of community-based human rights practice.

Many manifestations of spirituality, both from within and from outside traditional religious institutions, have explored and represented some of the most important ideas about humanity, community and our rights and responsibilities towards each other. It is easy to identify human rights traditions, though they may not be labelled as such, in all major religions (Hayden 2001). Many religious traditions have some form of the 'golden rule' ('do unto others as you would have them do unto you', in the translated words of the Bible) as an important basis for personal morality. This is closely related to the Kantian categorical imperative as discussed in Chapter 4, which is central to traditional understandings of human rights. Commonly there are traditions of respect for others, welcoming of the stranger and similar 'human rights' ideas expressed in the Bible, the Qur'an, the law of Moses, the teachings of the Buddha and other religious texts.

These ideas have far longer histories than the European Enlightenment. The exploration of these more religious origins of human rights concepts is important in helping to embed a culture of human rights at a community level, where not everyone will be by nature or desire a child of the Enlightenment.

For many people, the experience of community can itself be a spiritual experience. Institutional religions have long recognised this in traditions of celebrating the spiritual collectively in the religious service in a mosque, church, temple or synagogue. We can find our spirituality in communion with others, not just in individual personal experience, and for many people the communal experience of spirituality is the stronger. The Quaker meeting is an example: people simply coming together, even in silence, is a powerful experience in which the spiritual and the communal become one. Religious communities such as monasteries have often been represented as the ultimate form both of the spiritual and the communal.

However, this collective experience of the spiritual can also go beyond formal institutional religions. Making music together or dancing together, especially when these are more than refined artistic expression but become strongly emotional and passionate, can be profoundly spiritual experiences. This suggests that aspects of community cultural development, as discussed above, can also contribute to community spiritual development and can help to articulate and realise people's spiritual rights.

This is an important example of the link between spiritual development and cultural development. It is through cultural expression that we can have profound spiritual experiences, but it would be too limiting to say that the spiritual is simply a manifestation of the cultural. Spirituality can extend beyond the cultural, and in the current context a particularly important example is the connection with environmental development. Many people will link their spirituality with the natural world; this is particularly true of indigenous spiritual traditions, which emphasise the connection of humans with the rest of the natural world, but also of people who experience the spiritual in climbing a mountain, walking in the bush, looking at the ocean, surfing, sitting quietly beside a river, walking on a beach, contemplating a flower, being with animals, and enjoying other experiences of nature. In this sense, community environmental development can further the realisation of people's spiritual rights.

Because of the great variety of spiritual experiences, whether within or outside institutional religion, it is difficult if not impossible to be prescriptive about what is, or should be, involved in community spiritual development. It is an important aspect of community-based human rights, but it needs to start with the spiritual traditions within the community concerned (in modern urban society there will usually be several) and accept the diversity of spiritual experience. On this basis, community spiritual development then involves creating and allowing the space for people to experience their spirituality in their own way and validating the experience of the spiritual.

However, there is an additional layer required from a human rights perspective. As with all rights, spiritual rights must be circumscribed to ensure that their exercise does not impede rights held by others in the community. This means that spiritual rights must be understood in ways that respect the freedom and dignity of others, especially those with different spiritual traditions. Fundamentalist forms of spirituality that claim to know 'the truth' and also claim a duty to impose that truth on others, or to impose a form of religious law or moral code that restricts the rights and freedoms of others, cannot be allowed to flourish unchallenged in the name of spiritual rights.

Spiritual rights do not imply an 'anything goes' approach to religion, any more than civil and political rights imply total freedom of expression to say whatever one wishes regardless of the consequences for others. Like other rights, spiritual rights and their necessary limits need to be negotiated, discussed and ideally be the subject of genuine dialogue within the context of a community committed to human rights. This is often easier said than done, as fundamentalists cannot engage in dialogue. When you are convinced that you are right, you will not be prepared to listen to and learn from anyone else with a different view.

In general, however, people are open to dialogue in relation to the spiritual and many are genuinely interested in understanding other people's experience of spirituality if they can feel free from the fear that the other will try to convert them. Inter-faith dialogue has been a particularly fruitful area for human rights and this dialogue can take place at the community level.

Despite the difficulty of dialogue between religious faiths and secular humanism in relation to human rights, as discussed in Chapter 4, inter-faith dialogue shows up a number of commonalities across religious traditions in this respect, and this dialogue can be a powerful force for establishing a culture of human rights within a community, especially one in which different religious faiths are represented. It can ground community-based human rights in religious traditions with which community members are familiar, rather than in Western secular humanism which, while it is a familiar and comfortable world view for many people, is alienating and incomprehensible to others.

The spiritual, then, is an important component of human rights from below, even though it has been traditionally an area that has not been associated with human rights beyond a rather simplistic understanding of the right to freedom of religious expression. Seeing the spiritual as an important component of humanity, and of how we experience that humanity, requires that the spiritual be taken more seriously in understanding human rights, especially as many people experience spirituality collectively in some form of community. Articulating a spiritual basis to human rights, and to community, is not easy for a community worker from a Western secular tradition, but it is a challenge that is necessary if human rights from below is to address the full range of human rights and the human experience.

SURVIVAL RIGHTS

The final category to be considered in this chapter is that of survival rights. These are our rights for the things we need to survive: water, food, shelter and health care. They are the rights about which there is the least likelihood of disagreement and the rights that have the strongest claim to universality, as they clearly apply to all humans. They can also be important in the development of community-based human rights.

Food has always been important not only for survival but also as cultural practice. Cultures are partly defined by their cuisines and tasting different foods is one of the easiest and least threatening ways to experience 'multiculturalism'. The sharing of a meal is one of the most important communal activities in almost any culture, and often has associated with it important rituals or ceremonies. Successes, achievements or triumphs are commonly celebrated with a feast. The importance of food, food security, the sharing of food and so on suggests that it can be an important focus for community, and as it also represents a fundamental human right it can be an important focus also for community-based human rights.

Food security can be an issue even in developed nations (Riches 1997), and some important community development has taken place in conjunction with food banks and other forms of food relief. The Regina Food Bank in Saskatchewan, Canada, was a pioneer in showing how the right to food could be used as a basis for community development that involved people in cooking classes, understanding more about food and different culinary traditions, engaging as volunteers and making the food bank a thriving community centre rather than a place for a stigmatising handout. Thus the way in which a human right (to food) was met became the focus of community development and the enhancement of self-esteem.

While food security can be an issue in developed nations, in many poorer parts of the world it is a major human rights crisis. Many people regularly go hungry, and deaths from starvation or from diseases that could be readily prevented with adequate diet are a global scandal. The scandal is multiplied when one considers the gross overconsumption and waste of food in the wealthy West. While world hunger is an obvious focus for human rights-based community development in poor nations, it can also be a focus for communities in the West. NGOs such as Oxfam can readily provide educational material and also the capacity for communities in developed countries to raise funds for the relief of famine and starvation in other countries, as well as raising awareness and lobbying governments for more generous and appropriate aid programs.

On a more positive note, food can also become the basis for community development through, for example, cooperative buying, community gardens, community composting, permaculture and the like. The typical Western food cycle of supermarket–private consumption–waste disposal is not the only way and community development projects can focus on growing, purchasing, sharing and recycling. This can result in lower personal expenditure on food, healthier eating, bringing people together and reducing the environmental impact, while questioning conventional and wasteful ways that have more to do with reinforcing private consumption and supporting global food corporations than with community enrichment or sustainability.

Water can provide a similar focus for community activity. Securing a community's water supply, working out how limited supplies can be effectively shared, improving water quality and so on can often be achieved through community initiative and cooperation, rather than relying on a central authority. Although it does not as readily incorporate diversity (fresh water looks and tastes much the same everywhere, unlike food), it has the same significance. Conflicts over water supply seem likely to be a major issue in the twenty-first century, with increasing populations and decreasing water supplies. Community action in relation to water supply and treatment and engagement with issues such as desalination plants, recycled water, privatisation of water supply and bottled water has become a major arena for community action (Barlow 2007). Local community development from a human rights basis will need to address issues of water supply, quality and access, and this is a classic case for community-based human rights.

Shelter also has profound significance in many communities. The physical form of housing can either enhance or impede community interaction. There are issues of housing availability, addressing homelessness or housing inadequacy. There are issues of housing affordability, especially where state provision is inadequate and there is a reliance on the private market.

Further, there is the issue of housing design and its appropriateness in a particular cultural or climate context. For example, in Australian Aboriginal communities it is common for a number of relatives from another town to visit a family and the cultural expectation is that they will be housed by that family during their visit. The standard issue three-bedroom state-provided house, while fine for a nuclear family, is totally inappropriate for this purpose, and this has led to tension both between families and with state housing authorities who are agitated at the sight of twenty or so people sharing accommodation designed for four or five. Housing issues are often a source of tension and conflict in a community, and so a community adequately addressing what a right to housing means in the local context is an important project for community development.

Even in many parts of the so-called 'developed' world, housing rights have not been adequately met and there are people who are homeless. This has become a major human rights issue for many community workers. In poorer countries, there are many people without adequate housing, and housing is one of the most significant human rights issues needing to be addressed if people are to realise their humanity. In some countries, such as the Palestinian Territories, house demolition has been used as a form of intimidation and this represents a major human rights violation. The human rights issues raised by housing and the need for shelter are very real for many people, and it is an area where the world's human rights record is bleak indeed. In many communities this will be a major focus for community-based human rights work.

Housing can also be important in some communities where people wish to live together in a communal or semi-communal situation. This is not uncommon in indigenous communities, for example in North America, the Pacific and Aotearoa/New Zealand. It is also seen in residential retreats and in religious communities, where living together is an important expression of community. In this way, housing can itself become an expression of community.

Health care represents another basic right that is often denied in poor countries and also in the developed West. Perhaps the most extreme example of the latter is the USA where, in the world's richest country, many people cannot obtain access to adequate basic health care. The same phenomenon can be found, though in a less extreme form, in a number of other Western countries, especially where health care is partially privatised. However, the standard of health care in many poor countries represents a major global scandal. One need only consider that every few seconds, somewhere in the world, a child dies from a readily treatable disease to realise the enormity of the human rights abuse that is health care in the contemporary world.

As with other examples above, a community-based approach to human rights can articulate what kinds of health services would best meet the rights of people in a local community, rather than simply accepting a one-size-fits-all approach to health care provided by a central government. This can often mean a concentration on culturally appropriate health care for particular groups, such as indigenous people or recent immigrants, who are often not well served by mainstream services. The form that this can take will vary from one community to another, and this emphasises the need for a community development perspective in health as in other areas. Also, as was discussed in relation to food, rights-based community work can seek to raise awareness of health issues at a global level and determine a possible community response, possibly with the assistance of an NGO such as Médecins sans Frontières.

Finally, in the category of survival rights, we can consider the issue of natural disasters. Both planning for natural disasters and the community response after a disaster has occurred are human rights issues, and it is important for communities to ensure that survival rights are, as far as possible, protected. Some natural disasters can be anticipated, such as hurricanes or cyclones in the coastal tropics, earthquakes in areas near major fault lines, fires in bush areas prone to drought and floods in river plains where there can be heavy rainfall.

While such disasters cannot be predicted with accuracy in terms of their severity or when they will occur, they will inevitably come sooner or later and a community with an awareness of survival rights will seek to anticipate this and take appropriate action. Such action might be building cyclone-proof or flood-proof shelters (as has been done with some success in Bangladesh, where flooding is common), local building regulations in fire- or earthquake-prone areas, community education about what to do in the event of a natural disaster, the organisation of a local emergency service or keeping an inventory of skilled volunteers to be asked for help as needed. These can all be the focus of local community activity and are important for community-based survival rights.

When a community is hit by a natural disaster, whether anticipated or not, one of the important aspects of recovery is the ability of people in that community to help each other and to work together. It is commonly said that disasters bring out the best in communities, and many stories emerge of local people helping each other, often in circumstances of extreme adversity; for example, rescuing people from burning buildings or swollen rivers, sharing their houses with neighbours whose house has been destroyed, generously donating to relief appeals and so on.

This sort of community-based recovery is more likely to happen when there is already existing strength in the community, and so good community development before the event can pay dividends after the disaster. As an example, the Country Fire Authority, the body that coordinates volunteer fire-fighters in Victoria (Australia) in the event of a bushfire, has put some effort into encouraging and funding community development projects in fire-prone communities on the assumption that a stronger community will be better able to cope with both the event and the aftermath of a major fire. Understood from the point of view of survival rights and human rights from below, this is clearly human rights work, though it may not be so labelled by those involved.

CONCLUSION

This chapter has brought together, under the seven common dimensions of community development and human rights derived in previous chapters, some ideas for the practice of human rights from below. They are not prescriptions, but simply ideas that will always need to be contextualised in any particular situation. The important thing about these ideas is that they show how community development and human rights can be brought together, each informing the other and applied in communities. Further issues in relation to practice, where the idea of *practice* is discussed more specifically, will be considered in the final chapter.

7 | Practising human rights from below

IN THIS SECTION WE will examine the *practice* of human rights from below. It is important not only to understand human rights from below and the ideas that have been explored in previous sections, but also to think about what it means to enact this perspective of human rights. Here we will not only be concerned with what the 'human rights practitioner' might do – the advocate, the community development worker, the NGO worker – but also what human rights from below means for community members, engaged citizens, volunteers and others. One of the important aspects of a community development approach is that it is not confined exclusively to a community development worker but rather engages the entire community. Applying the same perspective to human rights from below implies that we are all concerned with working for human rights, whether paid or unpaid, activist, volunteer, citizen or engaged professional.

WAYS OF PRACTISING HUMAN RIGHTS FROM BELOW

Of the two fields discussed in this book – community development and human rights – community development has put more effort into considering the problematic of practice. In human rights, practice is often regarded as unproblematic – difficult, challenging and potentially dangerous, of course, but clear and straightforward in its nature. It is couched largely in terms of legal practice: advocacy, bringing cases to anti-discrimination tribunals or to courts, appealing to the United Nations. The actual skills involved in doing this are largely technical: knowing the relevant legislation, preparing documents, arguing a case and so on.

Human rights practice is seen as essentially this mix of technical skills grounded in a strong moral/value position in favour of human rights. Community development, however, sees 'practice' as more problematic and also more holistic, and this is an important component of human rights from below.

Traditional 'human rights work' has largely been understood from the perspective of advocacy. This is largely because of the legal tradition of human rights, as has been discussed in earlier chapters. Advocacy is what lawyers do best, and so understanding human rights from a legal framework is to privilege advocacy over other forms of human rights practice. However, practising human rights is much broader than advocacy. Advocacy is important and has played a vital role in the promotion and protection of human rights, but to understand human rights work only as advocacy is unnecessarily limiting. By using some of the ideas of community development practice, which is much broader and more holistic, we can significantly extend the practice of human rights from below.

It is worth mentioning, at this point in the discussion, some of the problems with an advocacy approach to practice. Advocacy involves advocating on behalf of another, a form of practice that is at the heart of the legal profession. But to speak on behalf of another can be disempowering. Concentrating on advocacy does not encourage people to speak up on behalf of themselves, but rather to assume that they are unable to do so.

This is the 'disabling' nature of professions, as discussed in the 1970s by Illich (Illich et al. 1977); professions define life as too complex and difficult for a person to negotiate it by themselves and they establish 'helping' professions to assist people, thereby disenfranchising and disempowering them. The technical, professional expert becomes essential if we are to live life the way it 'ought' to be lived, and the effect of this is to empower the professionals and disempower ordinary citizens. Advocacy can be understood in this way. A practice that speaks up on behalf of people, rather than helping them to speak up on their own behalf, is disabling (to use Illich's term) rather than empowering and, from the point of view of this book, is hardly compatible with human rights, especially the right to self-expression.

This does not mean that advocacy should never be used – clearly there are instances where, for various reasons, people are unable to speak out for themselves – but it is important to be able to justify such advocacy and, where possible, undertake other forms of practice as well that are aimed at helping people to advocate for themselves rather than rely on somebody else to do it for them.

HUMAN RIGHTS EDUCATION

It is interesting that human rights *education* is often thought of as separate from human rights practice. The latter is seen as being about gaining people their rights while the former is about teaching people about their rights. From a conventional human rights perspective this is fully understandable. The skills required of the two are very different, and if law is the natural profession for human rights practice, teaching is the natural profession for human rights education.

Reflecting the relative status of the two professions, human rights education has often been seen as the poor relation of human rights practice; something that is important but somehow secondary to the 'real' work of human rights activism. From the perspective of human rights from below, however, human rights education is at least as important as advocacy and arguably more so. Human rights from below require an active and engaged citizenry who understand some ideas of human rights and are able to articulate them in their local context; hence human rights education is paramount.

However, the conventional view of human rights education – teaching people about their rights – falls well short of what is required for human rights from below. Human rights education can readily reflect a top-down approach that does not incorporate the idea of citizens actively engaged in the definition of human rights. Such an approach might, for example, educate school students about the content of the Universal Declaration of Human Rights and the workings of the UN and other human rights bodies without any consideration of context or of possible critique of the Universal Declaration as simply one attempt (though an important one) to define human rights.

Such an approach to human rights education, loosely categorised as 'human rights are important, and this is what they are' is all too common, yet sends precisely the wrong messages about human rights if we are to adopt a perspective of human rights from below. It suggests that our human rights have already been defined for us by some authority that understands our rights better than we do ourselves, and that we should accept this definition uncritically. This approach to human rights education is usually couched in terms of a naive universalism; the universality of human rights is accepted as an article of faith, and to question this universalism is tantamount to questioning the value of human rights themselves.

Such an approach to human rights education is the equivalent of what Freire (1996) describes as the 'banking' concept of education, where what is taught is somehow transferred from the head of the teacher to the head of the pupil without transformation or critique. It implies that the educator knows what 'human rights' means and that the educator's task is to 'teach' this to the pupil/student. To treat human rights in this way is the antithesis of human rights from below.

Human rights education, therefore, requires a more active and critical role on the part of the learner, who is seen not as an empty vessel but rather as someone with experience, wisdom and knowledge. Human rights becomes an *arena* for education rather than a curriculum statement or specification of 'learning outcomes'. In this regard, the teacher and the learner enter more of an active dialogical relationship, as discussed in Chapter 5. The learning is two-way rather than one-way, each seeking to learn from the other's wisdom and to move forward together. Consciousness-raising, using the idea of human rights as a framework for exploration, becomes thus a critical component of human rights education from below.

This must be contextualised – rights need to be understood in the context of people's lived experience, especially their personal experience of human rights abuse or violation. This may include denial of the right to health care or education, denial of the right to freedom of expression, denial of the right to freedom of assembly or association, denial of the right to feel personally secure, denial of adequate income security or denial of the right to cultural expression.

But these are understood not in the context of a remote 'universal declaration' or bill of rights, but rather within people's day-to-day experience. This begins with people's personal stories, their hopes, disappointments, pain and experience of various forms of oppression, and then seeks to use 'rights language' to articulate their experience of the denial of their humanity in a way that asserts their rights, defined in their own way, and their claims on others (including the state) to help protect and realise those rights. It also means reflection on responsibilities, the perceived rights of others, and the way we are all linked in a network of mutual rights and duties.

This can still be done with reference to the Universal Declaration, bills of rights and other such documents, but only in the sense that they represent specific attempts to articulate humanity in particular contexts and at particular times. They are not given the status of holy writ, but can be examined to see to what extent they reflect the aspirations of the community, what they may have left out, what might be expressed differently, and what parts of them may have little relevance. This approach validates different aspirations for human rights and sees declarations, conventions and bills of rights as particular cases that have extra significance because of their legal status, but which do not represent the 'last word' in human rights.

This approach needs to be taken not merely in an individual sense, but preferably at a collective level ('our rights' rather than 'my rights'). Although rights can be understood individually, if we see rights and responsibilities as linked in human community then ultimately our understanding of rights is collective. As was argued in Chapter 5, human rights cannot be divorced from human community and so human rights education must be undertaken from within a community development framework, rather than seeing people as atomised individuals acting and experiencing their humanity alone.

Such consciousness-raising education cannot be undertaken in a value-free environment. Human rights are contentious and political – that is why they are so important – and human rights education that attempts to depoliticise human rights is both futile and ultimately irrelevant. This is important for the institutional and organisational auspicing of human rights education. Where an auspicing body is required to represent some form of 'political neutrality' or 'objectivity' or to be 'apolitical', it becomes difficult for it to engage in effective human rights education. Human rights education will inevitably be controversial and will threaten certain interests, often very powerful ones.

For this reason human rights education is often better undertaken by NGOs or community groups than by state education structures that are required 'not to be political'. Human rights *are* political; human rights education *is* political activity (though it may not necessarily be identified with the platform of any political party) and it will by its very nature be contentious. Human rights educators need to acknowledge that, and must beware of pretending that they are engaged in uncontroversial, objective and value-neutral education.

One of the most effective forms of human rights education is through modelling human rights. The old adage 'do as I say, not as I do' is bad education practice in any context, but quite disastrous when we are dealing with human rights. People whose schooldays are long behind them will often have only a vague memory of what they were taught, but will have a very clear recollection of how they were treated. It is how people are treated that makes a lasting impression: whether they were treated with kindness or cruelty, whether they felt listened to or not, whether their ideas were valued or ridiculed, whether they were discriminated against or accepted on their own terms and whether they were encouraged to think creatively or to conform.

Modelling human rights can make far more of an impression than simply teaching human rights content, and a school may teach human rights much more effectively if it forgets all ideas of including human rights in the curriculum but instead concentrates on dealing effectively and constructively with bullying, being inclusive, challenging discrimination, introducing democratic decision-making, valuing the ideas of all students and treating everyone with respect and dignity.

This, of course, can be extended beyond the school to include education at the community level, incorporating people of all ages. Any organisation claiming to embrace or promote human rights is surely obligated to practise what it preaches and to observe practices that are inclusive and treat people with respect and dignity. Unfortunately some NGOs, government bodies and corporations that claim to work for human rights do not model this very effectively in the way they treat staff, volunteers and community members. This comes from a separation of the goal of the organisation from its context, and a separation of the ends of the organisation and the means to achieve them. As was discussed in Chapter 2, means and ends cannot be so readily separated, and this is especially significant in seeking to implement human rights from below.

THEORY AND PRACTICE

The relationship between theory and practice is problematic and complex unless one accepts a naive and simplistic construction of each. Although this section does not deal with this issue in the depth it deserves, it will seek to identify some of the issues around the theory/practice dualism and to discuss approaches to theory and practice that may make sense for human rights from below.

'How to relate theory to practice' is a commonly discussed question in many areas of human services. This itself indicates something of the nature of the problem. The two, 'theory' and 'practice', are seen as separate and as potentially incompatible; hence the concern about how to 'relate' them. It is only a short step from this separation to seeing the two as binary opposites and we are back in the trap of modernity as discussed in earlier chapters. When theory and practice are seen in this way you can have one or the other; you can 'do' one or the other, but not both at once. Each in some way excludes the other and you are either a theoretician or a practitioner.

This is a very limiting view of 'theory and practice', and indeed the very use of the word 'and' in the phrase reinforces this separation. The relationship is clearly problematic and it needs to be thought through further. Unfortunately, this has not been evident in the human rights literature. The human rights field has been neatly and simplistically divided into two groups: the theorists, who write learned articles in journals about the finer points of philosophy or jurisprudence, and the activists, who seek to prevent human rights abuse.

Each group has something of a mistrust of the other. The theorists can see the activists as anti-intellectual, not appreciating the finer points of what they are doing, and as zealots who can sometimes make things worse rather than better because of their evangelical fervour about human rights. The activists, on the other hand, can see human rights theorists as indulging in the luxury of human rights scholasticism while there are urgent and serious human rights violations that require strong and immediate intervention. The usual way of thinking about this split between scholars and activists is exemplified by the following 1999 extract from the introduction to a human rights book by Hesse and Post:

> In the past, academics in traditional disciplines have unfortunately stood apart from the human rights community, separated by the line dividing advocacy from scholarship . . . we will have to efface these old distinctions and to strive for a fundamental rapprochement between academic disciplines and the human rights community. We will have to yoke the disinterested scholarship of the former to the moral and practical urgency of the latter. This will not be easy, but there is no alternative if we are to devise innovative and effective strategies to intervene in the new world order we now confront.
>
> Hesse & Post, 1999, p. 23

This need remains ten years on, but the quote is included here not just because of the important point it makes, but also because the very wording used by Hesse and Post, and the assumptions they make in posing the problem, are suggestive both of the nature of the problem and the difficulty of its solution.

First, there is an assumption of a 'line dividing advocacy from scholarship' which assumes that scholarship cannot be partisan; indeed, scholarship is defined as 'disinterested'. This is a narrow view of scholarship, based on some notion of quasi-scientific objectivity. It ignores the fact that much of the most important scholarship, especially in the field of human rights, has been strongly and unapologetically partisan. From Locke to Mill, Rousseau to Marx, Wollstonecraft to Arendt, Plato to Derrida, scholars have not only thought carefully about human rights and what they mean but have also advocated, often quite forcefully, what they see as a better form of society where rights can be respected.

These are hardly detached thinkers who disdain the 'real world'. They all sought to make a difference to that world, not only through their ideas but in many cases also through direct activism. Indeed, the idea of the detached scholar is at odds with the history of ideas and of political philosophy (Watson 2005) and it is probably fair to say that most of the significant contributions to 'human rights theory' have come from writers to whom such an ivory-tower existence was quite unacceptable. Human rights scholarship need not be the province of the detached philosopher; it can also be driven by the same sense of moral urgency that drives the activist. All scholarship, especially in a field like human rights, is value-based. From this perspective, to contrast 'disinterested scholarship' with 'moral and political urgency' makes no sense. The two need not be incompatible as implied by Hesse and Post.

The second point to note about the Hesse and Post quote is that it has loosely equated the 'human rights community' (that is, the activists/practitioners) with advocacy. The limitations of this view of human rights have already been discussed and so need not be reiterated, but it is worth noting that in this regard Hesse and Post, reflecting the dominant discourse of human rights, have limited their understanding of 'the human rights community' and the idea of human rights practice just as they have limited their understanding of 'human rights scholarship'.

Finally, Hesse and Post suggest that the way forward is to '. . . yoke the disinterested scholarship of the former [academic disciplines] to the moral and practical urgency of the latter [human rights community]'. To 'yoke' them together suggests that it is hardly a natural or easy union. They are seen as inherently in opposition and needing to be tied together, by force if necessary, so that they will be forced to go in the same direction. Such a linking is inevitably unstable and does not provide a sound basis for theory/practice that may overcome the divide in any sustainable way.

Hesse and Post have identified an important problem and one can only agree with them about the need for it to be resolved. However, in stating it they have reflected a number of the assumptions of the conventional human rights discourse, which demonstrate the inadequacy of the way the theory/practice issue has been conceptualised in human rights, and which are not held by Hesse and Post alone but are shared with many other writers about human rights. Both 'theory' and 'practice' have been inadequately and simplistically conceptualised, as has the relationship between them and what needs to be done to bridge the perceived gap.

Human rights from below suggests, and at the same time requires, a more sophisticated understanding of theory and practice. At the heart of this different approach is the assertion that theory and practice cannot be understood separately but are part of each other; in fact neither makes sense without the other. If practice is totally divorced from theory it leads to an unthinking anti-intellectualism. Frames of reference and critical reflection are gone and one simply does, for the sake of doing. The practitioner does not ask 'what' or 'why', but only 'how'.

Such practice, of course, is potentially dangerous. It can be counter-productive and will inevitably have unanticipated consequences, because without theory there can be no anticipation. The person who thinks that 'the right thing to do' and 'the right way to do it' are self-evident, and who has no time for reflection, critique and analysis, is likely to be ineffective at best and harmful at worst. Clearly practice requires something that might be called 'theory' – some set of principles, ideas, a frame of reference, the wisdom of experience – that can give shape to, and make sense of, the situation in which the practitioner finds her/himself.

Often such 'theory' will seem to be nothing more than 'common sense', and common sense as a basis for practice requires careful consideration. On the one hand, common sense is a reflection of the 'sense' of the common experience and can represent significant wisdom. If the idea of human rights from below is to incorporate the community development principles of wisdom and knowledge 'from below' (see Chapter 2), then there is a significant place for such 'common sense' in human rights practice. To assume that the only knowledge that 'counts' is the knowledge of the expert who can use big words to describe complex ideas is to marginalise the wisdom of the community and to privilege the expert in a way that human rights from below does not allow. Common sense, then, can be important.

However, it can also be limiting. The phrase 'it's just common sense' is often used merely to take the easy way forward and not to ask, or even consider, any difficult questions or alternative points of view. From the discussion in the previous chapters, it should have become clear that both human rights and community development are anything but simple, uncontroversial, straightforward ideas. The 'common sense approach' denies this complexity. Ideas that count as 'common sense' are invariably constructed from within dominant discourses of power and do not question those very discourses. Yet it is precisely the questioning of those discourses that is so important, and that a rethinking of human rights and community requires.

Common sense alone, therefore, will not suffice as a basis for practice. While everyday knowledge must be validated and drawn on for its contextual wisdom, this needs to be done in a way that opens up the practitioner, and the community, to other questions and formulations rather than in ways that close off such inquiry. Practice needs to be grounded in theory and inseparable from theory, but this does not mean that theory is reduced simply to 'common sense' or 'common knowledge'. On the contrary, it means that we have to search for uncommon sense, and uncommon knowledge, and use them to expand our world view and help us to ask new questions and seek new answers.

This need not be done in an elitist or restricting way. The challenge for community development is to find ways in which the development and use of 'theory' can be part of the community development experience as people from diverse cultural and intellectual backgrounds share their knowledge and wisdom ('common' or otherwise) with each other. Ideas are important and an anti-intellectual stance to human rights practice will not suffice. People engaged in human rights work are grappling with difficult and complex moral and political questions, whether they realise it or not, and their work will be more effective if they can recognise that.

From a community development perspective, 'theory' must not be seen in an elitist sense. Rather, 'theory' is developed as part of the process of community development and involves not just university graduates but everyone. Gramsci's (1957) classic notion of the 'street-level intellectual' is important here. It suggests that one need not separate the intellectual from the everyday, but should rather bring the two together; the engaged intellectual and the thoughtful activist become one and the same. From an academic perspective, this suggests that so-called 'grounded theory' where theory is built up from critical engagement with the lived experience, is important (Strauss & Corbin 1990).

From this perspective, 'theory' cannot be separated from human rights practice. It is an essential component of that practice. The practice is about learning as well as doing and the theory is about doing as well as understanding. This is the nature of a critical approach to social science, as discussed in Chapter 5, and such a critical paradigm is inherent in human rights from below. It does not mean that there is no place for larger-scale theory – the work of theorists such as Marx, Weber, Foucault and Derrida – but that these insights need to be made accessible to people in their everyday lives and need to be interrogated in the light of experience. At the same time, learnings and understandings of people – wisdom 'from below' – need to be validated and built as part of the developmental process.

Theory is not a static 'body of knowledge' – even in the physical sciences theory is always provisional and is constantly being tested, modified, expanded and developed – and it is the same in community development. Theory and knowledge are processes, part of an ongoing journey of discovery. No form of knowledge should be regarded as taboo. Knowledge from personal experience, from intuition, from the arts, from poetry and story-telling and from folk myths is as important as knowledge that is 'evidence-based' or that has been rigorously tested either in research studies or through the courts.

This idea of theory and practice as inseparable – 'praxis', to use the Marxist term – renders discussion of 'relating theory and practice' meaningless. The two are of necessity interrelated, and linking them should not be a problem. It is only a problem if we understand both theory and practice in their more limited, conventional sense as implied in the Hesse and Post quotation discussed above. However, from the more organic perspective described here, theory *is* practice and practice *is* theory. From a community development perspective both are incorporated in community processes and are owned by the community rather than by the expert, whether this is an 'expert' practitioner or an academic.

THE PROBLEM WITH 'HOW TO DO IT'

The organic connection of theory and practice described above, and the need for both to be contextualised consistent with the discussion in Chapters 5 and 6, means that there can never be simple 'how to do it' prescriptions about human rights practice from a community development perspective. This is because of the importance of process, as discussed in Chapter 2. Specifying, for example, 'community development in five easy steps' is a betrayal of the community development process in that it assumes that an expert knows more about the process than does the community itself. How a community will develop its ideas and processes around human rights from below will differ from one community to another and, while the general community development principles outlined in Chapter 2 will apply, any attempt to focus them into specific 'strategies' or 'tactics' must be contextualised.

This makes human rights 'practice' more problematic than is commonly thought. It can never be reduced to simple 'how to' steps that can be learned as a technical exercise. Rather, anyone working with human rights from below will be faced with unique situations requiring unique approaches. While there are obviously lessons that can be learned from other community-based human rights work (or human rights-based community work), each circumstance requires its own response. Rather than seeing the human rights worker as a technician, following a set of prescribed procedures, it is more useful to think of the human rights worker as a street-level intellectual who will bring a wide range of understandings, conceptual tools, frames of reference and resources to be applied in a particular and unique way.

This is more of a 'professional' than a technical response, but the term 'professional' has taken on pejorative meanings and is so associated with the use or misuse of power, with elitism and with the monopolisation of knowledge and skills that it is not a word that sits comfortably in any discussion of human rights from below. However, there are two aspects of professionalism that do belong with the form of practice described here. One is the maintenance of ethical standards, which has already been alluded to in the discussion of means and ends, and the other is the need to apply a wide range of knowledge and understanding uniquely in any one situation. Beyond these two, it is doubtful if models of 'professionalism' have much to contribute to human rights from below.

Hence there is a limited use for prescriptive 'how to do it' publications. These over-simplify and assume some commonality across different communities, which does not reflect the reality of practice. They emphasise a rational, quasi-scientific approach to working with communities when an analogy with art, rather than science, would be more appropriate. Human rights from below thus becomes more of a creative activity, and the importance of the creative has largely been ignored in the human rights literature (though it has been rather more significant in relation to human rights *education*). The idea of the creative human rights worker will be discussed later in this chapter, but the important point at this stage of the discussion is to emphasise human rights work as being more than merely technical, as implied in 'how-to-do-it' prescriptions. While there will inevitably be some technical components to human rights from below, it also requires imagination, creativity, risk, adventure, poetry, story-telling and other aspects of the creative.

DEDUCTIVE AND INDUCTIVE PRACTICE

In considering the different ways human rights practitioners go about their 'practice' it can be useful to draw a distinction between deductive and inductive ways of practising. This reflects the distinction between discursive and reflective understandings of human rights, as mentioned in Chapter 5.

Deductive practice, reflecting the discursive approach to rights, accepts the definitions of rights as contained in conventions, treaties, declarations and charters and seeks to find methods of practice that can turn those ideas into reality. It fits well with the states' obligations tradition of human rights and sees human rights practice as *implementing* human rights.

Inductive practice, on the other hand, fits more with the constructed rights tradition. It begins with the reality of a particular situation – such as a community issue, a family conflict or a complaint about discrimination – and, using more of a community development approach, identifies which rights issues are seen as important by the various actors. The actors are encouraged to articulate rights for themselves (possibly with reference to human rights charters and the like) and to find ways to have those rights realised.

The two contrasting approaches are exemplified in the case of human rights-based social work practice by two different books on human rights and social work by Reichert (2003) and Ife (2008), which take very different approaches to the same topic. Both forms of practice are important and useful, but in the context of human rights from below a more inductive approach to human rights practice is clearly appropriate.

COMMUNITIES DEFINING HUMAN RIGHTS

Central to the argument of much of this book has been the importance of communities themselves being able to define human rights. Having our rights defined for us by somebody else, it might be argued, is itself a human rights abuse. Hence it is important that people at a community level have some say in the definition of human rights if they are to have a sense of ownership of those rights, so that a 'culture of human rights' can be embedded in a local community.

This, however, does not imply that the Universal Declaration, UN covenants, national bills of rights and so on have no value. These documents are important, not only for their legal significance but also for their symbolic power. However, they are not the last word on human rights. They represent particular attempts that have been made to define human rights and, even though they claim some degree of universality, they were all made at particular times and in specific political and cultural contexts. People at a community level are entitled to look at them critically and to think about what human rights mean for them, in their particular context, rather than to accept them as 'holy writ'.

However, in encouraging communities and community groups to develop their own definitions of human rights, it is important to move the process beyond a narrow, inward-looking perception that only takes the community's interests into account. Claims of rights can be selfish and reflect self-interest. In a pluralist society, where the norm is for groups to advocate in their own interests (on the assumption that other interests will be advocated by others), there is a danger that a community defining rights will simply turn the process into the usual list of local 'demands' couched in rights language.

The idea of human rights, however, carries some notion of universality, despite the evident problems with universality discussed in Chapter 4. The idea of aspirational universality can be useful here: that human rights are what we would wish could be applied to all of humanity. (For a fuller discussion see Chapter 4.) This requires people to think beyond narrow self-interest and to adopt a more Kantian perspective. As discussed in Chapter 4, human rights will always carry both universal and contextual frames of reference.

In emphasising the local community, there is a real danger that the contextual will be so dominant that the universal will be lost. Therefore communities defining human rights need to think beyond their own borders and consider the rights and responsibilities of all. A statement of human rights generated at a community level must represent a broader view of humanity, and so some level of discussion about human rights in a more global context is necessary. The Universal Declaration can be a good basis for this discussion, as a community can think of questions such as what 'rights' are included, what are excluded and how they are worded.

THE HUMAN RIGHTS MATRIX

As has been made clear in this book, the concept of human rights is complex and contested. It is naive to think that a community can define human rights without having some understanding of the idea and thinking through the issues and dilemmas that this raises. The human rights matrix workshop is one way in which a community or community group can think through the idea of human rights and come up with their own definitions, for their own use.

Here are a number of sets of questions that can be posed for communities in thinking about human rights:

1 Questions about the cultural, religious, philosophical and ideological traditions and understandings of rights. These questions emphasise that there are different cultural and religious traditions in which human rights can be formulated, and that different philosophies and ideologies hold different ideas of what 'rights' mean.

2 Questions about individual and collective understandings of human rights, emphasising that rights can attach to either individuals or to groups, and that this affects the way we think about human rights.

3 Questions about human rights in the public and private domains: How do rights defined publicly transfer to the family or household?

4 The role of courts and legal processes in human rights: What rights are justiciable and what rights are not? What is the role of legal bills of rights? How are they enforced?

5 How do rights relate to the various structures and discourses of oppression such as gender, race, class, sexuality, age and (dis)ability? What groups are particularly vulnerable to human rights abuse? How does human rights work link to activist groups organised around these issues?

6 What is the link between rights and responsibilities? Who or what should be held responsible for achieving or protecting human rights? What are the responsibilities of the individual, the family, the community, the state, the private sector?

7 How can rights be understood intergenerationally? What are our responsibilities to the rights of future generations? What are our responsibilities to address human rights violations in the past?

8 What can be done in terms of education and consciousness-raising and in facilitating community awareness about human rights? What action might be taken to promote/protect/realise human rights?

Obviously the language of these questions would need to be changed, depending on the community or group. Use of terms such as 'justiciable', 'ideological' and 'discourse' could alienate many groups, though they are quite acceptable to others. The questions above simply give an idea of the kinds of topics that can be covered in helping a community or group understand some basic issues about human rights.

These questions can then be applied more specifically to each of the seven categories of rights discussed in Chapter 6: social, economic, civil/political, cultural, environmental, spiritual and survival. This, when set out as illustrated in the Appendix, produces a 'human rights matrix' of 56 cells, and this matrix can be the basis for an extended community workshop on human rights.

Working in small groups, people are asked to consider a specific set of rights in relation to one of the sets of questions above and then move to another. The whole process is described in the Appendix, including a fuller list of questions that might be used. It has proved to be a very effective way to construct a community workshop on human rights.

Such a workshop can easily take a full day, or could be extended to two days, depending on the time available. This serves to underline the complexity, and also the potential richness, of human rights.

All groups are asked to put their ideas on butcher's paper, or into laptop computers, and at the end of the workshop the ideas can be collated into a document that effectively becomes that community group's declaration of human rights. This is an excellent way for a community to achieve a sense of ownership of human rights, as well as of thinking through what human rights really involve.

It must be emphasised that this matrix is simply a framework. In different contexts it may be appropriate to change the questions and modify the process. As discussed early in this chapter, 'how to' approaches to community development usually do not work, and the matrix is presented here (and in the Appendix) simply as a process that has proved to be useful in practice and which should be modified as needed in any particular setting.

COMMUNITIES PROMOTING HUMAN RIGHTS

Community-based human rights implies more than just the definition of rights at a community level. It also requires that those human rights be promoted so that a culture of human rights can be achieved. This might be called community-based human rights education, which was discussed to some extent earlier in this chapter.

One of the important things to consider in community-based human rights education is the balance of 'good news' and 'bad news'. Human rights can often seem to be dominated by 'bad news' stories: torture, extra-judicial killings, disappearances, massacre, genocide, starvation, disease and other catastrophes. This can alienate many people. There is only so much bad news that people can take, and they may turn away from human rights as a result.

It is necessary to attempt to mix in some 'good news' stories of human rights, showing what can be achieved and celebrating human rights, so that there is some message of hope as well as of despair. However, the celebration of human rights can also be overdone, making people feel so good about 'celebrating the human spirit' that there is no sense of urgency to address immediate problems.

There is a need to have a judicious mixture of positive and negative so that a sense of hope and a sense of urgency can somehow be held together. For example, if there is a film showing about serious human rights violations in a particular country (bad news), the organisers could arrange for Amnesty International, Oxfam or some other group to have an information stall showing people what they can do to make a difference, or displaying some success stories (good news). Similarly, if there is a human rights festival celebrating the achievements of human rights (good news), there could be a display about major human rights abuses that need to be addressed (bad news).

Many human rights education projects only concentrate on the good news or the bad news, and each in its own way can result in disempowerment. However, juxtaposing 'good news' and 'bad news' in the one event can result in a creative dissonance; people are forced to temper both their hope and their despair and to ask some awkward questions and think about possible ways forward.

This need for balance also applies in dealing with human rights issues at a local level. There is a need both to celebrate what a community has achieved and also to highlight the problems and issues it faces; only by holding the two together is it likely that some form of appropriate action will eventuate. Celebrating achievements without confronting problems can lead to smug inaction and complacency while confronting problems alone can result in feelings of resignation and inability to achieve anything.

There are many ways in which human rights at a community level can be promoted. It is important to do this in ways that are consistent with a community's cultural traditions. For example, in a community that is obsessed with football one might want to organise a special football game, for example a game between refugee groups and longer-term residents, or between different religious faiths. Despite the apparent opposition that is set up in such a game, simply having a team can provide a group with much-needed community recognition. Participation in a game is a way of actually bringing people together, especially if a social event such as a barbecue or picnic is held afterwards and if families are encouraged to come and watch the game and participate in the social event.

In another community, such a football game would be completely inappropriate for various reasons. However, there may be other activities that could be organised: a music festival, a film festival, a community arts event, a theatrical production or story-telling. There might be, for example, a special evening devoted to a particular country or region, which is both a celebration of the culture and food of that country and an opportunity to focus on human rights issues within it.

Film can be a particularly powerful medium for human rights education, but again it is important to ensure that a human rights film festival, for example, has a combination of 'good news' and 'bad news' messages and also that avenues are provided for people who wish to take further action. Alternatively, film may be used in conjunction with other approaches, for example in conjunction with a festival to provide the 'bad news' counterpart to the 'feelgood' outcome of the singing and dancing.

In some contexts, competitions can be a good way to raise awareness, especially in schools. Human rights poetry competitions, short story writing, art competitions, photography competitions, dance competitions and so on can all be useful, especially if the emphasis is less on the actual winning of the competition and more on the educational component, both for the students who produced the work and for those who view or listen to the students' work. However, competitions have their disadvantages. With the inevitable announcement of 'winners' and therefore also, by omission, of 'losers', there is a message that runs counter to ideas of human rights and inclusiveness. This will be more important in some communities than in others and in some cases will make competitions inappropriate.

Some of these forms of human rights education can, inadvertently, concentrate only on human rights issues that are located elsewhere – in other countries or other communities. This can reinforce the idea of human rights as something that concerns 'them' rather than 'us', and can allow people to divert attention from their own engagement with human rights to concentrate on what is happening in the latest trouble spot to attract media attention. Again, it is a question of balance.

It is important to have a broader perspective of human rights than simply the local, and to recognise the severity of human rights violations in other countries. However, it is also important to focus attention on one's own community, its connection through globalisation to what is happening elsewhere, and its experience of human rights in the local context and the need for those rights to be realised. There is a danger in losing sight of either the local or the global whereas, in this era of globalisation when the local is global and the global is local (see Chapter 5), it is essential that understandings of human rights retain both.

The important point, from a community development perspective, is that there is no single approach that will work in all communities. Working out appropriate forms of community-based human rights education will depend on the nature of the community, its traditions, its culture, its resources and other factors. Determining an appropriate form of human rights education becomes itself a community development project and can involve different people from the community coming together to work out what is appropriate and achievable.

Sometimes it may be appropriate for a community to join a national or international program of human rights. For example, there is a UN program of 'Human Rights Cities' to encourage cities to identify as human rights cities and to meet criteria of what a human rights city would mean in practice. This may, for good reasons, be quite inappropriate for some cities (for example, a city that does not wish to claim an identity as a 'city' in isolation from the surrounding rural region), but for other cities it may be a very good way of developing a human rights consciousness and promoting community-based human rights.

The use of local media can be an important component of community-based human rights education. The inclusion of material in local newspapers, the production of a local newsletter, participation in a local radio station or using talkback radio and community television can all be useful in raising awareness about human rights and about how people might become involved. These are ways in which human rights issues can be presented as stories of people in that community, in a way that people can readily relate to.

Along with these conventional media, 'new media' (including the internet and the use of mobile phones) can, in communities with ready access to these technologies, be used to considerable effect. This can also be a way in which young people can become involved in community-based human rights, as they have far more expertise in these new media than most of the people who will be on local committees or local councils. They can be invited to design and implement human rights education strategies in ways of which their parents' generation (including this writer) is only dimly aware.

There are other ways in which human rights can be promoted at a community level, which are discussed in other sections of this chapter and in Chapter 6. Almost any of the initiatives discussed in other sections can be used to promote human rights education and awareness. Human rights education extends well beyond the school and formal education classes; indeed it might be argued that these are among the least effective of human rights education approaches in the local community context.

COMMUNITIES PROTECTING HUMAN RIGHTS

The protection of rights is an important component of community-based human rights. Here the community takes an active role in monitoring the activities of various institutions such as schools, hospitals, police, retailers, local government, local clubs and associations to ensure that they are consistent with human rights principles. These principles may be enshrined in legislation or bills of rights, or may be the community's own expectations as a result of a community development process as described above.

Documentation of human rights activities, however, is not enough. It is also important that this documentation be communicated to those who can take action accordingly, such as local officials, politicians, the media, school principals, police superintendents and community legal centres. Thus this aspect of community-based human rights requires both data collection/analysis and communication/advocacy skills.

In some communities this can only be undertaken with considerable risk; an example is the very courageous Iraqi students who sought to document human rights abuses in Iraq after the US-led invasion, including human rights abuses perpetrated by all sides in the conflict. Even in less dangerous situations there can still be an element of risk, since human rights monitoring by its very nature can question and scrutinise the activities of people with power who will not always welcome such attention and who may seek to act accordingly.

As with other aspects of community-based human rights, there is no 'right' way to undertake this work. It may involve using a camera, camcorder, sound recording, note-taking, analysis of documents, analysis of statistics, interviews or asking for submissions. Sometimes community groups can set up a 'people's inquiry', holding hearings and asking for people to give them information (see, for example Briskman, Latham & Goddard 2008). But all these activities can be appropriate in some situations and inappropriate in others. It is simply a matter of being aware of different possibilities and using whatever seems to be appropriate, or of using one's imagination and coming up with something different. This is also an area where a community group may need to seek expertise, for example in statistical analysis or in the preparation of legal submissions.

	Legislated requirements	Stated aims	Community expectations
Social rights			
Economic rights			
Civil/political rights			
Cultural rights			
Environmental rights			
Spiritual rights			
Survival rights			

Template for a human rights report card/human rights plan

One way in which this can be achieved is by producing a 'human rights report card' on which the activity of various local and other authorities can be monitored and compared with legislative requirements, the stated aims of the organisations concerned (in strategic plans or charters of customer rights, for example) or community expectations. These three sets of criteria, applied across the seven categories of rights described earlier, can produce a simple table that can be used as a template for a human rights report card, as shown above.

It is important to include the three categories of criteria, as the legislated requirements, the stated aims of organisations and the expectations of the community will not necessarily be the same and an organisation that may meet legislative requirements, for example, may not meet community expectations. In some instances it may not be possible to gauge community expectations, or the stated aims of an organisation may be vague, but this then can be used to find ways in which community expectations can be better identified (as part of a community development process) and organisations can be asked to be more explicit about their policies in relation to a range of human rights issues.

This 'report card' can be applied either to an organisation such as a school, a police district, a hospital or a local council or, more ambitiously, to a community as a whole. The categories may need to be modified, or some may need to be excluded, but that is normal for any community development process; ideas are always to be taken up and modified as necessary, never adopted uncritically. The organisation or community is then assessed on how well it has met the criteria – it may be allocated a score out of ten, or a letter grade, or some other grading – or it may simply be a case of pass/fail according to whether or not it has met the criteria. Out of this process can come a set of recommendations or an action plan that can be applied to encourage a better performance the following year. This template can also thus become a template for a human rights plan, where various objectives are identified that it is hoped will be reached, so that legislative requirements, stated aims and community expectations can be met.

In some cases, however, such a 'report card' and 'planning' approach may not be appropriate. These are, after all, the methods of modernist certainty and are more consistent with the world of Enlightenment modernity than with the postmodern world of community development. They are tools that have some use in an environment where techniques such as 'report cards' and 'planning' are seen as having validity, and they can help human rights-based community groups to speak the same language as local authorities and managers; in this sense they can be extremely useful. However, the temptation to think that they reveal some kind of 'truth' about human rights compliance must be resisted. They must always be seen in their political context. Like all other approaches discussed in this book, they must be used critically and only in circumstances where they are contextually appropriate.

HUMAN RIGHTS ACROSS COMMUNITIES

It is important to emphasise that community-based human rights does not imply that it is only the rights of people in that community, and the rights of that community itself, that must be considered. The idea of human rights requires that there be an extension beyond one's immediate environment to some notion of 'humanity', however problematic that word may be. The discussion above made reference to this, especially in relation to human rights education and the raising of awareness, and this needs to be extended to take account of human rights in an age of globalisation.

When the global is local and the local is global, as discussed in Chapter 5, there will be a global component of any human rights project undertaken at a community level. The discussion above about communities defining human rights emphasised that this definition should apply to the rights of all people, not just the rights of members of a particular community, and this aspirational universalism is key to ensuring that communities look beyond their own boundaries.

The literature about 'globalisation from below', discussed in Chapters 2 and 5 (Brecher & Costello 1994, Falk 1993), suggests that we need to understand globalisation not just as a movement in the interests of global capital, but also that an alternative globalisation can be articulated, one that is in the interests of people and communities at grassroots level and is concerned with the globalisation of social justice rather than the globalisation of profits. Modern communications technologies have made possible globalisation from above, as capital can be moved instantly through cyberspace, and the same technologies also make possible globalisation from below, as people and community groups have the opportunity to communicate their experiences, their successes and their frustrations, and to build coalitions and broad-based action as never before.

This has been used effectively by social movements, most particularly the environment movement, and it is very much part of human rights activism. Communities are now able to link with other communities, which may be on the other side of the world but which are experiencing the same problems, challenges and dilemmas. Technology now allows the dichotomy between local and global, like the dichotomy between universal and context (see Chapter 5), to break down. Community-based human rights is part of global human rights movements, is affected by them and can contribute to them.

By linking with other communities facing similar challenges, and also with other coalitions and NGOs, communities can take a global perspective while at the same time maintaining their local identity and dealing with local human rights issues. It is necessary to take action on both local and global levels, and communities can be engaged with both. The successful human rights NGO of the future will be one that is able to incorporate both the local and the global in this way. This was pioneered by Amnesty International which, before the days of the internet, developed a structure that was a global human rights movement and at the same time was strongly grounded in the local community group.

There are many possible examples of how this might work. The experience of twinning a community in one country with a community in another so that each can learn from the other's experience is common. Such initiatives are often taken by local government authorities and can provide a way in which interested citizens can readily participate. Internet web pages, discussion groups and so on are increasingly used for the exchange of information. It is also easy for individuals or communities to participate in mass movements around particular issues, largely generated through the internet.

It must also be remembered that not all the world is connected to the internet and that social movements that are internet-based, while powerful, also exclude many people and communities, often those experiencing the most severe forms of human rights abuse. Other ways of linking with communities internationally can include visits, letter-writing and working through international NGOs. These may sound old-fashioned, but for many people in the world they are all they have. It is important that community-based human rights not work exclusively in a way that only serves to reinforce the 'digital divide'.

THE COMMUNITY-BASED HUMAN RIGHTS PRACTITIONER

This final section is concerned with the community-based human rights practitioner. It must not be thought, however, that this term only applies to someone who is employed to work for human rights at a community level, as such an exclusive understanding is to reify 'practice' into something precious and exclusive. Anyone can 'practise' community-based human rights: the employed human rights worker, the community activist, the professional in a related field (such as a community-based social worker, a lawyer in a community legal centre, a community health nurse, a teacher or a police officer), the volunteer, or the concerned citizen who may claim no 'expertise' in human rights but who, from the point of view of community development as discussed in Chapter 2, has considerable wisdom and expertise to contribute.

From a community development perspective, not only can anyone be involved in human rights, but it is also important to maximise the number of people involved. In this sense, the term 'practitioner' refers to anyone working for human rights at a community level, paid or unpaid, whatever their qualifications.

KNOWLEDGE, VALUES AND SKILLS

A useful framework for discussing practice is to think of it as comprising three components: knowledge, values and skills. Each of these is important in its own right and each also interacts with the others. Good practice must incorporate all three.

Someone who has knowledge and values but no skills is of limited use. They become the characteristic 'armchair revolutionary' who is good at thinking about what needs to be done but does not actually do anything very effectively. While ineffective, at least they are unlikely to cause much harm.

Someone who has values and skills but is lacking in knowledge becomes the unthinking pragmatist, with a mistrust of anything that looks like 'theory' and a strong anti-intellectual stance that favours 'common sense' over other knowledge that may be harder to access or to understand. Such a person may well do harm, unintentionally, because of their lack of critical understanding of what they are doing and of the context within which they are doing it.

Worst of all, however, is the person with knowledge and skills but no values. This is the technician, who is not concerned with the moral or ethical issues about what they are doing and about why and how they are doing it. This results in amoral, instrumental, technocratic practice where efficiency and effectiveness are valued but where value issues are not addressed; this is potentially the road to Auschwitz.

Knowledge, values and skills interact and the interactions between them provide many of the most problematic, but also the most interesting, aspects of 'practice'. The intersection between values and knowledge has been of major concern in the philosophy of science and the philosophy of social science, evident in vigorous debate about whether research can be 'objective' and value-free. Unless one takes a rigidly positivist position, which is now rare in the social sciences, knowledge and values are clearly not independent of each other. Rather, each affects the other.

Our knowledge is value-based. Values determine what knowledge we think is important, how we gather that knowledge, how we interpret knowledge and indeed how we 'construct' our knowledge of the world. Even though some research proceeds as if it is an objective exercise, the very way that 'objectivity' is constructed is itself value-based.

And similarly, just as values affect knowledge, knowledge affects values. The acquisition of knowledge can make one reassess one's values, and anyone who takes an open attitude to knowledge – a willingness always to learn – carries with that an open attitude to values – a willingness to rethink a value position in the light of new understandings.

This intrinsic link between knowledge and values is important in relation to human rights. No human rights 'knowledge' is ever value-neutral. Indeed human rights is an area that is always strongly value-laden, and there should be no need to apologise for that. Humanity is, after all, a matter of values, not just 'knowledge of the human'.

Human rights is also an area where knowledge can have a profound impact on values. Many human rights activists were first motivated to action by knowledge: the sight of refugee families being turned away, the knowledge of massacres or genocides in Rwanda, Dili, Srebrenica, Cambodia, Sudan or other troubled places, the knowledge of imprisonment without trial or the knowledge that millions of children die of preventable diseases. The community-based human rights practitioner cannot separate knowledge and values, nor should they try. But an examination of the interplay between knowledge and values, and the exploration of how that plays out at the community level, can help to develop a more critically reflective approach to practice that takes neither knowledge nor values for granted but seeks to interrogate each in terms of the other.

The relationship between knowledge and skills has already been discussed in relation to theory and practice and so need not be reiterated here. It will be recalled from the discussion earlier in this chapter that theory and practice cannot be understood in isolation from each other, and that the two are inevitably interrelated. Each in fact needs the other in order to make any sense, and any community-based human rights practitioner will be constantly seeking to understand each in relation to the other and to enact the problematic theory/practice relationship.

The relationship between skills and values raises the question of whether the skills of a community-based human rights worker can ever be merely technical and value-neutral. It is hard to maintain such an argument when the skills are being exercised towards the end of human rights, which is unambiguously value-laden, being grounded in some construction of the 'value of humanity'.

Here also it is important to recall the discussion of means and ends (see Chapter 2), where it was argued that it is not possible to separate means and ends in community work. To the extent that skills represent the 'means' in human rights work, with the achievement of human rights as the 'end', this suggests that a clear distinction cannot be made between skills and values. Skills in human rights work cannot be value-neutral. The skills must themselves incorporate human rights principles, and are thus necessarily value-laden. In Chapter 6 it was suggested that it is important for any human rights-based organisation to observe human rights in the way it carries out its work, and the same applies to any case of community-based human rights practice. Just as Kant and Gandhi would argue that the end does not justify the means and that a corrupt means will corrupt the end, human rights work that does not itself observe human rights principles is self-defeating. The skills and processes used by a human rights worker must inevitably be themselves grounded in the values of human rights, and hence skills and values are inevitably linked.

KNOWLEDGE

There are many knowledges that are relevant to community-based human rights. One area of knowledge is the 'traditional' human rights field: knowledge of the various international, regional, national and state human rights instruments, how they operate and the legal ways in which people can act to ensure that their human rights are protected and realised, or to seek redress for rights that have been violated.

However, from the point of view of human rights from below, this is only the beginning. It is also important to have some understanding of the more theoretical and philosophical issues around human rights, as discussed in Chapters 3 and 4, as the view of human rights implied in community-based work is that they are constantly being reconstructed and are always problematic, rather than being inscribed on tablets of stone or in international law. It is important for people at a community level to engage with some of these issues as they struggle to articulate human rights in their context, and so a community-based human rights worker needs to be familiar with these philosophical and theoretical issues and be able to pose questions around them.

Knowledge of community development, and ideas of community, are also essential for the community-based human rights worker. Community is as problematic a concept as human rights, and there are dangers when a community worker simply accepts an idea of 'community' as straightforward, self-evident and non-problematic.

There is a rich body of theory about community and communities, and about community development, that is of obvious relevance for anyone wishing to 'practise' community-based human rights. Although, as was shown in earlier chapters, the ideas of community and human rights are inextricably linked, they have been theorised and conceptualised separately, and so there are two bodies of traditional theory that are relevant. In Chapter 5 an attempt was made to bring the two concepts together as an initial formulation of community-based human rights, or human rights from below, and these ideas also need to be addressed by the community-based human rights worker.

There is also a whole area of knowledge that is local and contextualised. This is knowledge about the community itself: its history, its culture, its demographics, its resources, its potential, its traditions and idiosyncrasies, its physical location, its natural environment and its built environment. This may be easy for a locally based community worker who has lived in that community, though even for such a worker there can be blind spots. For example, the worker may be largely unaware of the culture and traditions of certain immigrant or indigenous groups within that community. It is a mistake to assume that a local person automatically knows everything about the community in which they live, especially in urban communities with high mobility and cultural diversity.

A further area of knowledge that can be important is more general knowledge about the wider environment. Examples include knowledge about political structures and processes and knowledge about a range of broader social issues, whether these be child protection, domestic violence, poverty, crime, economic concerns, refugees and asylum seekers, climate change or police corruption. These all reflect the environment of the community; the more informed a worker is, the more they are able to work with these issues as human rights matters at a community level. To this can be added knowledge of wider resources, such as funding sources, academics, educational institutions, trainers and facilitators.

These different forms of knowledge can come from a variety of sources. There are, obviously, formal education qualifications that are relevant, such as a degree in community development, or human rights, or some related field or profession. However, there are other sources of knowledge that are equally important, and it must never be thought that only people with a relevant degree can work in community-based human rights. These sources of knowledge include reading, the considerable resources of the internet, informal discussions with colleagues and friends, and simply the experience of living in a community and attempting to implement human rights.

One very important component of a worker's knowledge is knowing what you don't know. However knowledgeable a worker may be, there will always be gaps and areas of relative ignorance. Here a worker will need to seek expertise from elsewhere and also seek additional knowledge. A community worker never 'knows it all', and to wait until one is fully qualified or fully equipped to undertake community work is to wait forever. Community work is an ongoing process of learning, formal and informal. As well as the continuing development of knowledge, it is also about growing wisdom that comes from experience and reflection.

VALUES

The values that are important for the practitioner are obviously those values that are consistent with human rights, however those rights are constructed, and this perspective must pervade every aspect of human rights from below. As was discussed in Chapter 2, means and ends cannot be separated in this regard, and hence human rights must inform the way that a human rights worker goes about their job rather than merely the outcomes they hope to achieve; ethics is an essential component of human rights work. This includes valuing colleagues and community members, using inclusive and respectful processes and ensuring that the rights of all people involved can be both protected and realised.

The values of community-based human rights also include ideas of social justice. These are closely connected with human rights and other values that have been discussed in this book such as the value of diversity, ecological values of both diversity and interconnectedness (which will always be held in tension), sustainability and integrity.

Where can a worker derive and develop these values? The development of values is a complex and contested issue, involving socialisation (both during and after childhood), experience, education, emotion and inspiration. These will be mentioned again below, but at this stage it is important to remember that, like knowledge, the process of developing one's value position is a never-ending one. It is therefore important for a community-based human rights worker to be critically aware of their values and to be always open to dialogue, clarification and the experience of new challenges.

SKILLS

There are many skills that can be brought to bear on the practice of human rights from below, and there is not a single 'skill set' for a community human rights worker. Different workers will bring different strengths to the role and so will work in different ways. These skills include: advocacy, consensus-building, education, communication, consciousness-raising, group facilitation, interpersonal skills, use of the media, working with conflict, negotiation, public presentation, writing, research, data analysis, organising and record-keeping. Some of these skills will come naturally to any community worker, while others will have to be developed in some way. With some skills a worker may have to conclude 'that's just not me' and find someone else who can do a particular task.

Skills in community work cannot be 'learnt' in the conventional sense. Rather than learning skills, it is more helpful to think about *developing* skills. Most of the skills mentioned above cannot be simply taught and step-by-step manuals are of little use. Rather, the idea of *developing* skills suggests that the community worker grows and is transformed in the process. Indeed the process of skill development is not unlike the process of community development; it cannot be rushed, it must proceed at its own pace and the outcome cannot be rigorously specified. Hence for the community development teacher it is important to provide the environment in which skill development can take place, and nurture the process rather than inhibit the learning process with objectives and outcome statements.

One of the best ways of learning skills is to watch others and to work collaboratively with others. This does not mean slavishly copying everything another worker does, but rather reflecting on how they do their work and what ideas might be gained from the work of another. Working collaboratively in a team or a partnership creates an opportunity to try things out together, for one worker to mentor another, and for mutual constructive critique.

SHARING KNOWLEDGE, VALUES AND SKILLS

An important community development principle is that knowledge, values and skills should be shared, rather than jealously guarded under the guise of monopolistic professionalism. This is part of the empowerment aim of community development, by which it is hoped that people from the community will develop their own knowledge, values and skills so that they can fill many roles themselves rather than relying on a community development worker to do it for them.

Thus, for example, in planning the lobbying of a politician it may be that only the paid community worker has the necessary experience and confidence to fill that role effectively. However, a good community worker will ensure that other community members are part of a delegation, rather than simply making the presentation to the politician alone. They will also discuss the meeting with the other community members with the aim that next time other people will be able to do the lobbying. The same can be done with media releases, interviews, surveys, meeting facilitation and so on. Each activity should be seen as a learning opportunity. That way responsibility is shared, confidence and self-image are developed and the community becomes stronger.

The above example is one of sharing skills, but the same can apply to knowledge and values. Knowledge can be shared through discussion groups, film and DVD, computer access and simple informal discussions, for example while making the coffee for a community meeting. The sharing of values can be more problematic, but environments can be created where people are able to talk about their values, about what they think is important, their hopes, dreams and fears. A human rights focus provides a ready opportunity to discuss values, since statements of human rights are value statements and it would be impossible for a community or group to go through a process such as the 'human rights matrix' without a good deal of sharing of value positions and reflection on the values and ideology behind human rights.

Indeed it could be argued that, if human rights are incorporated into community development, people have a right to be able to develop knowledge, values and skills so that they can more adequately articulate and advocate for their own rights and the rights of others. Hence the sharing of knowledge, values and skills at all stages of community-based human rights is not only a sound community development principle, but is also a form of human rights practice.

THE ONGOING JOURNEY

The issue of process and outcome has been discussed in Chapter 2. It is important here to emphasise the importance of process in community development and in human rights from below. It is in the process, the ongoing journey, that we work out what human rights mean and how we can go about achieving them. It is a journey that will never have an end-point. Attempts to define humanity as the ideal, perfectible human lie in ruins in the smashed gas chambers of Auschwitz, while attempts to create the perfect ideal community similarly lie in the ruins of Stalinist communism. The history of the twentieth century surely tells us of the dangers of these twin ambitions for the perfect human and the perfect community. This is the logical end-point of Enlightenment modernity, and community-based human rights needs to avoid such false idealism.

It is not the end that is important but the journey; and it is on the journey, in discovering new pathways and directions, in working things out as we go, with a sense of moving but not in the hope of ultimate 'arrival', that the rich potential of community-based human rights can be realised. The nature of human rights is that it will always be a work-in-progress, as 'humanity' is reconstructed in different times and different contexts. For example, the construction of humanity at the time of the Universal Declaration did not include the important interconnection with the natural world that now has become such a vital imperative for any understanding of 'the human'. This construction will surely continue to change in future eras.

The ongoing journey is a journey of shared humanity. As discussed in Chapter 5, the idea of a shared humanity as opposed to a common humanity makes the human, and hence human rights, a continuing project. Sharing means that we contribute what we can and take what we need. In an ongoing process of contributing what we can to our understanding of 'humanity', and taking what we need from the similar contributions of others, humanity becomes dynamic rather than static and we no longer need be so concerned with reaching the ultimate end-point in a quest for the realisation of a single ideal human. The same also applies to community; it cannot be static and an end to be achieved, but rather it is an ongoing journey of excitement, hopes, disappointments, dreams, magic and enchantment, with new and potentially exciting avenues opening up if we are only able to trust the process and abandon the modernist search for certainty.

Human rights have tended to be understood as universal, despite the manifest problems with naive universality as discussed in Chapter 4, while community has tended to be understood as contextual, despite the influences of global capital, global culture and global media. Bringing the two together, as community-based human rights or human rights from below, requires each to be understood in terms of the other and demands the kind of synthesis of universality and context that was discussed in Chapter 4. It therefore is a promising way forward for one of the most perplexing issues confronting human rights. The tension between the universal and the contextual, and the need to incorporate both, is central to any understanding of community-based human rights.

The other central feature for community-based human rights, which has been an ongoing theme in this book, has been diversity. Both the idea of the human and the idea of community must incorporate diversity if they are to fulfil the ambitions of human rights from below as outlined here. This challenges the modernist project of conformity and uniformity and locates human rights from below as part of the project seeking a world view of sustainability and diversity, rather than growth and sameness, as a vision for the future of humanity.

INSPIRATION AND HOPE

One of the major problems for people seeking significant social, economic and political change in the contemporary world is that traditional ideologies, which held out a hope for a better future, have been largely discredited. Socialism has been discredited by Stalinist communism. Social democracy has, in the English-speaking world at least, become identified with the 'third way' of British Labour and become thoroughly compromised by the pragmatics of 'spin'. Market ideology and laissez-faire capitalism has become discredited by the global financial crisis of 2008–09.

Traditional religions appeal to fewer people in the secular West, other than those attracted by the simplicities of fundamentalism. The humanist alternative, promised by the Enlightenment, has also been discredited by the wars and genocides of the twentieth century and by the colonialism which, while reaching its peak in the nineteenth century, remains powerful even into the twenty-first. It is not easy for people to relate to a promise of a better world, or a light on the hill, when so many of these promises have turned out to be false. Human rights itself, if too firmly attached to Western secular humanism, will be similarly discredited and needs an alternative vision.

Where, then, can the community human rights activist turn for some form of inspiration and hope? Vague talk about 'the triumph of the human spirit' no longer seems adequate, powerful though that sentiment may be. Throughout this book it has been suggested that the core ideas of human rights and community development – the *human* and *community* – need to be rethought, and that each can be rethought in terms of the other. Clearly there needs to be a break away from the constraints of Enlightenment modernity towards an alternative world view that affirms diversity, that transcends the tension between universal and contextual, that seeks sustainability rather than increasing consumption and growth, and that requires a new contract with the non-human world. The ecological crisis suggests that, in the longer term, there is probably no alternative to such a change if some form of 'human civilisation' that respects community and humanity is to survive.

For such a radical rethink, sources of inspiration are more likely to come from the margins than from the centre. While the sciences are clearly important, they do not represent the only way to view the world. And some of the traditional sciences, especially economics and the 'social sciences', have become more part of the problem than part of the solution.

Mary Midgley (2001) uses the analogy of a map. The same part of the earth can be represented in many different maps. One map may show roads and railways, one may show physical features, one may show vegetation patterns, one may show population density, one may show geological forms, one may show language patterns, one may show political and administrative boundaries, one may show objects of strategic significance for the military, one may show places of recreation, amusement and retail outlets, and so on. They all show this same piece of the world in different ways, each is 'accurate', but each looks very different and none is more 'valid' or 'true' than any other.

The sciences provide us with certain 'maps' of our social world. They are useful for some purposes, but there are other maps that are just as valid and that are more useful for other purposes. If it is 'humanity' that is of concern, then surely it is important not merely to subject 'the human' to scientific study, but also to utilise the disciplines that have made 'the human' and its problematic nature their focus of study, namely the humanities. Philosophy, history, literature, poetry, art, music, film and theatre have much to say about humanity and its problems, and these are too often ignored when human rights or community development are seriously discussed and researched.

Yet it is these disciplines that are particularly good at helping us 'think outside the square', challenging our preconceptions and providing the outrageous and apparently impossible ideas that are the ones we actually need. The humanities have had a lot to say about human rights – one need only think of Picasso's *Guernica*, Wilfred Owen's poetry, Dylan's songs, Havel's plays, Shostakovich's symphonies, Dickens' novels, Hobsbawm's historical writings, the philosophy of Kant and countless other examples of philosophers, historians, writers, poets and artists who have profound things to say, not just about human rights but about humanity, about the natural world and about community.

The above examples are all from the Western tradition, of course, but they are matched by great thinkers and creative artists from other cultural traditions: Arabic and Latin American poets, African musicians, Indigenous Australian artists, Chinese and Indian philosophers. Yet the mainstream human rights discourse largely omits, or at best marginalises, them. They are seen as peripheral to the 'main game', whereas perhaps they should be seen as central to the main game of human rights and community.

From a community development perspective, moving away from the apparent constraints of 'high culture', it is often through the creative arts expressed at a community level – street theatre, local artists, theatre workshops, local musicians, community video, story-telling festivals, and so on – that the most transformative moments can be reached.

This is not to deny the importance of more traditional knowledge forms in human rights and community development. Lawyers, sociologists, politicians and economists all have important contributions to make, as do the physical scientists in this era of ecological crisis. However, it is also important for the community-based human rights worker to seek insight from other sources; to dream, to read poetry, to listen to music, to watch films and to use these media to help ask and answer important questions about humanity and community. Artists can often ask the questions that others will not or cannot, and artists can also point the way to some outrageous 'answers' that others cannot dare to suggest.

Human rights work, in the context of human rights from below, must be creative. When there are no simple text-book solutions, the practitioner has to be able to come up with creative alternatives, to use the imagination and to draw inspiration from various sources. Creativity is often discouraged within the managerial, technocratic and legal discourses within which most human rights workers are forced to operate, but creativity is needed in order to open those very discourses up to scrutiny, to imagine alternatives and to act on them. By engaging with the community in a community development approach, a human rights worker will find the inspiration and hope that is lacking in the managerial, ordered world of top-down modernity.

One of the most important ways forward for human rights, and especially for community-based human rights, is to open up. This means opening up to other sources of knowledge, wisdom and inquiry, beyond the traditional boundaries of the discourse. It means opening up to other people, other disciplines, other ideas. It also means opening up to new directions, not seeing human rights as a linear progression towards an ultimate goal but as discovering myriad possibilities for action and understanding. Human rights from below suggests that many of these possibilities are there at the community level, if only we have the courage and imagination to see them and follow where they lead.

Appendix
The human rights matrix

OUTLINE FOR A WORKSHOP

1 Introductions, etc. are made. The facilitator outlines the program for the workshop.

2 The facilitator gives a presentation of the different dimensions of human rights, identifying the seven dimensions used in the horizontal axis of the matrix.

3 The facilitator gives a presentation of ideas about the cultural, religious, philosophical and ideological origins of human rights, emphasising diversity.

4 Participants break into seven groups (or multiples of seven for larger groups). Each group is allocated one category of rights (social, economic, etc.) and asked to apply the ideas from the previous presentation to that category of rights. Each group is given a set of questions about the cultural, religious, philosophical and ideological traditions of human rights, as listed on the next page, and asked to put their ideas on butcher's paper.

5 Each small group briefly reports back to the whole group, allowing time for questions and suggestions from others.

6 The facilitator gives a brief presentation on individual and collective ideas of rights.

7 Each group is then assigned a different category of rights (for example, the group that first had social rights might be allocated economic rights) and given a new set of questions related to individual/collective rights, and the process is repeated.

This process (steps 3 to 5) is repeated until all eight sets of questions have been applied to all seven categories of rights; that is, all 56 sections of the matrix have been completed and there are 56 pieces of butcher's paper (or more if there are more than seven groups).

The next task is to take the 56 pieces of butcher's paper and collate the ideas into a single document, though still using the same headings. This would ideally be done by a small group selected from the larger group, though in other circumstances it might be better done by the facilitator, depending on time and other factors. This document can then become the group's own declaration of human rights. It can be used in ongoing discussions and the development of action plans, or there may be a further process seeking to make amendments to it.

If appropriate technology is available, and the group is sufficiently computer-literate, laptops can be substituted for butcher's paper and the process can gradually build up a matrix that is stored electronically and shared among all the groups.

The entire process will last for at least one full day, ideally two. However, abbreviated versions may be developed if time is short, or if the group is too small to be divided into seven.

QUESTIONS FOR DISCUSSION

(wording to be changed as appropriate for any particular group)

1 Cultural, religious, philosophical and ideological traditions and understandings of rights

There are different constructions of human rights from different world views, shaped by culture, philosophy, religion and ideology.

a How is each set of rights understood in different cultural traditions?

b How is each set of human rights understood in different religious traditions?

c What are the philosophical bases for these rights, in both Western and non-Western thought?

d How are these rights related to different political philosophies/ ideologies, e.g. liberalism, socialism, conservatism, anarchism, green ideology, neoliberalism, etc.?

2 Individual and collective understandings of rights

Human rights can be understood both as individual rights (the rights of an individual person) and as collective rights (the rights of a group).

a How can each set of rights be understood individually, as a right 'belonging' to a particular person?

b How can each set of rights be understood collectively, as rights 'belonging' to a community, social group, cultural group, nation or society?

c For each set of rights, what are the tensions between the individual and collective understandings?

3 Rights in the private/domestic and public/civil domains

Human rights apply not only in the public sphere but also in the domestic sphere, e.g. the right to freedom of expression in civil society and the right to freedom of expression within the family.

a How can each set of rights be understood as applying within the private domain of the family or household?

b How can each set of rights be understood as applying within the public domains of the community, workplace, state or civil society?

c What are the implications of this distinction for people whose lives are largely confined to the domestic sphere, e.g. many women and children, people dependent on carers, the carers themselves?

4 Rights and protection through courts and legislation, justiciability, etc.

a To what extent are these rights justiciable (i.e. can be protected, guaranteed or realised through legal processes: laws, courts, legal action, prosecutions, etc.)?

b How might their justiciability be strengthened?

c What are the limits to their justiciability?

d Do legal constructions of these rights limit the way we understand these rights and the way we act to secure them?

5 Rights and oppression: class, gender, race, age, disability, sexuality

Human rights violations are more frequent and more serious among oppressed or disadvantaged populations.

a How do the structures and discourses of class, race, gender, ethnicity, age, disability, sexuality, etc. impact on the protection and realisation of each set of rights?

b What special measures need to be taken to safeguard the human rights of vulnerable or powerless groups, in relation to each set of rights?

c What is the relationship of human rights work to social movements committed to overcoming structures and discourses of disadvantage?

6 Responsibilities: individual, family, professional, community, civil society, state, world

All rights imply responsibilities, and the realisation and protection of human rights make no sense if the corresponding responsibilities are not specified and enacted.

a There is no point in having human rights if they are not exercised. With each set of rights, what are the responsibilities to ensure that they are actually exercised?

b What is the obligation of a person or group claiming a right to exercise that right *responsibly*, in relation to each set of rights?

c What is the responsibility of the private citizen to ensure that other citizens are able to exercise their rights within each category?

d What is the responsibility of the professional (e.g. teacher, medical practitioner, priest, lawyer, health worker, engineer, architect, development worker) to ensure that each set of human rights is both promoted and protected in the course of their work?

e What is the responsibility of the community to ensure that each set of rights can be realised or protected?

f What is the responsibility of the state to ensure the protection and realisation of each set of rights?

g What is the responsibility of business to ensure the protection and realisation of each set of rights?

h What is the responsibility of regional and global bodies to ensure the realisation of each set of rights?

7 Intergenerational responsibilities to past and future generations

The responsibilities that go with human rights do not only exist in the present. We acknowledge responsibility for human rights violations in the past, and a responsibility to future generations.

a For each set of rights, are there human rights violations in the past that impose responsibilities on the present? If so, what are those responsibilities and who should meet them?

b For each set of rights, are there responsibilities on present generations to safeguard the human rights of future generations? If so, what are those responsibilities and who should meet them?

8 Education, facilitating dialogue, consciousness-raising, community awareness, action

Human rights will only be realised if people are aware of them, and of their role in constructing, claiming, protecting and facilitating the rights both of themselves and of others.

a For each set of rights, how much active public debate is there around the meaning of those rights, their realisation and their protection?

b How can community awareness of each set of rights be improved?

c How can individuals and groups be encouraged to become involved in debating, discussing and constructing their own view of rights?

d For each set of rights, what are the important groups that need to engage in dialogue about those rights and what they mean?

e For each set of rights, what is the role of government, community groups, educational institutions and business groups in raising awareness about human rights?

f For each set of rights, what actions might be taken in this community to ensure that they are protected, respected or realised?

THE MATRIX

	Social rights	Economic rights	Civil/political rights	Cultural rights	Environmental rights	Spiritual rights	Survival rights
Examples of rights in each category: (not exhaustive lists)	Family life, privacy, recreation/leisure, education, choice of partner, lifestyle, sexuality, housing	Basic living standard, earn a living, work, social security, savings, choice of spending	Free speech, free assembly, vote, fair trial, stand for office, join organisations, join union, strike	Cultural expression, cultural practices, clothing, religious expression, intellectual property, land rights	Pollution free, poison free, wilderness, beauty, sustainability, access to land	Choice, religious expression, rituals, experience nature, personal fulfilment, sacred land/objects	Life, food, water, shelter, clothing, health, safety
Cultural, religious, philosophical and ideological traditions and understandings of rights							
Individual and collective understandings of rights							
Rights in the private/domestic and public/civil domains							

Rights and protection through courts and legislation, justiciability etc.					
Rights and oppression: class, gender, race, age, disability, sexuality					
Responsibilities: individual, family, community, civil society, state, world					
Intergenerational responsibilities to past and future generations					
Education, facilitating dialogue, consciousness-raising, awareness, action					

References

Ackerly, B. 2008, *Universal Human Rights in a World of Difference*, Cambridge University Press

Adger, W.N., Paavola, J., Huq, S. & Mace, M.J. (eds) 2006, *Fairness in Adaptation to Climate Change*, Cambridge Mass.: MIT Press

Alinsky, S. 1969, *Reveille for Radicals*, New York: Random House

Alinsky, S. 1971, *Rules for Radicals: A Practical Primer for Realistic Radicals*, New York: Random House

Angle, S. 2002, *Human Rights and Chinese Thought: A Cross-Cultural Inquiry*, Cambridge University Press

Appelbaum, D. 1995, *The Vision of Kant*, Shaftesbury Dorset: Element Books

Armstrong, K. 2000, *The Battle for God: Fundamentalism in Judaism, Christianity and Islam*, London: Harper-Collins

Ashworth, G. 1999, 'The silencing of women' in Dunne, T. & Wheeler, N.J. (eds) *Human Rights in Global Politics*, Cambridge University Press

Aziz, N. 1999, 'The human rights debate in an era of globalization' in Van Ness, P. (ed.), *Debating Human Rights: Critical Essays from the United States and Asia*, London: Routledge, pp. 32–55

Baldissone, R. 2009, *A time of openings: beyond modern fundamentalisms*, Perth: Curtin University of Technology (unpublished PhD thesis)

Barlow, M. 2007, *Blue Covenant: The Global Water Crisis and the Coming Battle for the Right to Water*, Toronto: McClelland & Stewart

Bauer, J. & Bell, D. (eds) 1999, *The East Asian Challenge for Human Rights*, Cambridge University Press

Bauman, Z. 1993, *Postmodern Ethics*, Oxford: Blackwell

Bauman, Z. 1995, *Life in Fragments: Essays in Postmodern Morality*, Oxford: Blackwell

Bauman, Z. 2001, *Community: Seeking Safety in an Insecure World*, Cambridge: Polity Press

Beardsworth, R. 1996, *Derrida and the Political*, London: Routledge

Beetham, D. 1999, *Democracy and Human Rights*, Cambridge: Polity Press

Bello, W. 2002, *Deglobalization: Ideas for a New World Economy*, New York: Zed Books

Bentham, J. 2001, 'Anarchical fallacies: a critical examination of the Declaration of Rights' in Hayden, P. (ed.) 2001, *The Philosophy of Human Rights*, St Paul: Paragon House

Boal, A. 1979, *Theatre of the Oppressed*, London: Pluto Press

Bobbio, N. 1996, *The Age of Rights* (trans. A. Cameron), Cambridge: Polity Press

Bornstein, D. 2004, *How to Change the World: Social Entrepreneurs and the Power of New Ideas*, Oxford University Press

Boucher, D. & Kelly, P. (eds) 1998, *Social Justice: from Hume to Walzer*, London: Routledge

Brecher, J. & Costello, T. 1994, *Global Village or Global Pillage: Economic Reconstruction from the Bottom Up*, Boston: South End Press

Brems, E. 2003, 'Protecting the rights of women' in Lyons, G. & Mayall, J. (eds), *International Human Rights in the 21st Century: Protecting the Rights of Groups*, Lanham Md: Rowman & Littlefield

Briskman, L., Latham, S. & Goddard, C. 2008, *Human Rights Overboard: Seeking Asylum in Australia*, Melbourne: Scribe

Bronk, R. 2009, *The Romantic Economist*, Cambridge University Press

Brown, C. 1999, 'Universal human rights: a critique' in Dunne, T. & Wheeler, N.J. (eds), *Human Rights in Global Politics*, Cambridge University Press

Bryant, B. (ed.) 1995, *Environmental Justice: Issues, Policies and Solutions*, Washington DC: Island Press

Brysk, A. (ed.) 2002, *Globalization and Human Rights*, Berkeley: University of California Press

Bryson, L. 1992, *Welfare and the State: Who Benefits?*, London: Macmillan

Bryson, L. & Mowbray, M. 1981, 'Community: the spray-on solution', *Australian Journal of Social Issues*, 16 (4), pp. 255–67

Buber, M. 2002, *Between Man and Man*, London: Routledge

Calhoun, C. 1995, *Critical Social Theory: Culture, History and the Challenge of Difference*, Oxford: Blackwell

Caney, S. & Jones, P. (eds) 2001, *Human Rights and Global Diversity*, London: Frank Cass

Carroll, J. 2004, *The Wreck of Western Culture: Humanism Revisited*, Melbourne: Scribe

Carter, A. 1999, *A Radical Green Political Theory*, London: Routledge

Cassese, A. 1990, *Human Rights in a Changing World*, Philadelphia: Temple University Press

Castells, M. 1997, *The Information Age: Economy, Society and Culture*, vol. 2, *The Power of Identity*, Malden Mass.: Blackwell

Chile, L. (ed.) 2007, *Community Development Practice in New Zealand: Exploring Good Practice*, Auckland: Institute of Public Policy, AUT

Considine, M. & Painter, M. (eds) 1997, *Managerialism: The Great Debate*, Melbourne: Melbourne University Press

Craig, G. 2007, 'Community capacity-building: something old, something new...?' *Critical Social Policy*, 27 (3) pp. 335–59

Craig, J. 1993, *The Nature of Co-operation*, Montreal: Black Rose

Crotty, M. 1998, *The Foundations of Social Research: Meaning and Perspective in the Research Process*, Sydney: Allen & Unwin

Dalacoura, K. 2003, *Islam, Liberalism and Human Rights*, London: Tauris & Co.

Daly, H. 1997, *Beyond Growth: The Economics of Sustainable Development*, Boston: Beacon Press

Davis, M. (ed.) 1995, *Human Rights and Chinese Values: Legal, Philosophical, and Political Perspectives*, New York: Oxford University Press

Diamond, J. 1998, *Guns, Germs and Steel: A Short History of Everybody for the Last 13,000 Years*, London: Vintage

Diamond, J. 2005, *Collapse: How Societies Choose to Fail or Succeed*, New York: Viking

Diesendorf, M. & Hamilton, C. (eds) 1997, *Human Ecology, Human Economy: Ideas for an Ecologically Sustainable Future*, St Leonards NSW: Allen & Unwin

Douzinas, C. 2000, *The End of Human Rights*, Oxford: Hart Publishing

Douzinas, C. 2007, *Human Rights and Empire: The Political Philosophy of Cosmopolitanism*, Abingdon, Oxon: Routledge-Cavendish

Doyal, L. & Gough, I. 1991, *A Theory of Human Need*, London: Macmillan

Drengson, A. & Inoue, Y. (eds) 1995, *The Deep Ecology Movement: An Introductory Anthology*, Berkeley: North Atlantic Books

Durkheim, E. 1933, *The Division of Labor in Society* (trans. G. Simpson), New York: Free Press

Dyer, G. 2008, *Climate Wars*, Melbourne: Scribe

Eckersley, R. 1992, *Environmentalism and Political Theory*, New York: SUNY Press

Ekins, P. & Max-Neef, M. (eds) 1992, *Real-Life Economics: Understanding Wealth Creation*, London: Routledge

Falk, R. 1993, 'The making of global citizenship' in Brecher, J., Childs, J. & Cutler, J. (eds), *Global Visions: Beyond the New World Order*, Boston Mass.: South End Press, pp. 39–50

Falk, R. 2000a, *Human Rights Horizons: The Pursuit of Justice in a Globalizing World*, New York: Routledge

Falk, R. 2000b, 'Global society and the democratic prospect' in Holden, B. (ed.), *Global Democracy: Key Debates*, London: Routledge, pp. 162–78

Falk, R., Ruiz, L. & Walker R. (eds) 2002, *Reframing the International: Law, Culture, Politics*, New York: Routledge

Fay, B. 1975, *Social Theory and Political Practice*, London: Allen & Unwin

Fay, B. 1987, *Critical Social Science*, Cambridge: Polity Press

Foucault, M. 1970, *The Order of Things*, London: Routledge

Foucault, M. 1986, 'Truth and power' in Rabinow, P. (ed.), *The Foucault Reader: An Introduction to Foucault's Thought*, Harmondsworth: Penguin Books

Freeman, M. 2002, *Human Rights*, Cambridge: Polity Press

Freire, P. 1972, *Cultural Action for Freedom*, Harmondsworth: Penguin Books

Freire, P. 1985, *The Politics of Education: Culture, Power, and Liberation* (trans. D. Macedo), Westport Conn.: Bergin & Garvey

Freire, P. 1996, *The Pedagogy of the Oppressed*, Harmondsworth: Penguin Books

French, M. 1992, *The War Against Women*, Oxford: Blackwell

Gale, F., Bolzan, N. & McRae-McMahon, D. (eds) 2007, *Spirited Practices: Spirituality and the Helping Professions*, Crows Nest NSW: Allen & Unwin

Galtung, J. 1994, *Human Rights in Another Key*, Cambridge: Polity Press

Gandhi, M. 1964, *Gandhi on Non-Violence: Selected Texts from Mohandas K. Gandhi's 'Non-Violence in Peace and War'*, Merton, Thomas (ed.), New York: New Directions Publishing

Garkawe, S., Kelly, L. & Fisher, W. 2001, *Indigenous Human Rights*, Sydney: Sydney Institute of Criminology Monograph Series no. 14

Gastil, J. 1993, *Democracy in Small Groups: Participation, Decision Making and Communication*, Philadelphia: New Society Publishers

George, V. & Wilding, P. 1994, *Welfare and Ideology*, London: Harvester Wheatsheaf

Gewirth, A. 1996, *The Community of Rights*, University of Chicago Press

Goodale, M. (ed.) 2009, *Human Rights: An Anthropological Reader*, Oxford: Blackwell

Goodale, M. & Merry, S. (eds) 2007, *The Practice of Human Rights: Tracking Law Between the Global and the Local*, Cambridge University Press

Goodin, R. 1995, *Utilitarianism as a Public Philosophy*, Cambridge University Press

Gramsci, A. 1957, *The Modern Prince, and Other Writings*, New York: International Publishers

Hamilton, C. 2003, *Growth Fetish*, Crows Nest NSW: Allen & Unwin

Havel, V. 1991, *Vaclav Havel: Open Letters*, London: Faber & Faber

Havel, V. 1992, *Summer Meditations: on Politics, Morality and Civility in a Time of Transition*, London: Faber & Faber

Hayden, P. (ed.) 2001, *The Philosophy of Human Rights*, St Paul: Paragon House

Held, D. 2006, *Models of Democracy*, 3rd edn, Stanford Calif.: Stanford University Press

Henderson, H. (with Simran Sethi) 2006, *Ethical Markets: Growing the Green Economy*, White River Junction Vt: Chelsea Green

Herbert, G. 2003, *A Philosophical History of Rights*, New Brunswick NJ: Transaction Publishers

Hesse, C. & Post, R. (eds) 1999, *Human Rights in Political Transitions: Gettysburg to Bosnia*, New York: Zone Books

Hines, C. 2000, *Localization: A Global Manifesto*, London: Earthscan

Hobbes, T. 1968, *Leviathan*, Harmondsworth: Penguin

Honoré, C. 2005, *In Praise of Slow*, London: Orion Books

Hopkins, R. 2008, *The Transition Handbook: Creating Local Sustainable Communities Beyond Oil Dependency*, Sydney: Finch Publishing

Howland, C. (ed.) 1999, *Religious Fundamentalisms and the Human Rights of Women*, New York: Palgrave

Hunt, L. 2007, *Inventing Human Rights: A History*, New York: Norton

Ife, J. 2002, *Community Development: Community-based Alternatives in an Age of Globalisation*, 2nd edn, Melbourne: Pearson

Ife, J. 2006, 'Human rights beyond the three generations' in Porter, E.J. & Offord, B. (eds), *Activating Human Rights*, Oxford: Peter Lang, pp. 29–46

Ife, J. 2007, 'Cultural relativism and community activism' in Reichert, E. (ed.), *Challenges in Human Rights: A Social Work Perspective*, Columbia University Press, pp. 76–96

Ife, J. 2008, *Human Rights and Social Work: Towards Rights-based Practice*, rev. edn, Cambridge University Press

Ife, J. & Tesoriero, F. 2006, *Community Development: Community-based Alternatives in an Age of Globalisation*, 3rd edn, Melbourne: Pearson

Illich, I., Zola, I., McKnight, J., Caplin, J. & Shaiken, S. 1977, *Disabling Professions*, London: Marion Boyars

Ishay, M.R. (ed.) 1997, *The Human Rights Reader*, New York: Routledge

James, R. 2001, *Practical Guidelines for the Monitoring and Evaluation of Capacity-Building: Experiences from Africa*, occasional paper no. 36, Oxford: INTRAC (The International NGO Training & Research Centre)

Keck, M. & Sikkink, K. 1998, *Activists Beyond Borders: Advocacy Networks in International Politics*, Ithaca New York: Cornell University Press

Kennedy, M. & Kennedy, D. 1995, *Interest and Inflation Free Money: Creating an Exchange Medium that Works for Everybody and Protects the Earth*, Gabrioloa Island, BC, Canada: New Society Publishers

Kenny, S. 2006, *Developing Communities for the Future: Community Development in Australia*, 3rd edn, South Melbourne: Thomson

King, M.L. 1969, *Where do we Go from Here: Chaos or Community?* Harmondsworth: Penguin

Klein, N. 2007, *The Shock Doctrine: The Rise of Disaster Capitalism*, London: Allen Lane

Knudtson, P. & Suzuki, D. 1992, *Wisdom of the Elders*, Sydney: Allen & Unwin

Korey, W. 1998, *NGOs and the Universal Declaration of Human Rights: 'A Curious Grapevine'*, New York: Palgrave

Kristol, I. 1989, '"Human rights": the hidden agenda' in Laqueur, W. & Rubin, B. (eds) *Human Rights Reader*, rev. edn, New York: Meridian

Kumar, K. 1995, *From Post-Industrial to Post-Modern Society: New Theories of the Contemporary World*, Oxford: Blackwell

Laber, J. 2002, *The Courage of Strangers: Coming of Age with the Human Rights Movement*, New York: Public Affairs

Larsen, M. 2000, 'Imperialism, colonialism, postcolonialism' in Schwarz, H. & Ray, S. (eds) *A Companion to Postcolonial Studies*, Malden Mass.: Blackwell

Lauren, P. 1998, *The Evolution of International Human Rights: Visions Seen*, Philadelphia: University of Pennsylvania Press

Levinas, E. 1998, *Entre Nous: Thinking of the Other*, New York: Columbia University Press

Levinas, E. 2006, *Humanism of the Other*, Urbana: University of Illinois Press

Lewis, J. (ed.) 2003, *The New Rights of Man: An Anthology of the Events, Documents and Speeches that have Shaped Western Civilisation*, London: Robinson

Locke, J. 1967, *Two Treatises of Government*, Cambridge University Press

Lovelock, J. 1987, *Gaia: A New Look at Life on Earth*, Oxford University Press

Lovelock, J. 2006, *The Revenge of Gaia: Why the Earth is Fighting Back – and How We Can Still Save Humanity*, London: Allen Lane

Lovelock, J. 2009, *The Vanishing Face of Gaia: A Final Warning*, Camberwell Vic.: Allen Lane

Lyons, G. & Mayall, J. 2003, 'Stating the problem of group rights' in Lyons, G. & Mayall, J. (eds), *International Human Rights in the 21st Century: Protecting the Rights of Groups*, Lanham Md: Rowman & Littlefield

MacCulloch, D. 2003, *Reformation: Europe's House Divided 1490–1700*, London: Penguin

Macy, J. 2007, *World as Lover, World as Self: Courage for Global Justice and Ecological Renewal*, Berkeley Calif.: Parallax Press

Mandela, N. 1994, *Long Walk to Freedom: the Autobiography of Nelson Mandela*, Boston: Little Brown.

Mander, J. & Goldsmith, E. 1996, *The Case Against the Global Economy and for a Turn Towards the Local*, San Francisco: Sierra Club Books

Marshall, P. 1992, *Demanding the Impossible: A History of Anarchism*, London: Harper Collins

Marx, K. 1954, *Capital: A Critique of Political Economy*, vol. 1, Moscow: Progress Publishers

Max-Neef, M. 1991, *Human Scale Development: Conception, Application and Further Reflections*, New York: Apex Press

McCashen, W. 2004, *Communities of Hope: A Strengths-based Resource for Building Community*, Bendigo: St Luke's Innovative Resources

McCowan, L. 1996, *A Social Work Approach to Post-Genocide Trauma Recovery for the Rwandese Community*, Newcastle NSW: University of Newcastle

McKibben, B. 2008, *The Deep Economy: The Wealth of Communities and the Durable Future*, New York: Holt Paperbacks

McLaren, P. & Lankshear, C. (eds) 1994, *Politics of Liberation: Paths from Freire*, London: Routledge

McLaren, P. & Leonard, P. (eds) 1993, *Paulo Freire: A Critical Encounter*, London: Routledge

Meadows, D., Meadows, D. & Randers, J. 2004, *Limits to Growth: The Thirty Year Update*, London: Earthscan

Meckled-García, S. & Çali, B. (eds) 2006, *The Legalization of Human Rights: Multidisciplinary Perspectives on Human Rights and Human Rights Law*, Abingdon, Oxon: Routledge

Meeker-Lowry, S. 1996, 'Community money: the potential of local currency' in Mander, J. & Goldsmith, E. (eds), *The Case Against the Global Economy and for a Turn Towards the Local*, San Francisco: Sierra Club Books

Meijer, M. (ed.) 2001, *Dealing with Human Rights: Asian and Western Views on the Value of Human Rights*, Utrecht: HOM

Midgley, J. 1997, *Social Development: The Developmental Perspective in Social Welfare*, London: Sage

Midgley, M. 2001, *Science and Poetry*, London: Routledge

Mill, J.S. 1906, *On Liberty*, London: Everyman's Library

Mitchell, A. 2008, *Seasick: The Hidden Ecological Crisis of the Global Ocean*, Millers Point NSW: Murdoch Books

Monshipouri, M., Englehart, N., Nathan, A. & Philip, K. (eds) 2003, *Constructing Human Rights in the Age of Globalization*, Armonk New York: M.E. Sharpe

Moussalli, A. 2001, *The Islamic Quest for Democracy, Pluralism and Human Rights*, Gainesville, Fla: University Press of Florida

Naess, A. 1989, *Ecology, Community and Lifestyle*, Cambridge University Press

Nancy, J.-L. 1991, *The Inoperative Community*, Minneapolis Minn.: University of Minnesota Press

Nicholls, A. 2006, *Social Entrepreneurship: New Models of Sustainable Social Change*, Oxford University Press

Nirmal, C. 2000, *Human Rights in India: Historical, Social and Political Perspectives*, New Delhi: Oxford University Press

Northcott, M. 2007, *A Moral Climate: The Ethics of Global Warming*, London: Darton Longman & Todd

Orend, B. 2002, *Human Rights: Concept and Context*, Peterborough Ont.: Broadview Press

Paine, T. 1994, *The Rights of Man/Common Sense*, London: Everyman

Parekh, B. 1999, 'Non-ethnocentric universalism' in Dunne, T. & Wheeler, N.J. (eds), *Human Rights in Global Politics*, Cambridge University Press, pp. 128–59

Peet, R. & Hartwick, E. 2009, *Theories of Development: Contentions, Arguments, Alternatives*, 2nd edn, New York: The Guildford Press

Pereira, W. 1997, *Inhuman Rights: The Western System and Global Human Rights Abuse*, Penang: The Other India Press, The Apex Press and Third World Network

Peterson, V. & Parisi, L. 1998, 'Are women human? it's not an academic question' in Evans, T. (ed.), *Human Rights Fifty Years On*, Manchester University Press

Plummer, J. 2000, *Municipalities and Community Participation: A Sourcebook for Capacity Building*, London: Earthscan Publications

Pogge, T. 2008, *World Poverty and Human Rights: Cosmopolitan Responsibilities and Reforms*, 2nd edn, Cambridge: Polity Press

Pojman, L. 2006, *Terrorism, Human Rights and the Case for World Government*, Lanham: Rowan & Littlefield

Postman, N. 1993, *Technopoly: The Surrender of Culture to Technology*, New York: Random House

Rajagopal, B. 2003, *International Law from Below: Development, Social Movements and Third World Resistance*, Cambridge University Press

Ray, L. 1993, *Rethinking Critical Theory: Emancipation in the Age of Global Social Movements*, London: Sage

Rees, S. & Rodley, G. (eds) 1995, *The Human Costs of Managerialism: Advocating the Recovery of Humanity*, Sydney: Pluto Press

Reichert, E. 2003, *Social Work and Human Rights: A Foundation for Policy and Practice*, New York: Columbia University Press

Rendel, M. 1997, *Whose Human Rights?* Oakhill Staffordshire: Trentham Books

Reynolds, H. 1998, *This Whispering in Our Hearts*, St Leonards NSW: Allen & Unwin

Riches, G. (ed.) 1997, *First World Hunger: Food Security and Welfare Politics*, New York: St Martin's Press

Roberts, P. 2004, *The End of Oil: On the Edge of a Perilous New World*, Boston: Houghton Mifflin

Roemer, J. 1999, 'Does democracy engender justice?' in Shapiro, I. & Hacker-Cordon, C. (eds), *Democracy's Value*, Cambridge University Press

Rosenau, P. 1992, *Post-Modernism and the Social Sciences: Insights, Inroads and Intrusions*, Princeton University Press

Rothman, J. 1974, 'Three models of community organisation practice' in Cox, F., Erlich, J., Rothman, J. & Tropman, J. (eds) *Strategies of Community Organization: A Book of Readings*, 2nd edn, Itasca Ill.: F.E. Peacock

Rousseau, J. 1968, *The Social Contract*, Harmondsworth: Penguin

Said, E. 1993, *Culture and Imperialism*, New York: Random House

Said, E. 1995, *Orientalism*, Harmondsworth: Penguin

Samuel, R. 1975, *Village Life and Labour*, London: Routledge

Sarantakos, S. 1998, *Social Research*, 2nd edn, South Yarra Vic.: Macmillan

Saul, J.R. 2002, *On Equilibrium*, Camberwell Vic.: Penguin

Saward, M. 1998, *The Terms of Democracy*, Cambridge: Polity Press

Schumacher, E.F. 1973, *Small Is Beautiful: A Study of Economics as if People Mattered*, London: Blond & Briggs

Schmale, W. (ed.) 1993, *Human Rights and Cultural Diversity*, Goldbach, Germany: Keip

Schwarz, H. & Ray, S. (eds) 2000, *A Companion to Postcolonial Studies*, Malden Mass.: Blackwell

Seed, J., Macy, J. & Fleming, P. 2007, *Thinking Like a Mountain: Towards a Council of All Beings*, Gabriola Island, BC: New Catalyst Books

Seidman, S. (ed.) 1994, *The Postmodern Turn: New Perspectives on Social Theory*, Cambridge: Cambridge University Press

Sellars, K. 2002, *The Rise and Rise of Human Rights*, Phoenix Mill: Sutton

Shearman, D. & Smith, J.W. 2007 *The Climate Change Challenge and the Failure of Democracy*, Westport Conn.: Praeger

Shragge, E. 2000, *Community Economic Development: In Search of Empowerment and Alternatives*, 2nd edn, Montreal: Black Rose

Shiva, V. 2005, *Earth Democracy: Justice, Sustainability and Peace*, London: Zed Books

Sim, S. 2004, *Fundamentalist World: The New Dark Age of Dogma*, Cambridge: Icon Books

Sinclair, R. 1988, *Democracy and Participation in Athens*, Cambridge University Press

Smillie, I. 2001, 'Capacity building and the humanitarian enterprise' in Smillie, I. (ed.), *Patronage or Partnership: Local Capacity Building in Humanitarian Crises*, Bloomfield Conn.: Kumarian Press

Spratt, D. & Sutton, P. 2008, *Climate Code Red: The Case for Emergency Action*, Melbourne: Scribe

Stiefel, M. & Wolfe, M. 1994, *A Voice for the Excluded: Popular Participation in Development, Utopia or Necessity?* London: Zed Books

Strauss, A. & Corbin, J. 1990, *Basics of Qualitative Research: Grounded Theory, Procedures and Techniques*, Newbury Park Calif.: Sage

Tascón, S. 2009, 'Australia's border protection: morphing racial exclusion into terror[ism]', in Wynterdyk, J. & Sundberg, K. (eds), *Transforming Borders in the Al Qaeda Era*, London: Routledge

Tascón, S. & Ife J. 2008, 'Human rights and critical whiteness: whose humanity?' *International Journal of Human Rights*, vol. 12, no. 5

Taylor, C. 1989, *Sources of the Self: The Making of Modern Identity*, Cambridge University Press

Terkel, S. 2004, *Hope Dies Last: Keeping the Faith in Difficult Times*, New York: New Press

Thoreau, H.D. 1983, *Walden and Civil Disobedience*, Harmondsworth: Penguin

Tönnies, F. 1955, *Community and Association* (trans. C. Loomis), London: Routledge

Touraine, A. 1995, *Critique of Modernity*, Cambridge Mass.: Blackwell

Tutu, D. 1999, *No Future Without Forgiveness*, London: Random House

Uhr, J. 1998, *Deliberative Democracy in Australia: the Changing Place of Parliament*, Cambridge University Press

Uhr, J. 2000, 'Testing deliberative democracy: the 1999 Australian republic referendum', *Government and Opposition*, 35 (2), pp. 189–211

Van Ness, P. (ed.) 1999, *Debating Human Rights: Critical Essays from the United States and Asia*, London: Routledge

van Ufford, P. & Giri, A. 2003, *A Moral Critique of Development: In Search of Global Responsibilities*, London: Routledge

Watson, P. 2005, *Ideas: A History from Fire to Freud*, London: Phoenix

Williamson, T. 2003, *Making a Place for Community: Local Democracy in a Global Era*, London: Routledge

Wilson, R.A. & Mitchell, J. (eds) 2003, *Human Rights in Global Perspective: Anthropological Studies of Rights, Claims and Entitlements*, London: Routledge

Wittgenstein, L. 1974, *Tractatus Logico-philosophicus* (trans. D.F. Pears & B.F. McGuinness), London: Routledge & Kegan Paul

Wollstonecraft, M. 1975, *A Vindication of the Rights of Women*, Harmondsworth: Penguin

Woodiwiss, A. 2006, 'The law cannot be enough: human rights and the limits of legalism' in Meckled-García, S. & Çali, B. (eds), *The Legalization of Human Rights: Multi-disciplinary Perspectives on Human Rights and Human Rights Law*, Abingdon, Oxon: Routledge

World Commission on Environment and Development 1987, *Our Common Future*, Oxford: Oxford University Press (the 'Brundtland Report')

Yankelovich, D. 1999, *The Magic of Dialogue: Transforming Conflict into Cooperation*, London: Nicholas Brealey

Young, R. 2001, *Postcolonialism: An Historical Introduction*, Oxford: Blackwell

Zarsky, L. (ed.) 2002, *Human Rights and the Environment: Conflicts and Norms in a Globalizing World*, London: Earthscan

Index

CPSIA information can be obtained
at www.ICGtesting.com
Printed in the USA
LVOW10s1034241117
557421LV00027B/1547/P